RED
DWARF

PROGRAMME GUIDE

RED DWARF

PROGRAMME GUIDE

by
Chris Howarth & Steve Lyons

Virgin

This edition published in 1997 by
Virgin Books
an imprint of Virgin Publishing Ltd
332 Ladbroke Grove
London W10 5AH
First published in 1993

Reprinted 1993 (twice), 1994 (twice), new edition 1995
This edition reprinted 1998

Photo section credits:
Photographs on pages 4, 6, 8, 11, 12 (bottom) and 14 by Mike
  Vaughan
Photographs on pages 2, 3, 12 (top) and 13 (top) by Oliver Upton
Photographs on pages 1 and 15 © BBC
Photograph on page 13 (bottom) © Peter Walsh

ISBN 0 7535 0103 1

Cover illustration by Alister Pearson

Typeset by Galleon Typesetting, Ipswich

Printed and bound in Great Britain by Mackays of Chatham PLC

CONTENTS

For Liz Guest

ACKNOWLEDGEMENTS

The Authors would like to say a great big thank you to the following:

Rob Grant and Doug Naylor.

John Albineri, Chloë Annett, Charles Augins, Chris Barrie, Suzanne Bertish, Mel Bibby, Stephen Bradshaw, Mike Butcher, Ed Bye, Craig Charles, Paul Cornell, Lee Cornes, Kate Cotton, Brian Cox, Matthew Devitt, Andy de Emmony, Howard Goodall, C. P. Grogan, Tony Hawks, Hattie Hayridge, Jonathan Head, Don Henderson, Graham Hutchings, Kathleen Hutchison, Danny John-Jules, John Knight, Andrew and Catherine Liddell, Denis Lill, Robert Llewellyn, Norman Lovett, Jason Lythgoe, Mac McDonald, Keith Mayes, Jim Marshall, Chrissie Moses, Helen Norman, John Pomphrey, David Ross, Gary Russell, Maggie Steed, Mike Tucker, Lisa Wardle, Peter Wragg and Sophie at Egmont (who's finally got around to watching an episode).

AUTHORS' NOTE

What you are holding in your hands is yet another revised edition of the *Red Dwarf Programme Guide*. Ultimately the blame for this must lie with Grant Naylor Productions, who will insist on making new episodes, thus rendering our book out of date. Bearing in mind those of you who've already purchased previous editions, we've done our best to avoid making this latest work the same as before but with a new bit tacked on to the end, and have tried to make it as different as possible while at the same time retaining all the crucial stuff. For example we've cut down on information regarding the T-shirts and added plenty of facts, trivia and interview material about the episodes themselves (apologies to T-shirt buffs out there). Oh, and we've also changed the cover and given the chapters some naff new titles, so that bookshops will think it's a different publication entirely and order more copies.

Chris Howarth and Steve Lyons
Planet of the Nymphomaniacs, 1997

SECTION ONE:

MISSION BRIEF

'This is an SOS distress call from the mining ship *Red Dwarf*. The crew are dead, killed by a radiation leak. The only survivors were Dave Lister – who was in suspended animation during the disaster – and his pregnant cat, who was safely sealed in the hold. Revived three million years later, Lister's only companions are a life form who evolved from his cat and Arnold Rimmer, a hologram simulation of one of the dead crew.'

Well, actually Lister had one more companion: *Red Dwarf*'s super-intelligent computer, Holly, from whom the preceding paragraph is quoted (he delivered it at the beginning of episodes 2–6). Even so, it does sound like a bleak premise for a comedy series, doesn't it? 'The entire human race is wiped out – with hilarious consequences.' And yet, from its humble beginnings as an unregarded BBC 2 sitcom which almost didn't make it on to the screen at all, *Red Dwarf* has grown into a cult science-fiction phenomenon. It has spawned videos, tie-in novels, factual books, an official fan club – oh, and lots of the inevitable crappy merchandise that we'd rather not go into right now. At the time of writing, there is even a feature film under consideration. *Red Dwarf* is consistently BBC 2's top-rated programme and its special effects have won it several awards, consistently putting its competitors to shame. And it has evolved, too, so that its most recent episodes are hardly recognisable to fans of the original series.

Red Dwarf is the creation of Rob Grant and Doug Naylor, who, after leaving college in Liverpool, formed a writing partnership and began work on the Radio 4 sketch shows

Cliché and its sequel, *Son of Cliché*. For the latter they created 'Dave Hollins – Space Cadet', an ongoing series-within-a-series, which was destined to be remembered as a sort of embryonic version of their later television success. Hollins (voiced by the comedian Nick Wilton) was the last human alive; his one companion in the vastness of space was the computer Hab (a not-very-subtle spoof of *2001*'s Hal, played by Chris Barrie).

Soon enough, Rob and Doug were writing for television: *Carrott's Lib* in 1984 (on which, incidentally, they worked with Chris Barrie again) and then the satirical puppet show *Spitting Image*, for which they became head writers (and, yep, there was Chris again, here utilising his talents as an impressionist). Perhaps their most notorious accomplishment of this period, though, was their penning of the lyrics to the number-one smash hit 'The Chicken Song'. In the meantime, though, they were working on a long-term objective: a television sitcom to call their own. Rob, in particular, wanted to write science-fiction, and there seemed to be one obvious starting point for both ambitions. And so, after much discussion, they found their thoughts turning back to a certain Mr Hollins.

Of course, Rob and Doug were keen to make *Red Dwarf* as distinct an entity as possible from its predecessor. Dave Hollins became Dave Lister and Hab became Holly, but these were only cosmetic changes. If the transition into thirty-minute television episodes was to be successful, it was clear that the cast had to be expanded. Rather than dilute their original premise, which required the pivotal figure to be the last human being alive in the universe, the writers chose to make the additional characters nonhuman. Rimmer, the hologram of a dead man, was created first. Rob and Doug coined the word 'hologramatic' (sometimes spelt 'holo-grammatic') to describe his peculiar state of existence (the dictionary would suggest 'holographic'). He was followed by a representative of a race of cats which had evolved into humanoid form. Like Lister, the Cat was the last of his kind. Another semi-regular character at this stage was Kristine Kochanski, the navigation officer after whom Lister had unsuccessfully lusted and whose death he couldn't accept (later on in the series, Rob and Doug decided that his attitude was a little immature, and they amended the story to suggest that Lister and Kochanski had had a brief affair). Kochanski was included merely as an icon: a romanticised ideal to give Lister some reason for living. However, she was destined to become far more important to *Red Dwarf* than that. Another decision which would later be reversed was Rob and Doug's resistance to the temptation of including a robot in a central role. Rob in particular considered this to be a science-fiction cliché.

The pilot script for *Red Dwarf*, subtitled 'a situation comedy in space', was written in 1983, halfway up a Welsh mountain in a cottage belonging to Doug Naylor's father. It was more or less completed in a week – despite a traumatic incident in which the writers nearly drove the fast way down said mountain one night – but was subsequently rewritten six times before it was perfected. It was then handed to producers John Lloyd and Paul Jackson – who, between them, were responsible for most of the alternative comedy programmes around at the time, including such classics as *Blackadder* and *The Young Ones*. Both were decidedly impressed with it. It even seemed likely, for a time, that they might work together on the project, but such an unprecedented co-production was destined not to be. The task of selling *Red Dwarf* ultimately fell to Paul Jackson alone.

Initial attempts to find a home for the show proved fruitless, partly because of Rob and Doug's insistence that – rather than lose valuable minutes of air time for the sake of a few commercials – the show must be made by the BBC. Their faith in the potential of *Red Dwarf* as a thirty-minute, ongoing sit-com even led its creators to turn down an offer to include it as part of the highly respected *Film on 4* series. Ultimately, their confidence turned out to be justified, and Paul Jackson did indeed persuade the Manchester-based BBC North-West (now simply BBC North) to commission a series of six episodes.

The next stage was to assemble a cast – and, once again,

things didn't go quite as planned. Rob and Doug had always envisaged if not classically trained then, at the very least, established 'legitimate' actors portraying their characters, and indeed several high-profile people did audition (the one whose involvement has been publicised is Alfred Molina, who tried out for Rimmer). What they eventually got – and in fact selected themselves – was a poet, an impressionist, a dancer and a stand-up comic. But these choices were inspired: the performances of the regulars would prove to be as instrumental in the series' eventual success as the innovative scripts.

The first to join the cast was comedian Norman Lovett, who originally auditioned for the part of Arnold Rimmer but was signed up as the ship's computer Holly instead. Danny John-Jules was the next to be enlisted: dressing as the Cat for his interview and arriving in character, he made a positive impression from the start. The Cat had always been envisaged as a black character, and Paul Jackson had once thought that Craig Charles (with whom he had worked on *Saturday Night Live*) might be the one to play him. In fact, he sent a copy of the script to Craig for his appraisal of the Cat's character, being worried that the idea of a sharply dressed, cool black guy might be considered a bit of a racial stereotype. Craig liked it and wanted to be part of the show, so Paul ended up recommending him for the all-important role of Dave Lister. Rob and Doug agreed that he was perfect, even though they had intended the character to be somewhat older (and they had never envisaged him as a Liverpudlian). The line-up was completed with the addition of the seemingly ubiquitous Chris Barrie as the hologram Rimmer. Chris seems such an ideal choice that it is perhaps surprising to learn that he first tried out for the part of Lister. The episode 'Body Swap' gives us some idea of how he might have played him.

Finally, with the cast assembled, things were ready to roll. Studio time was booked and sets assembled at the BBC's Oxford Road studios in Manchester: from this humble cradle, a cult TV phenomenon was about to be born. Over the next decade, *Red Dwarf* would grow in both popularity and technical sophistication. Holly would change sex, leave the series and return with his original head, while the cowardly Rimmer would develop into an unlikely hero and depart. The crew would lose *Red Dwarf* and find it again, and the absence of the service mechanoid Kryten from the series would eventually seem inconceivable to its viewers. In perhaps the most startling development of all, Lister's one-time lover Kristine Kochanski would be returned to him alive and well, albeit with origins in a parallel dimension. No aliens would be discovered – the writers would stick to their self-restricting, but highly original, edict that the human race should be alone in the cosmos – but the '*Dwarf*ers' would face all manner of manmade and natural phenomena from time holes to rampaging Simulants and alluring GELFs to Despair Squids to a bread-obsessed toaster, as well as situations arising from their own peculiar origins and their relationships with each other.

What follows is an in-depth look at these developments – and at all the incarnations of the greatest comedy science-fiction series of all time . . .

SECTION TWO:

CREW ROSTER

LISTER

Full name: David Lister.

He picks his ears clean with tin-openers, he trims his toenails with his teeth, he thinks fresh vegetables are for health psychos and he sprays the contents of sugar puff sandwiches round his bunk room. A barely human, grossed-out slimeball, Dave Lister has the unearned distinction of being the last man alive in a Godless universe. Pity the universe!

Lister was discovered on 26 November 2155, by a man named Frank, beneath the grav-pool table of a bleak Liverpool drinking establishment called the Aigburth Arms. His parents were never located, the only clue being that the baby was dumped in a cardboard box on which they had scrawled OUROBOROS. This was taken to be a misspelling of 'Our Rob or Ross', but the child's adoptive parents christened him David anyway. He was estimated to be about six months old, so they provided him with a nominal birthday (we know that he's an Aries). But sadly, this new-found family was not to last: tragedy struck Lister when, at the tender age of six, his stepfather passed away. At the time, he was too young to fully understand what that meant and he confesses that he saw the event primarily as a way of getting concerned relatives to contribute towards his Lego collection. He was told only that his father had gone to the same place as his goldfish, and as a consequence, the young Lister spent many fruitless hours with his head down the toilet, reading him the football results. Eventually, he was taken to see a child psychologist, who helped him to cope with the loss, but even now, he clings to the only photograph of the man that he ever had – and that shows only his leg, the focus of the picture being on his dog, Hannah.

From then on, Lister was brought up by his grandmother, with whom he lived from the ages of eleven to fourteen. She was an enormous woman, whose stockings used to rub together when she walked – and, under her care, Lister began to grow too, so that his school nickname for a time was Fat Boy. Nor did Gran do much to further his educational prospects: she even nutted the headmaster when Lister came bottom of the class in French. It is fair to say, though, that he came bottom in most other subjects too, simply because he was unwilling to learn. In Biology lessons, for instance, the only task to which his skills were ever applied was to turn to page 47 of the text book and draw little beards and moustaches on all the sperms that were pictured there. And outside school, his 'education' was provided mainly by his friend Duncan, who taught him, for example, the art of using mirrored toe-caps to look up girls' skirts. Lister was deeply upset when, at the age of ten, Duncan and his family had to move to Spain because of his father's job – a bank job.

Even deprived of Duncan's tutelage though, Dave Lister had already realised one integral thing about himself – he hated working! He would much rather sit back with ten cans of lager and a curry, and he resented the intrusions of the more unpleasant realities of life. All he wanted from his existence was to just slob about and generally have a good time; while other twelve-year-olds were busy considering which exams would shape their future, Dave Lister was busy going scrumping – for cars! – and losing his virginity to Michelle Fisher on the tenth hole of the Bootle Municipal Golf Course. He did make a token attempt to better himself, by moving to art college once school had finished, but even that didn't last. Having believed the option to be an easy one, Dave was appalled to learn that lectures regularly started first thing in the afternoon! Ninety-seven minutes after enrolling, he had had enough, and he left.

Lister was forced to leave home when his grandmother was killed in a car accident. The people who drew the chalk outline had to go back for a second piece, and this prompted him to lose weight himself for fear of likewise ending up as a double chalker. He moved into a flat and, at the age of seventeen, found himself a part-time job as a trolley parker at the Mega-Mart. The pay wasn't very rewarding, but cashier number four was – until her husband found out and arranged for the hapless Lister to stumble, stark naked, out of a crate of tinned asparagus in the middle of the Bootle Players' amateur production of *The Importance of Being Earnest*. The incident changed him for life, leaving him with an intermittent fear of being trapped in confined spaces. In the meantime, he solved some of his money problems by stealing items from a local hotel to furnish his new residence. Not just the normal bars of soap and sachets of coffee, though. With a little help from his friends, Lister managed to lower the bed out of the hotel window!

By now, he had realised that his future lay in exploiting his own musical genius. The author of such instant classics as 'Om' and 'The Indling Song', Lister was keen to pursue a career as a rich and famous rock star – and he became the lead singer of a three-piece band called Smeg and the Heads, who managed to find themselves a few gigs in local pubs. When he wasn't working or performing, Lister could often be found indulging in his all-time favourite hobby. He was a massive fan of Zero Gravity Football, supporting in particular the London Jets team, whose Roof Attack player, Jim Bexley Speed, was his absolute hero. He even managed to get his photograph taken with the player, who seems rather less than impressed in the shot.

Meanwhile, Lister's evenings were generally spent throwing his wages away at the Aigburth Arms. He monopolised the very pool table under which he was first found, and earnt himself the nickname Cinzano Bianco because, once he was on the table, no one could get him off.

When he wasn't drinking, he was often out courting, although most of the girls he fell for were either heartbreakers or moral garbage on legs. Presumably falling into the former category, Lise Yates became the love of his life for a time, but he broke off the relationship himself when he felt she was trying to tie him down. He later regretted that move.

All in all though, as his early twenties came and went, Lister was beginning to realise that he wasn't very happy with his life. Problem number one: He now knew that Smeg and the Heads weren't going to become an international success, simply because they were totally crap. Problem two: Having spent eight years as a trolley attendant, he was beginning to worry about being tied down to a career! It was time for a change of direction.

For Lister, that change meant joining the Space Corps, and leaving Liverpool – and Earth – far behind him. So, by age twenty-five, he found himself assigned to the Jupiter Mining Corporation vessel *Red Dwarf*, as Third Technician David Lister, number RD52169. It was a post that he might have quite enjoyed (although, in keeping with his habitual aversion to work of any kind, he did request sick leave due to diarrhoea on no less than five hundred occasions during his eight months with the company), if not for the presence of one Second Technician Arnold Rimmer. Not only did he have to share a bunk room with Rimmer, but he also had to work for the man. Rimmer was in control of the ship's spectacularly unimportant Z Shift, the most important task of which was to ensure that the ship's vending machines didn't run out of Fun-Size 'Crunchie' bars, and life with him was not exactly Lister's idea of fun. The feeling was very much mutual.

For spick and span Rimmer, living with Lister was a nightmare. He sang, he clicked, he hummed, he deluded himself considerably about his guitar-playing abilities, and his chirpy, gerbil-faced optimistic approach to life drove Rimmer round the bend. Worse, he seemed to live on a non-stop diet of beer and vindaloos, and goodly amounts of these substances often 'decorated' his bunk-mate's meticulously crafted revision timetables. Breakfast for Lister consisted generally of last night's flat lager, sometimes in milkshake form, sometimes hot with croutons. And his clothes had to be seen to be believed. Lister's socks were capable of setting off the sprinkler system, and one of them was actually identified by the ship's computer Holly as a totally new lifeform. 'If you'd put Napoleon in quarters with Lister,' contended Rimmer, in defence of his own various failings, 'he'd still be in Corsica peeling spuds.'

The two were obviously not destined to hit it off, but for Lister at least, the Space Corps had its compensations, the biggest of which came in the form of Navigation Officer Kristine Kochanski. It was love at first sight – for Lister if not for his intended – and over the next few months, for the first time since his dreams of rock stardom had fallen down around his ears, he began to actually plan a future for himself. He would marry her, he decided, and they would have two sons, Jim and Bexley (both named after Jim Bexley Speed, of course). He would take her back to Earth with him, where they would start a farm on Fiji, breeding cows, sheep and horses. They would even open a chain of Hot Dog and Doughnut Diners, and they would certainly live happily ever after. Of course, he hadn't actually mentioned this glorious vision of the future to Kochanski yet – but he still had hope, even when a brief, three-week affair (during which they didn't even make love) ended with her throwing him over in favour of a catering officer. He even composed three love songs for her, although he could think of only two words that rhymed with Kochanski (and he used 'underpantski' twice).

There was, too, a very special place in Lister's dream for one other. Frankenstein was a pregnant cat he had picked up during planet leave on Titan, and which he had smuggled on board *Red Dwarf*. He kept her hidden in his quarters, away from prying eyes, feeding her with his regular milk ration, and bending her sympathetic ear with the intimate details of his wonderful plan, and of her position by his side when he achieved his ambitions.

The dream lasted no longer than eight months. It was then that Hollister, the ship's captain, discovered the cat's presence, and ordered Lister to hand her over. He refused. His punishment was to be placed in stasis for six months, until the end of the voyage – but as we all know, he actually remained there for slightly longer. Three million years later, Lister awoke to find himself the last human being alive – and the rest, as they say, is history.

Lister has precious little to remind him of his past now; just a few souvenirs from the pre-accident days, a tattoo on his inner thigh reading 'I love Petersen' (he doesn't – but that's what happens when you get drunk with your mates), a parallel universe counterpart of his lost love and a creature which evolved from Frankenstein's litter. Even his long dreamed of sons, Jim and Bexley, no longer see him, living as they do with their 'father', Dave's female equivalent in a parallel universe (and giving birth to them is an experience he doesn't wish to repeat).

You might think that being cast adrift in space with no responsibilities at all would be an ideal situation for someone who proudly lists his occupation as 'Bum' – and, indeed, at the age of twenty-eight (or thereabouts), Lister still walks around smelling like a Balti house laundry basket and has to surrender his cap to the service mechanoid Kryten for a monthly scraping. He has grated onions on his cornflakes and his vindaloo mania has ensured that only two of his taste buds still work. He possesses at least two super-hero costumes for the purpose of making love in and thinks of his ability to open lager bottles with his anus as his greatest achievement – but at least he now accepts that his guitar-playing sounds like the pained squeals of a monkey being stretched across a tennis court, although this doesn't stop him from subjecting his shipmates to it regularly. But, despite all this, Dave Lister has risen to his effective command position on *Red Dwarf* with unexpected strength, courage and even intelligence.

And when things are at their very worst, Lister still has the future to look forward to. Actually, he has several futures. In one, he and the rest of the crew become time-travelling epicures, although Dave accidentally loses his body in the process, becoming a talking brain in a dreadlocked tank. In another, his second son Bexley returns to *Red Dwarf* and dies in an explosion in the drive-room. A far more optimistic view of things to come sees a bearded, early-thirties Lister travelling back in time to marry Kristine Kochanski. Of course, she'll be wiped out three weeks later – but those three weeks will be brilliant! And rumour has it that he and a parallel-universe Kochanski may even conceive a child (though it will be an in-vitro fertilisation), and leave him in a cardboard box beneath a certain pool table in a twenty-second century pub. Perhaps best of all, future echoes have shown him that he might live to be 171 (although he'll pick up a cybernetic arm along the way). As for his long-stated objective, to return to Earth at last . . . well, only time can really tell.

CRAIG CHARLES was already known as a comedian and a poet, primarily from *Saturday Night Live*, before being cast as Dave Lister. However, it is with *Red Dwarf* that he is most closely identified, and it was arguably because of the show that his career has really taken off. He has presented many series, from *Them and Us* to the virtual-reality gameshow *Cyberzone* to the more recent *Funky Bunker*, and he also recently starred in the title role of the Channel 4 sit-com *Captain Butler*. He co-wrote his first book – *The Craig Charles Almanac of Total Knowledge* – in 1993, but still has one unfulfilled ambition. Craig always wanted to be a professional footballer, and he nearly made it too: he played with both Tranmere Rovers and the Liverpool Youth Team.

RIMMER

Full name: Arnold Judas (not Jonathan, as he'd have us believe!) Rimmer.

To Kryten, he was 'an incompetent vending machine repairman with a Napoleon complex'. To the Cat, he was 'the human equivalent of a visible panty line' – and the man's own description of himself as a 'Tosspot by Royal Appointment' was pretty close to the mark too. And yet, despite all evidence to the contrary, this sad specimen of humankind was destined for great things, albeit posthumously. His name was Arnold Rimmer, and his life ended on the Jupiter Mining Corporation vessel *Red Dwarf* during a radiation accident. But his new 'life' began when the ship's computer, Holly, chose him above all others to resurrect as a Class One hologram, sustained by a mobile light bee and maintained by a great deal of *Red Dwarf*'s power supply, to keep his once and future bunkmate sane. Alas, Rimmer's characteristic make-up of arrogance and neuroses, coupled with enough charm to fill his little finger – almost – remained absolutely unchanged.

Even when he was alive, Rimmer had not been the ideal person with whom to spend eternity. He was fixated on his ambition to become a Space Corps Officer, and even the tiny bit of power he enjoyed as the Second Technician in charge of *Red Dwarf*'s Z Shift (which consisted of himself and Lister) was excuse enough for him to throw his weight around. He knew he was destined for better things, despite the officers' refusal to accept his proposal for a new Space Corps salute. After all, in a previous incarnation, he had risen to the heights of being Alexander the Great's chief eunuch – or so Donald, his hypnotherapist, claimed. Unfortunately, his own death and the near extinction of the human race suggested that Rimmer would never achieve the fame that, in his eyes, he richly deserved. Hence his spare time was generally occupied by loud complaints about how unfair life had been to him (even his final words had been 'Gazpacho soup!' – a reference to his worst humiliation and an indication of how much it consumed him). Rimmer could never accept responsibility for his own failures. He even considered himself a good technician, although the dispensing machines maintained by him tended to give out oxtail soup and orange juice instead of Coke. And everybody around him became a target to be blamed for his own inadequacies.

Bad as that must have been, it certainly wasn't the worst that life with Rimmer had to offer. No, there were also his rather esoteric interests and his habit of waxing lyrical, and at great length, about them. He was writing the definitive history of pockets, for a start, and as the treasurer of the Hammond Organ Owners' Society, his unending recitals of Reggie Wilson 'classics' were more than could be borne. He was a great fan of twentieth-century telegraph poles and morris dancing, and his tales of a 'Risk' campaign against his Cadet School training officer Caldicott gave the word 'boredom' a new meaning. To a confirmed slob like Lister, Rimmer's obsession with tidiness must also have niggled. Everything had to be 'ticketty-boo' and 'licketty-split': his overstarched pyjamas were always neatly folded, his nocturnal boxing gloves tidied away and his collection of shoe trees was given names like Mon-Tree and Tues-Tree to ensure that they all received equal use. Even his ship-issue condoms had name tags sewn into them.

Rimmer never found the knack of making himself liked. He was the sort of person, according to Lister, who had to organise his own surprise parties. And his love life was just one disaster after another – from Sandra at Cadet School, to Carol McCauley (the recipient of his secret love letters) to a girl called Lorraine who, initially overwhelmed by the techniques Rimmer had learnt from his book on 'Picking up Girls by Hypnosis', eventually moved to Pluto to avoid a second date. For a long time, the nearest he got to a sexual liaison was with one Fiona Barrington, in his father's greenhouse – and even then, his illusions were shattered by the realisation that he had his hand in warm compost. In all of Arnold Rimmer's life, he only ever had sex once. The experience lasted for twelve minutes – including the time it took to eat the pizza – and was shared with one Yvonne McGruder, who has since dominated his dreams (usually clad in a skimpy peephole bra). As Lister is quick to point out, not only was McGruder the ship's female boxing champion, she was also concussed at the time, and she believed Rimmer to be somebody called Norman. Other than her, Rimmer's only 'intimate friend' was a blow-up doll called Rachel, and even she now has a puncture.

Still, as Lister has grown to realise, once you look under

the almost unbearable surface, there is plenty about Arnold Rimmer with which you can't help but sympathise. Certainly, as a child, he was somewhat lacking in love and encouragement. Rimmer was the youngest and least able of four children, and was particularly despised by his elder brothers, John, Frank and Howard. When the Rimmer clan played at being the Three Musketeers, Arnold was always 'allowed' to be the Queen of Spain – and when the others weren't actively ignoring him, they were planning even worse fates for their kid brother. Arnold tried to turn a blind eye to their cruelty – even when they planted a landmine in his sand pit, he passed it off as a harmless practical joke gone wrong – but deep in his heart, he was beginning to realise that he wasn't exactly Mister Popular.

Neither was school any haven. Rimmer's nickname at Io House was 'Ace' – but no matter how many times he let the other boys beat him up, they would never use it, preferring instead to refer to him as 'Bonehead'. Indeed, in all of the school, Rimmer only ever had one person he could truly call a friend, and then, only if you ignored the fact that said friend, one Porky Roebuck, had once thrown him into the septic tank. In the end though, even that solid friendship was destined to come to an abrupt end. Its cessation occurred during a Space Scout camp, when Porky led a gang of boys in trying to eat the hapless young Arnold. His life was only saved by the timely intervention of the Scout mistress, Yakka Talla Tulla – and after that, relations between Arnold and Porky became somewhat strained.

Even animals never showed any friendship towards Rimmer. His favourite and much adored pet, a Lemming, sadly had to die when it bit him on the finger and refused to let go until he had smashed its brains out against the wall. The incident deeply upset young Arnold, primarily because of the severe damage which was suffered by his helicopter wallpaper as a consequence.

As unhappy as his life was, Rimmer received no encouragement or support whatsoever from his parents. His mother didn't suffer fools gladly – and Arnold was certainly that!

Eventually, she gave up on him altogether, becoming more interested in keeping her numerous men-friends happy – and on the odd occasion that she did actually speak to him, she addressed him exclusively as 'Rimmer'. It says something about Mrs Rimmer's personality that, when a Psy-Moon gave form to Arnold's consciousness, it portrayed her as a huge, blood-sucking leech. Uncaring as she was though, she was nothing compared to Mr Rimmer Senior. Rimmer's father had been refused entry to the Space Corps because he was one inch below the regulation height. Frustrated at this failure, he was determined that his sons should pursue the career that he never could, and he followed this ideal even to the point of having them stretched on a rack. By the time he was eleven years old, Arnold's brother Frank was six foot five in height. Mealtimes too were a nightmare. Each night, Mr Rimmer quizzed his sons on Astro-Navigation theory. Only those who answered his questions correctly were allowed to eat – so naturally, poor Arnold nearly died from malnutrition.

Despite all this, Arnold Rimmer wanted nothing more than to please his father and to win the approval he had never had – but no matter what he did, it was never good enough. With all three of his brothers happily enrolled in the Space Corps Academy (his oldest brother, John, was a Test Pilot by the time Arnold was seven), he became nothing more than a bitter disappointment to both his parents. They let it show, too – particularly his father, who did nothing to ease Arnold's guilt at his failures by blaming him for the four strokes he suffered.

In the end, Rimmer could stand his home life no longer. At the age of fourteen, he took his parents to court and legally 'divorced' them. From then on, he rarely saw either of them again – although they had to pay him maintenance until employment age, and he did have access to the family dog every fourth weekend. It is not known exactly where Arnold resided at this time in his life, although he presumably stayed in the vicinity of both his home and his school. It was not until a few years later – at the age of sixteen, in fact – that he moved away from both altogether and attended Saturn Tech, where he took a maintenance course. He also found as many ways as he could to occupy his spare time; he took a film course at night school, and became a member of the Io Amateur War-Gamers, the Recreators of the Battle of Neasden Society and the Love Celibacy Society, plus of course, Cadet School and the aforementioned Hammond Organ Owners Society. He even joined the Samaritans, although his association with them proved to be extremely short-lived. All five of the people he spoke to on his first morning went on to commit suicide – and one of them was a wrong number, who phoned to check the cricket results! The event made the newspapers who, with their typical subtlety, christened the day 'Lemming Sunday', whilst Rimmer, disheartened, moved to pastures new.

In between all this, he had managed to keep in touch with his mother, albeit only by the occasional letter. As for his father . . . well, the only link he had to him was the Javanese camphorwood chest which was the only thing, other than his disapproval, that he had ever given to his youngest son – and even that now has a guitar-shaped hole in it, thanks to a certain D. Lister Esq!

To give him credit though, Rimmer just kept on trying. Despite suffering a life which, in his eyes, was plagued by bad luck, bad company and the wrong sort of background, he clung to his ambition: to become a Space Corps officer and to make his father proud of him. When he was unable to gain access to the Space Corps Academy, he joined the Jupiter Mining Corporation vessel *Red Dwarf* as a lowly third technician, convinced that he could take a few exams and climb the ranks that way. Eleven attempts at Engineering and thirteen at Astro-Navigation later, he was beginning to realise that it wouldn't be that easy. Indeed, after almost fifteen years of service, he had only four things to show for his efforts: his promotion to the dizzying heights of Second Technician (the second lowest rank on the ship), his bronze and silver swimming certificates, his collection of four medals (Three Years Long Service, Six Years Long Service, Nine Years Long Service and Twelve Years Long Service) and his unfortunate death thanks, in part, to his own inefficient repair to a drive-plate.

Thanks to Holly, he came back, his personality reduced to an algorithm and reproduced electronically. He still made life hell for his crewmates, dividing his time between such projects as the production of his own death video (complete with self-performed poetry readings), the arranging of *Starbug*'s alphabet soup supplies into alphabetical order and an impossible quest for alien beings that might fashion him a new body. Alas, the merest sign of an alien presence – or, indeed, of danger of any sort – was likely to send him cowering under a table with a collander on his head. Even he once confessed that the bravest thing he had ever done was setting fire to one Stinky Bateman's turn-ups in third-form prep. This doesn't stop him from visualising himself as a bold warrior, of course: it is simply another of his misfortunes that he has been reincarnated within the body of an abject coward. He can't stand the sight of blood (unless it's Lister's), he's particularly prone to stress-related disorders even in hologram form and he's no good at anything practical, as was proven in school when it took him five terms to make a tent-peg. Rimmer's primary contributions to the ongoing mission were the pernickety enforcement of Space Corps Directives and the changing of the blue/red alert bulb every so often. But, despite all that, there was still reason for hope.

Even Rimmer can know true love, as his dalliance with Nirvanah Crane showed. When he sacrificed his ideal life aboard the holoship *Enlightenment* for her sake, we saw a side of Rimmer that even he had never dreamt existed. And when faced with evil future versions of the *Starbug* crew, and only two choices – to surrender or to fight a suicidal battle against them – he discovered an untapped seam of courage within himself, announcing that he was 'better dead than smeg!' Perhaps his fortuitous encounter with Legion – who upgraded his intangible hologramatic form into a hard-light equivalent – had bolstered his reserves. But the catalyst that really brought Rimmer's better qualities to the fore was the second appearance in his life of his braver, smarter, more handsome other-dimensional equivalent, Ace Rimmer.

Arnold had never liked Ace: with his long hair and bacofoil

jacket, he looked like a reject from a Gay Pride disco, and he probably wore women's underwear too. But this Ace was one in a line of millions of Arnold Rimmers who had taken on the role of the dashing hero and given the multiverse hope – and he wanted Arnold to follow him. At first, Rimmer wasn't convinced. After years of failure, he had finally accepted that he would never amount to much. And yet so many other versions of himself had done it before him – and an encounter with an emotion-leeching emohawk had shown him that a burgeoning hero was within him, if only he could rid himself of his bitterness, negativity and snidiness. Arnold Rimmer left our universe in his new Ace persona, with all but Lister believing that he had died. But first, he attended his own funeral, at which he was posthumously promoted to first officer of *Red Dwarf* in recognition of his spectacular success in following Holly's original directives of keeping the last human being alive sane. Arnold Rimmer's third life was beginning, and only time will tell if this can be the one for which he has always longed.

CHRIS BARRIE began his performing career as an impressionist at the Comedy Store in London in early 1982. From then on, it was only a matter of time before his talents were spotted for both radio and television. On the former, he lent his voice to Rob Grant and Doug Naylor's creation Hab – Holly's forerunner – in *Son of Cliché*, while his debut on the latter was in Jasper Carrott's 1983 *Election Special*. More work with Carrott followed, as well as a long, successful stint on *Spitting Image*, giving voice to such luminaries as Ronald Reagan, George Bush and Prince Charles. Indeed, his work on this series ended only when a direct recording clash with *Red Dwarf V* prevented him from doing both. Chris originally read for the role of Lister in *Red Dwarf*, but was awarded that of its other major protagonist, Rimmer, instead. He has since shot to fame as Gordon Brittas – another unpleasant character with likable depths – on the BBC 1 sitcom, *The Brittas Empire*. He left *Red Dwarf* after only four episodes of its seventh series, but has expressed an interest in returning.

CAT

Full name: Cat (though if he had any need for a middle name he's sure it would be 'superficial').

He's vain and narcissistic; he's also selfish, self-centred and shallow. He possesses no tact whatsoever and he has an ego the size of a planet. But he is a cat, after all, and he considers these to be his best features.

Anyway, he has proved himself consistently useful to the *Red Dwarf* crew's mission: on at least two occasions in his lifetime, he has had plans taken up by the others, and his quivering nostril hairs can detect danger even through the void of space. He's an excellent pilot, and when something needs doing, you don't have to tell him twice. Well okay then, maybe you do.

If the Cat had any understanding of the concept of gratitude – which he most certainly doesn't – then he'd have Dave Lister to thank for his very existence. The race of Cat people to which he belongs evolved over the course of three million years in the cargo hold of *Red Dwarf* because Lister hid his unquarantined pregnant pet cat Frankenstein there, safely away from the Cadmium 2 radiation that killed the rest of the crew. As a species *Felis sapiens* is virtually indistinguishable from *Homo sapiens* – only the tell-tale fangs and six nipples give them away – though it's highly unlikely that the Cat would ever want to be mistaken for a human, or a 'monkey' as he sees them. Sadly it is more than likely that the Cat is the last survivor of his race. Religion proved to be the downfall of felinekind – they made the fatal mistake of worshipping Dave Lister, or Cloister the Stupid as they knew their God. The story of Cloister is revealed in the Cats' Holy Book, which tells of how Cloister was frozen in time, but would one day return to take his people to the promised land of Fuchal, and of The Holy Mother Frankenstein whose miraculous virgin birth spawned the Cat race. Like many myths it had a basis in truth, but the concept of heaven as a hot dog and doughnut diner sparked off a holy war that would last for thousands of years. One faction vehemently believed that red cardboard hats should be worn, the other thought they should be blue (ironically, the hats were in fact meant to be green). Eventually, after countless casualties on both sides, two arks were constructed to take the Cats to Fuchal. Believing that a laundry list used to line Frankenstein's basket was actually a star chart, the Cats in one ark were killed when their vessel collided with an asteroid. The other ark flew out into infinity never to be seen or heard from again. Only the sick and the lame remained on *Red Dwarf*, left there to die. In time Cat was born, to a cripple and an idiot. Cat had never suspected that his father was a jellybrain, but when he later found out, it at least explained why he'd eaten his own feet.

The Cat never had a formal education. He did attend Kitty School but, as there was no one else around, he had to teach himself there. This wasn't easy, as he knew nothing to start with. The lessons were long and slow, particularly on Thursdays when he had double nothing. However, he did learn how to read the Cat People's language of scents and how to break at least one of their Sacred Laws: the one that stated 'It is a sin to be cool'. The Cat never did have much time for a religion which, in deference to Cloister, rejected coolness in favour of slobbiness. Indeed when he did finally meet up with his 'God', Cat was decidedly unimpressed. After all, what kind of God would choose *that* face? And surely any deity worth his salt would be able to perform such a simple miracle as turning a bowl of Krispies into a woman.

In the days before Lister was brought out of stasis the Cat had the companionship of an old blind priest, but he much preferred to hang out with his own shadow which at least looked nice – he thought they made a good team. The Cat devoted all of his time to doing his favourite things – eating, sleeping, looking good, investigating things and making some of them his own with the aid of a scented spray (you can imagine what a cat would use to mark his territory with, but at least this cat bottled it first), and searching for sex. He never found any of course, there being no women on

Red Dwarf, but nevertheless he diligently slinked around the mining ship, armed with a megaphone and a bouquet of flowers, in an endless search for lady cats. If he'd believed for one minute that his quest was in vain he's sure he'd have gone crazy.

Life for the Cat changed considerably when Dave Lister was released from the stasis booth and Arnold Rimmer was resurrected as a hologram. In Lister he found a friend with whom he was able to waste time in a multitude of pointless pursuits like 'Durex Volleyball', 'Junior Angler' and 'Unicycle Polo'. Yet despite their friendship the Cat's nature prevented him from actually caring very much about his new buddy. On one occasion when Lister contracted a virulent form of flu, and as a result collapsed, the Cat left him lying in the corridor – though he obviously thought enough of the human not to steal his shoes. Rimmer, on the other hand, he took an almost instant dislike to and time has done little to change his opinion. However, the hologram did prove useful once, when the Cat discovered his all time best ever find in the whole of that particular day, and the find in question turned out to be the cigarette supply that Rimmer had thought safely hidden from his bunk mate. In return for keeping the location secret, Cat was given instructions on the working of the food dispenser. However, his initial – greed-motivated – fish binge resulted in a severe bout of food escape, but he did have the last laugh when he revealed to Lister where the cigarettes were anyway.

The Cat may not be all that bright – Commander Binks from the Holoship Enlightenment suggested that, as a race, *Felis sapiens* were about half as smart as the domestic cats they evolved from – but he certainly hates to be corrected, it really gets his feckles up. Despite his lack of brain power Cat does try now and again to come up with ideas for extracting himself and the others from tricky situations – everything from laser cannons to jet powered rocket pants – all highly inventive and all equally non-existent.

Kristine Kochanski once opined that the wall was more capable of formulating an intelligent opinion than he was.

That doesn't worry the Cat, though. He doesn't do the 'w' word if he can help it, and he resented even the small role he was forced to play when *Red Dwarf* was lost and its crew was cast adrift in *Starbug*. If he was meant to work, he'd be a dog! He would far rather be engaged in one of his nine or ten daily naps, which are essential if he is to have enough energy for his main snooze. His waking hours he likes to spend eating (either fish or chicken, perhaps the occasional mouse if he can catch one and indeed absolutely anything else unless it has been prepared by Lister), preening and attempting to fulfil his sole ambition of getting his end away. Naturally the Cat doesn't lack confidence, only women; he knows there can't be any female in the universe who wouldn't go for him or he'd have read about her in 'Ripley's believe it or not'. His body, he contends, is the sort that would make men wet and so, rather than leave it to medical science, he intends that it should go to the Louvre. Though it might sound as if the Cat is the unreliable type as far as women are concerned, that isn't strictly true and as soon as he finds the seven or eight that are right for him he'll be only too willing to settle down. In the meantime, he'll have to make do with a large amount of optimism and an equal number of fantasies and, judging by some of those, included in his harem would be Marilyn Monroe, a mermaid – top half fish, bottom half woman, naturally – and Wilma Flintstone. As for the rest, well, scanty-armour-clad Valkyries with cleavages you could ski down are a distinct possibility. Unfortunately the first time Cat actually did meet a real woman things didn't progress in the manner he'd anticipated. Although he knew he really wanted to do something to her, he just didn't know quite what it was.

Apart from female pussies (and himself) the great love of Cat's life is his collection of suits; he makes them all himself and even uses his tongue to launder them. If it were possible he'd like to have a wardrobe so massive that it crossed an international time zone, then he could easily make the thirty-six changes of clothes necessary in any given day, without fear of repetition. To say that being fashionable is vital to the

Cat is the understatement of the millennium; without style his life would have no meaning. He was shocked when he met his sandal wearing higher self; when the aesthete explained that he found clothes to be a distraction from the pursuit of spiritual and intellectual fulfilment, Cat responded with his own personal philosophy affirming that spiritual and intellectual fulfilment were a distraction from the pursuit of clothes. A prime example of the importance placed in remaining dapper at all times occurred when he badly injured his leg and was more worried about the red blood clashing with his apricot trousers than he was about his damaged limb; indeed when he learnt that there was a danger of gangrene setting in, he brightened – green with apricot, he could probably pull that off. One of the worst experiences of the Cat's life occurred when his body was 'borrowed' by Rimmer. If it wasn't bad enough seeing his prized possession being abused he also had to spend time trapped in 'Trans-am wheel arch nostril's' own comparatively unlovely holographic form. But it was an encounter with the Despair Squid and its hallucinogenic ink that proved to be a near fatal ordeal for the normally unshakable Cat. When it led him to believe that he wasn't the universe's coolest feline with a terminal case of sexual magnetism, but was actually the singularly uncool and unattractive Duane Dibbley with a penchant for white socks, bri-nylon shirts, cardigans and anoraks, the belief drove him to the point of suicide. Luckily the whole nightmarish incident was nothing more than a hallucination and the Cat too shallow to have sustained any lasting psychological harm. And once this minor fashion predicament was behind him Cat was easily able to resume his self-appointed *Red Dwarf* post as most handsome guy on the ship.

DANNY JOHN-JULES sees himself primarily as a musician, and has starred in many productions including *Starlight Express* and *Carmen Jones*. He even appeared in *Cats*, perhaps an omen of what was to come. Perhaps his most notable regular role (apart from the Cat) is that of Barrington in Tony Robinson's *Maid Marian and Her Merry Men*; however, he has also turned up in series from *Runaway Bay* to *The Bill*, and telefantasy shows such as *The Tomorrow People* and *The Demon Headmaster*. He certainly made an impression at his audition for *Red Dwarf*: he turned up in character and in costume, and showed his interviewers what had to be the definitive Cat there and then.

HOLLY

Full name: Holly.

Red Dwarf, a spaceship the size of a town, takes some running and that's where Holly, a tenth-generation AI hologrammic computer with an IQ of 6000 comes in, or at least he did once. Not even a computer as complex and sophisticated as Holly undoubtedly was when first constructed is impervious to the eroding ravages of time. Even before *Red Dwarf*'s three million year jaunt into endless space began, Holly was not new; already the Jupiter mining corporation had started fitting their vessels with eleventh-generation computers with IQs in the region of 8000. One such machine was Gordon, of the Scott Fitzgerald whose vast intellect made Holly seem like a mere abacus. Nevertheless, *Red Dwarf*'s dauntless computer was prepared to take on his brighter digital kinsman in a game of postal chess. Not surprisingly, Gordon fared better in the contest, but as only one move was ever actually made Holly did not disgrace himself with his own performance.

With *Red Dwarf* lethally contaminated with Cadmium 2 radiation, Holly had little option but to take the mining ship out of the solar system and away from where it could do any harm to humans. Since its sole surviving crew member was safely sealed in stasis Holly was entirely alone. For an ordinary computer, programmed simply to carry out the functions needed to keep the ship operational and not give it a lot of thought, several million years of solitary space travel

might not have caused too many problems. But for Holly –
not only in possession of Artificial Intelligence, but with an
almost human personality too – the loneliness and boredom
proved a little too much to bear. Indeed if it weren't for the
amusement provided by his collection of singing potatoes the
computer believes that he might well have gone insane. To
pass the time he read everything that was ever written. This
comprehensive knowledge enabled him to state with complete authority that the worst book ever written was *Football
– it's a funny old game* by Kevin Keegan. The novels of
Agatha Christie, however, did provide a certain amount of
pleasure. Such was their appeal that later on Holly decided to
have them erased from his memory banks so that he could
read them all again, though once they had been deleted he
wasn't sure why he'd actually made the request – he'd never
heard of Agatha Christie.

By the time the radiation levels had dropped sufficiently to
release Dave Lister from stasis, Holly had gone decidedly
peculiar. But even in this inferior state the new-found companionship of Lister and subsequently Rimmer and the Cat
was not capable of providing anything approaching either
intelligent or stimulating conversation. And so Holly busied
himself with further tedium relieving projects such as 'Hol
Rock', his innovative decimalised music, and compiling his
comprehensive A–Z of the Universe. Unfortunately his plan
to build a perfect replica of a woman capable of abstract
thought had to be abandoned when even the nose proved to be
too much of a challenge.

Despite his lack of brain power Holly was quite hurt by
the fact that *Red Dwarf*'s small crew considered him a
senile gibbering wreck only useful for telling the time. He
decided to teach them a lesson for not appreciating him more.
He devised Queeg 500, the mining ship's imaginary back-
up computer. At first the efficient Queeg seemed an ideal
replacement for Holly – who Rimmer considered ought to be
put out of his misery and blown away like a blind old
incontinent sheep dog. However, the harsh regime imposed
by the 'back up' soon became unpopular and Holly was

eagerly welcomed back into the fold, greatly pleased with the success of his massive 'jape'.

Back in favour once more, Holly was able to devote more time to getting everyone back to Earth. Travelling at the speed of light was not one of his favourite things and so, to avoid the navigational chaos that generally ensued, he developed the 'Holly Hop Drive', a device theoretically capable of instantaneous travel to anywhere in the universe. When the drive was put into operation, the others were convinced that the ship hadn't actually moved 'a smegging inch' but in fact it had traversed the fifth dimension into a parallel universe, a universe dominated by women. The experience of meeting his female counterpart, Hilly, proved a little too much for the crazed computer and he fell – appropriately enough – madly in love. Before this only a Sinclair ZX81 had put a spark in his circuits, but Hilly was the real thing and upon returning to his rightful universe Holly found he was unable to cope without her. His original countenance had been personally selected from the billions available because it resembled that of the greatest and most prolific lover who ever lived – although the bald pated middle-aged features prompted Rimmer to opine that he must have worked in the dark a lot – but Holly now decided to forego the face that had served him well for three million years and perform a head sex change on himself so that he might resemble his lost love, Hilly.

The operation was successful and he became a she, but although baldness was no longer a problem, computer senility certainly was. Her competence to run the mining ship properly was severely doubted in some quarters and not without some justification. There was the little incident with the auto-destruct sequence and the bomb and then there were the five black holes which turned out to be specks of grit on the scanner scope. It might also be worth mentioning the little problem with the DNA modifier but, as Holly herself pointed out, that was a mistake any deranged half-witted computer could make.

Things came to a head (no pun intended) when an ion

storm had rather an extreme effect on Holly's circuitry. As a consequence she could no longer even count without banging her head against the screen. Drastic measures needed to be taken and the thoughtful Kryten decided that an intelligence compression process was the desirable alternative. Unfortunately the operation, designed to restore the computer's IQ to its original 6000 at the cost of a reduction in operational run time, was a little too successful and it didn't take much of Holly's new IQ of 12,000 to work out that, with a remaining life span of just over three minutes, she'd better switch herself off. It was just lucky that as a consequence of sealing up a time spewing white hole the whole procedure never actually took place. The effects of the ion storm were negated too, so although Holly was no longer a genius who knew absolutely everything – from the meaning of life to the winners of the double in 1994 – her counting abilities were back to normal, including her longstanding blind spot with 7s and 2s.

One final reversion was in store for Holly, when nanites kidnapped *Red Dwarf* and discarded all excess matter from it. They repaired the computer's core program so that she became a he once again. Having done this, they decided that he was no use at all and ripped him out of the ship, abandoning him on a deserted planetoid. There he remained for several hundred years, until his former shipmates finally recovered him. Fortunately, this second enforced period of loneliness seems to have had little effect upon him, beyond the odd memory lapse. Restored to full command of *Red Dwarf*, he's back and ready to kick bottom.

NORMAN LOVETT began his career in comedy in his early thirties, performing his 'hang-dog' stand-up routine on the same bill as new wave bands such as 999 and the Clash. A stint in the Comedy Store followed, with television roles coming shortly thereafter. Before *Red Dwarf*, he appeared as Ruby Wax's floor manager in *Don't Miss Wax*, writing his own material for the part. Afterwards, he starred in his own BBC 2 series, *I, Lovett*. He initially auditioned for the part of Arnold Rimmer, but ended up playing the *Red Dwarf* computer instead. He left the role after two years, because the pressure of living in Edinburgh, rehearsing in London and filming in Manchester became too much. His replacement as Holly was HATTIE HAYRIDGE, who had already portrayed the computer's female equivalent in 'Parallel Universe'. Hattie had been a secretary for eight years, but she made an impromptu stage appearance at a comedy club when she couldn't stand it any more. The club's management were so impressed that they gave her an immediate booking, and she was soon to be seen performing a series of comic monologues on *Advice Shop*. She left *Red Dwarf* when its writers decided that Kryten's arrival had made Holly superfluous and wrote out the character for the sixth series. She still works primarily as a stand-up comedian, and she has recently released her autobiography, *Random Abstract Memory*. Finally, fan pressure forced a reconsideration of Holly's status, and Norman Lovett returned to the role in the final episode of the seventh series, 'Nanarchy'. Whether this return will be a permanent one is yet to be seen.

KRYTEN

Full name: Kryten 2X4B 523P.

He may be a pompous, ridiculous-looking, mother-hen-clucking, irascible buffoon – and he may have been voted 'the big-eared ugly one' by his own spare heads – but it's very unlikely that the *Red Dwarf* crew would have survived without the abilities, the intelligence and above all the domestic skills of their service mechanoid, Kryten. He is amply qualified for the job: he is a Bachelor of Sanitation, having studied – among other things – Lavatorial Sciences at Toilet University (Toilet University is actually a piece of software in his core programming, but he still had to do a written exam to prove it had been properly installed). He also served aboard the *Nova 5*, an Earth ship engaged in a stellar mapping mission, although the slight accident that resulted in the deaths of the crew could be seen as a hiccup in his resumé. Not that the passing away of Jane Air, Anne Gill and Tracey Johns stopped Kryten from performing his programmed functions. When Professor Mamet created the Series 4000/Series III androids in the twenty-fourth century (c.2340), she imbued them with an abiding belief in Silicon Heaven, an electronic afterlife in which they would someday find reward for their faithful and diligent service to humankind. But the real reason that Kryten performed his menial tasks with such enthusiasm, refusing to believe that his charges were now mere skeletons as he waited for someone to respond to the ship's distress beacon, was simply that he took great pleasure in them.

With only countless reruns of the soap opera *Androids* providing any respite, the mechanoid remained in a state of self-induced enslavement for countless millennia, until finally the distress call was heeded – by the crew of *Red Dwarf*. Despite the fact that none of his rescuers were actually doctors, Kryten was eventually persuaded that his decomposed mistresses were indeed dead. He was devastated, his artificial life no longer had any meaning; without masters the android philosophy 'I serve therefore I am' was no longer germane. The only option he could see was to activate his shut-down disc.

Kryten needn't have worried, however. Rimmer was only too glad to have someone other than the rebellious Skutters dance attendance to his every whim. The horrible hologram was more than willing to provide a duty list that would have taken even the most dynamic series 5000 a couple of centuries to complete, let alone a clapped-out antique like Kryten. The situation would have endured were it not for Lister's violent opposition to the concept of 'masters and servants'; he was determined that Kryten should become his own android, and so began the foundation course in advanced rebellion. It was a slow and difficult process but with the help of films such as *The Wild One*, *Rebel Without a Cause* and

Easy Rider, Kryten was able to break his programming and simulate some of the qualities he so admired in humans by becoming deceitful, unpleasant and offensive.

Apart from the escape he found in watching *Androids*, Kryten took delight in his down-time dreams – especially the one in which he had a garden of his own to nurture and watch grow. Now that he finally had his freedom there was nothing to stop him from making his desires become reality. On a space bike, borrowed from Lister, he set off in search of an S3 planet on which he could cultivate both his plants and his ambitions.

In the fields of hoovering and washing up Kryten was without equal, but the art of space bike riding was to prove a little too tricky for the novice droid cyclist. The bike collided with an asteroid and this time there was to be no lucky escape; Kryten's metal and plastic body was extensively damaged. Fortunately, after some time spent lying around in bits and pieces, the 'noid was once again salvaged by the *Red Dwarf* crew. Although Lister wasn't a fully qualified engineer and his attempts at repair would invalidate Kryten's guarantee, he did his utmost to restore the parts into a fully functional whole. The head was irreparable, but as the series 4000 is supplied complete with spares Lister simply fitted a replacement. Although managing to get the android into a state of working order, Lister's technical inexperience coupled with the severity of the crash made it impossible to re-create Kryten's original personality. His new traits were not too far removed from those of his old self, indeed if not for the freshly developed Canadian accent it's possible that no one would ever have noticed the difference.

One unfortunate side effect of the accident and subsequent repair was the undoing of many of Lister's instructions in dissent. He was forced to resume the lessons in lying and insubordination. Kryten found lying in particular difficult to come to terms with. In Lister's company he could manage it easily, but any attempt in the presence of others was futile until the act of being dishonest was required in order to save his own life. Despite the fact that their series 4000s had received the award for 'Android of the year' five times on the trot, Diva-Droid International were in business to make a profit. Sometime in the dim and distant past, Kryten had reached his expiry date and a replacement had been promptly dispatched from Earth. The model selected to take the place of the 'slow, stupid and ugly' Kryten was a Hudzen 10 – a highly advanced super android, programmed to become violent should his predecessor-to-be put up any resistance.

Kryten had no intention of presenting any opposition. When he learnt of Hudzen's imminent arrival, he was quite prepared to activate his shut-down disc, for he had served his human masters well and now had a lasting and peaceful existence in 'Silicon Heaven' – the afterlife machines were programmed to believe in – to look forward to. But at a surprise party thrown by the others, he discovered for the first time that the employment of time in a profitless and non-practical way really could be fun and he decided that he wanted to experience more of it. Although waking up with a 45 per cent dehydration level, a 2 per cent recall of the previous evening and a 91 per cent embarrassment factor – in other words a raging hangover – the mechanoid was determined not to be dismantled by his would-be replacement. And fortunately, the now quite deranged Hudzen was easily induced to crash and consequently shut down after hearing Kryten's 'untruthful' revelation that 'Silicon Heaven' was actually a myth.

However, Kryten needed to fall in love to discover that, in certain circumstances, lying could actually be a noble thing. When he first met Camille he believed that, like him, she was a series 4000 mechanoid – albeit the more upmarket GTi model with slide back sun roof head and realistic toes. They hit it off immediately, he loved the perfumed aroma of the WD40 on her neck hinges and she thought he made the most romantic calculations. The old cliché that 'love is blind' was certainly applicable in this instance for even after learning that Camille was actually a tentacled green blob, Kryten still thought she was cute. Of course he was no oil painting himself, resembling at best a huge, half-chewed, rubber-tipped pencil and at worst a novelty condom for the enormously endowed. Sadly, despite overcoming the problems inherent in mixed relationships, the affair was doomed to failure; the arrival of Camille's husband Hector was enough to terminate Kryten's short-lived stint in happiness mode. She was quite prepared to leave her amorphous spouse and remain on *Red Dwarf* with her android admirer, but Kryten knew it wasn't for the best. Without his wife at his side Hector would not have the resolve to complete his research into a cure for their condition, so Kryten lied once again in order that his love would leave him.

After learning both to enjoy life and to experience the emotion of love, Kryten had but one wish – to become human. Though he believed it to be an impossible goal, the discovery of a DNA modifier actually allowed him to realise his dream. Using the organic part of Kryten's brain as a blueprint, the highly advanced technological device was able to transform the android into a fully functional flesh and blood human. Ironically, Kryten's new features resembled those of Jim Reaper, the Diva-Droid employee who had once described him as ugly.

Despite relishing his new-found humanity, Kryten was disappointed with the accompanying body. Particularly unsatisfactory were the eyes. He'd always been extremely fond of his old 579s with the automatic 15F stop corneas and the new ones not only didn't have a zoom function but couldn't even manage quantel. But it was the overlarge and ugly appendage that suddenly appeared in the vicinity of his old groinal socket that really disgusted him, especially as it refused to behave itself when he was reading an electrical appliance catalogue. Kryten had a problem: although he looked human, his thought processes were still those of a mechanoid. Making the most important decision of his life he elected to return to his mechanical form.

It was a more confident Kryten that emerged from the operation. Thanks to Lister's influence he was no longer the guilt-ridden slave that he had been assembled to be. He had broken his programming to such an extent that he was able to take his place with the others of the *Red Dwarf* crew as an equal, although admittedly a significantly more intelligent, resource-ful and capable equal. In time he would even overcome his deep-rooted belief in the falsehood of 'Silicon Heaven'.

One incident did shake his belief system though, when his master Dave Lister turned out to be an earlier model android and technically inferior to him. After years of scrubbing out gussets and offering to pointlessly sacrifice his own life for the crew's sake, the revelation was almost too much to bear, and Kryten took out his bitterness by turning his one-time icon into a downtrodden slave. When he discovered that the whole thing was an illusion caused by *Starbug* passing through a pocket of unreality, he had a lot of apologising to do.

More recently, the balance of power has been upset again by the arrival of the high-ranking and extremely capable Kristine Kochanski. Her arrival filled Kryten with unfamiliar feelings of resentment. The crew of the *Nova 5* had left him, and before that those of the SS *Augustus* had died of old age. Now he feared that Lister too would be lost to him, stolen by this woman with all the in-and-out bits that he likes so much. As a result, Kryten became very bitter and irascible towards the new crew member, particularly when she 'borrowed' his friends to go off gallivanting in Artificial Reality. An incident involving ketchup on lobster was the final straw: Kryten's nega-drive, the repository of all his negative emotions, was overfilled and his head exploded. Although repaired, he was distraught to learn in the process that Professor Mamet had created the entire 4000 series of mechanoids as caricatures of John Warburton, a fellow bio-engineer who had jilted her the day before their wedding (Warburton used to allow his nega-tive emotions to build until he blew his top, too). Kryten was ridiculous because he had been designed to be ridiculous. However, with Lister's encouragement, he began to accept that, by breaking his programming, he has managed to evolve beyond a joke. He has even begun to appreciate Kochanski more, since she saved Lister from the epideme virus. Kryten's growth as an emotional being continues. But he still has a head shaped like a novelty condom.

* * *

Kryten was originally played by DAVID ROSS, who has appeared in a multitude of series from *Coronation Street* to *Leave it to Charlie* to *Yanks Go Home* to the acclaimed drama serial *GBH*. He has worked extensively at the National Theatre and earned a certain amount of notoriety for appearing nude on stage throughout Alan Bleasdale's play *Having a Ball*. He was introduced to Rob Grant and Doug Naylor while working in radio, and later recruited into the *Red Dwarf* team. Rob and Doug were impressed by his performance in his debut episode, 'Kryten', and decided to make him a regular for the following season. However, David was appearing in *A Flea in Her Ear* at the Old Vic and was unavailable. He did return eventually, to play Talkie Toaster in 'White Hole' – but in the meantime, a new mechanoid was needed. The producer Paul Jackson had seen ROBERT LLEWELLYN playing a robot in *Mammon, Robot Born of Woman* during the 1988 Edinburgh Festival, and suggested him for the job. Robert had made his debut as both a writer and an actor during the early eighties, when he joined a theatre company called the Joeys. His more recent credits include a series of comedy lectures which started with 'The Reconstructed Heart', two autobiographies and a book called *Therapy and How to Avoid It*, which he co-wrote with Nigel Planer. He also guest-starred in Craig Charles's Channel 4 sitcom *Captain Butler* and was the only member of the *Red Dwarf* cast to appear in the ill-fated pilot episodes of the proposed American series. However, he sees himself more as a writer than as an actor: he even co-wrote the *Red Dwarf* episode 'Beyond a Joke', with Doug Naylor.

KOCHANSKI

Full name: Kristine Kochanski (although she may have a middle name beginning with Z).

Kochanski isn't like her shipmates. In fact, that's putting it mildly. She's bright, intelligent and witty. She likes opera and knows her cheeses, she eats low-fat yoghurt and thinks that crystalline formations are 'faberoo', and her jokes are about things like the third-largest city in Vietnam and Bath in the nineteenth century. She actually remembers things from school and her greatest accomplishment definitely isn't a line on a loo wall somewhere marking her highest ever pee. A more unlikely addition to the motley crew of *Red Dwarf* could scarcely be imagined – and indeed, given half a chance, she'd leave it like a shot. Kochanski does have at least one thing in common with Dave Lister, though: she is the last human being alive in the universe. Her universe, that is. Kochanski's dimension is very much like ours, but there are one or two variations. For a start, she looks quite different from the Kristine Kochanski whom our Lister once loved and lost (though he fancies her like mad anyway). She doesn't even have a Scottish accent, although she was brought up in the Gorbals, the trendiest part of Glasgow (Rimmer had always considered her counterpart in this universe to be a 'snooty cow').

As a child, she was spoilt rotten. Her rich parents forked out the cash to buy her a pony – Trumper – and to send her to Cyberschool for eleven years. Here, she was given the best possible education from Artificial Reality teachers and she formulated many close Artificial Reality friendships. Kochanski's idea of a good time was conversing with the Bennett family in an AR simulation game called Pride and Prejudice World. She went on to Cadet School and finally joined the Space Corps (studying astro-glaciers in her first year) as an upwardly mobile young officer. And she found herself serving as the navigation officer on board the Jupiter Mining Corporation vessel *Red Dwarf*. It was here that she met Dave Lister – the Dave Lister of her dimension, that is, although at this point he seems to have been very much like his counterpart here. They enjoyed a brief relationship, which Kochanski broke off when she decided she couldn't spend her entire life hanging out in her boyfriend's bunk eating delivery curries and having fantastic sex. She had gone out with him on the rebound anyway, and she now went back to her previous partner, a chef named Tim.

There was still a spark there, though – and this, combined with Kochanski's guilt over hiding from Lister behind a 'Dear John' note, motivated her into meeting him in the locker room as he returned from planet leave on Mimas. This decision was to cause the most crucial divergence between her reality and ours. As Kochanski made her apologies, Lister's pet cat Frankenstein put in an unscheduled appearance – and, as an officer, she was clear about her duty. She had to confiscate the dangerous animal and disintegrate it. But, deep down, Kochanski had always been a bit of a softie – films like *Gone With the Wind* and *Now Voyager* had always made her cry – and, when it came down to it, she couldn't do the deed. She hid Frankenstein instead. And so it was that, when the ship's computer Holly detected the presence of the cat, it was Kochanski and not Lister who was blamed and sentenced to eighteen months in stasis. And it was Kochanski, not Lister, who emerged from the cubicle an incredible three million years later to find herself entirely alone in the universe. Holly chose to keep Kochanski sane by resurrecting her old flame, Lister, as a hologram, and this proved to be a wise choice. The experience of existing only in an intangible form forced this Lister to become more caring and sensitive. He eventually turned into the kind of man who enjoyed shopping for shoes and talking about relationships, and Kochanski realised that she loved him now more than ever. He didn't even care that she made a sound like a rusty gate when she was making love. To her, he was the human equivalent of a pot of cottage cheese with pineapple chunks in it: gorgeous. But then it all went wrong. Investigating a dimensional tear, Kochanski and her crew came face to face with their parallel-universe counterparts, and a sudden attack by a GELF ship sundered the linkway and left her stranded on the wrong side of non-space. Suddenly, Kochanski had swapped the comfort of her own refined lifestyle for a version of *Starbug* which resembled a big skip with thrusters, and on which she didn't even like to breathe in. Not only was shopping no longer an option, but even a decent bath was difficult to come by. She was forced to take showers.

To give Kochanski her due, she did try to fit in. She even learnt what 'off-side' was – and she introduced her new shipmates to Pride and Prejudice World, although her attempts to acquaint them with the complexities of opera-based games fell rather flat. But how could she ever completely belong on a ship where the fourth most popular pastime was watching her knickers going around in the laundry room? Apart from having to deal with the under-stimulated libido of a slobby, uncouth version of Dave Lister (his version of Kochanski was no longer any good to him, unless he needed her to grit paths with in the snow), she had to suffer the jealousy of the android Kryten, who considered her a bossy old trollop and was terrified that she would lure his master away from him with her curvy in-and-out bits. Kochanski had to put up with numerous pernickety lectures on the proper place of the salad cream bottle (the fridge, apparently, rather than the cupboard) and the importance of not putting pants in the sock drawer.

Despite all this, Kristine Kochanski has consistently proved herself to be the most capable and resourceful person on board either *Starbug* or the recently recovered *Red Dwarf* (not a difficult feat, admittedly). Her skill in rescuing Kryten from the hands of a rogue Simulant was not fully appreciated at the time, and the Cat has trouble working out what she's talking about on most occasions. But her plan to save Lister's life from the epideme virus was positively inspired, and even Kryten had to admit that she wasn't just 'a bit of a madam' after that. As she settles into a life that she wouldn't have chosen, and slowly gains the respect of her fellows, Kochanski is becoming perhaps the most valuable member of the mission. But still she has one eye ever open for the dimensional tear which will lead her back to her home, her boyfriend and her life.

The first Kochanski was played by Altered Image's former lead singer, CLAIRE GROGAN. However, her foray into acting was complicated by the fact that a Clare Grogan was already on Equity's books, and Claire was forced to appear as C. P. Grogan (her middle name is Patricia). She remembers turning up for her first make-up session, only to find a photograph of her namesake on the mirror! She is now more commonly seen as herself on such shows as *Never Mind the Buzzcocks*, but she still gets a lot of fan attention from *Red Dwarf* despite appearing in only a few scenes. When the decision was taken to include Kochanski as a regular, Doug Naylor chose to give the part to a more experienced actress, and to alter the character so that she would fit more neatly into the established team. CHLOE ANNETT had appeared in such series as *Byker Grove*, *Cadfael*, *The Ruth Rendell Mysteries* and *Jeeves and Wooster* during her six years in acting, and *Red Dwarf* was only one of the two leading telefantasy roles in which she made debuts in 1997. The other was, ironically, a character named Holly, as whom she starred alongside Michael French in the BBC's semi-SF cop show, *Crime Traveller*.

SECTION THREE:

SHIP'S
LOG

RED DWARF I

It was something of a minor miracle that *Red Dwarf* ever got made at all. After sitting on the pilot script for three years the BBC eventually commissioned a full series in 1986. With five further scripts delivered, rehearsals began; two days into rehearsal there was a BBC electricians' strike. Expecting the strike to be a short-run thing, the production team continued with the rehearsing schedule, with the assumption that the delayed episodes could be slotted in elsewhere in the recording run. Eventually it became apparent that that wouldn't be the case: *Red Dwarf* was put on indefinite hold. It would be six months before the BBC gave the go-ahead for the production to be remounted.

The first episode of *Red Dwarf* was broadcast on BBC 2 on 15 February 1988. It wouldn't be unfair to say that the series was not a massive overnight success, at least in the opinion of the press reviewers. The early episodes were slower-paced than now and concentrated more on the relationship between Lister and Rimmer. Viewed in retrospect – with the personalities of the protagonists now familiar – season one is funnier and more entertaining than it might have seemed at the time. Some of the production values were disappointing: the sets in particular were rather cheap and tacky; and the uniforms were very basic, consisting of simple cotton shirts and trousers. On the plus side, Peter Wragg's effects were superb as was Howard Goodall's music – especially the closing theme, sung by Jenna Russell.

Appearing only on a very semi-regular basis in the show's early days was Kristine Kochanski played by C. P. Grogan.

Regulars: Rimmer – Chris Barrie. Lister – Craig Charles. Cat – Danny John-Jules. Holly – Norman Lovett. Written by Rob Grant and Doug Naylor. Produced and directed by Ed Bye. Developed for television by Paul Jackson Productions.

1: THE END

Broadcast date: 15 February 1988.

Guest cast: Robert Bathurst (Todhunter), Paul Bradley (Chen), David Gillespie (Selby), Mac McDonald (Captain Hollister), Robert McCulley (McIntyre), Mark Williams (Peterson – spelling later changed), C. P. Grogan (Kochanski).

Introducing Dave Lister and Arnold Rimmer – work-mates and room-mates on the mining ship *Red Dwarf*, with the only drawback being that they can't stand each other. Lister just wants to slob around and enjoy George McIntyre's funeral – and his subsequent welcome back party as the ship's computer, Holly, resurrects his mind in a hologramatic body. Rimmer on the other hand is cramming for an important exam – yet another attempt at passing Engineering. Sadly, neither of their plans are to come to fruition. Even as Rimmer is being carried out of the examination room on a stretcher after a nervous breakdown, Lister is summoned to see Captain Hollister. Holly has discovered the unquarantined cat that he has smuggled on board. Lister is given a choice: hand over Frankenstein, or spend the remaining eighteen months of the voyage in stasis. To him, it is no choice at all – the cat remains at liberty and Lister is frozen in time. However, Lister's incarceration has unexpected consequences. Unaccompanied on his maintenance rounds, Rimmer makes a mistake which ultimately causes a massive leak of Cadmium 2 radiation. The entire crew of the ship is killed with only one exception. Shielded from the radiation in stasis, Lister survives and is awakened by Holly when the danger is over. Unfortunately, this is some three million years later, during which time *Red Dwarf* has been heading directly away from Earth. If he is to survive the voyage home, Lister needs somebody to keep him sane. Holly is capable of sustaining only one hologram at a time, and for reasons best known to himself, he chooses to resurrect Arnold Rimmer. Lister's sanity is perhaps more truly saved, however, by the presence of a third person on the ship. Safely sealed in the hold, Frankenstein has given birth to a litter – and over the last three million years, the species has evolved. What confronts Lister and Rimmer now is an example of *Felis sapiens*: a humanoid Cat, from a race which worships Lister – or rather, Cloister the Stupid – as its God. Lister's destiny is clear. He may have been deprived of the love of Kristine Kochanski and of his dream of a farm on Fiji, but he still has his cat, and now he's the deity of an entire race. So the Earth can look out . . . Lister's on his way home!

- The original pilot script described Lister as being forty-one years old, and Holly – quite prophetically – as female. These details were changed during casting. Less significantly, perhaps, Lister was to have spent seven billion years in stasis (instead of a comparatively conservative three million) and George McIntyre's funeral song was not 'See Ya Later Alligator', but rather 'Heaven is Ten Zillion Light Years Away' by Stevie Wonder. The number of crew members on *Red Dwarf* was established as 129 rather than 169 (but, as this changed in 'Justice' anyway, it hardly seems to matter), and a scene in which Lister performed 'funerals' for his crewmates was dropped.
- Craig Charles was alarmed to discover a testicle peering out of his pants during the scene in which he feeds Frankenstein; fortunately, an earlier – albeit slightly inferior – take was available for use.
- The Cat's pink suit – his main costume for the first series – is seen for the first time. 'That was copied from an old suit of

my father's, that he got married in,' says Danny John-Jules. 'Originally, when the designs first came out, they weren't really right for my character, so I brought one of my suits in to let them have a look at it. It was roomier, with more of an outrageous cut.' The original, however, was in black. 'I personally wouldn't dress like [the Cat],' Danny confides, 'but I think he is the best-dressed person on television.'

- Rob Grant and Doug Naylor were disappointed with the *Red Dwarf* sets, and particularly with the uniform-grey colour scheme, which even encompassed lager cans and cigarette packets. In retrospect, though, Doug says: 'The fact that the series looked so cheap and the sets were wobbly and it was all grey actually won us a lot of friends, because people felt sorry for it. I think if we'd gone into it all hi-tech and glossy, we might have gone down the toilet right there and then.'

2: FUTURE ECHOES

Broadcast date: 22 February 1988.

Guest cast: John Lenahan (Toaster), Tony Hawks (Dispensing Machine).

As Holly turns *Red Dwarf* around and heads back towards Earth, strange things begin to happen. The mirror reveals images of events that haven't yet occurred and a photograph inexplicably shows Lister with twin sons. The explanation for what is happening is simple – or at least, according to Holly it is. The ship has broken the light barrier and as a consequence, the crew are seeing random future echoes – images of things that are yet to come. Things take an ominous turn when, in one such vision, Rimmer sees Lister die horribly in an accident in the drive room. He is actually quite amused by this turn of events, and he takes pleasure in assuring his companion that the future cannot be changed. Of course, Lister has to try. Having seen the Cat break a tooth in one of the echoes, he sets his mind to preventing the injury, thus changing the course of the future. Too late, he realises the accident's cause. He tackles the Cat in an effort to prevent him from sinking his teeth into one of his robot goldfish and the ensuing fall actually causes the mishap he had hoped to prevent. The future seems inevitable – and never more so than when Holly announces that there is an emergency in the drive room. Come in number 169, your time is up. But Lister is determined to meet his fate kicking and screaming. Nobody then is more surprised than he when the emergency is diverted without the fatal consequences that were predicted. A version of Lister from the far future sheds some light on the situation. The man who Rimmer saw die in the drive room was actually Bexley, one of Lister's sons – and Lister himself certainly has plenty more years left in him. As for Rimmer's future, well, he isn't letting on about that. So that just leaves one more conundrum. How, with no women on board the ship, does Lister get twin sons? He doesn't know, but he's certainly looking forward to finding out.

- Doug Naylor, in particular, was keen on varying the 'dull' end credits wherever practical. This episode features the first such variation, as we see Lister's photograph of his own future self with twins slowly developing over the customary shot of *Red Dwarf*'s scoop.
- Lister's access code for the food machine is RD52169. In later episodes, he offers the codes 169–12–14–16 ('Balance of Power') and 000169 ('The Inquisitor') for other uses, all indicating that – as there were 169 people aboard *Red Dwarf* (at least, at this point in the series) – he is the lowest of them bar none.
- In retrospect, Rob Grant and Doug Naylor weren't happy with Lister's casual acceptance of his future son's death. When they adapted portions of this episode into their first novel, they reserved the unpleasant fate in the drive room for a grandson instead, to make it one step more distant. Even so, they chose never to mention the incident again in either format.

- Dave Lister's oft-mentioned twin sons, Jim and Bexley, are seen for the first and only time. 'Those babies wouldn't stop crying,' complains Craig Charles, 'and one was sick all down my arm. And the other one pissed in my hand!' As a result, he had to improvise the line, 'Stop crying and say cheese, boys!'

3: BALANCE OF POWER

Broadcast date: 29 February 1988.

Guest cast: Rupert Bates (Trout la Crème and Chef), Paul Bradley (Chen), David Gillespie (Selby), Mark Williams (Peterson), C. P. Grogan (Kochanski).

Rimmer is relishing his new-found position as the senior officer on board *Red Dwarf*, despite the fact that Lister is determined not to actually obey him. Rimmer's solution is to take hostage every cigarette on the ship, promising to return one for every day that his subordinate follows orders. However, that is certainly not the only bone of contention between the two. Lister is unhappy with Rimmer's presence altogether, and wonders why Holly couldn't have re-created somebody he actually liked. Kristine Kochanski would have been ideal, he decides, but in this too, Rimmer blocks his desires. After all, Holly can only sustain one hologram at a time, and there's certainly no way he's allowing Lister to turn him off and bring Kochanski back. Apart from anything else, he fears he would never be turned back on again – and he's probably right. So the hologram disks, like the cigarettes, have been removed to a safe place. Eventually, Lister hits upon the answer. All he has to do to get his own way is to become Rimmer's superior. Unlike himself, Rimmer has a moral code that will force him to obey the every wish of an officer, even if that officer be Dave Lister. Rimmer of course is hardly worried. After all, if he couldn't pass his Engineering exams and become a Space Corps officer, what hope could Lister have? Every hope, as it turns out – for Lister has no intention of passing the Engineering exams at all. He is studying to become a chef – the easiest exam available, but one which will result nevertheless in automatic promotion. Holly duly sets the exam and Rimmer can only watch as the balance of power looks set to alter. Finally, it is all too much for Rimmer. Even as the exam commences, Lister's heart's desire arrives in the teaching room. It is Kristine Kochanski, in hologram form at least. Rimmer has given in. Or has he? Lister becomes suspicious when 'Kochanski' tells him that she doesn't really like him at all and that she would never dream of going out with him. It doesn't take him too long to work out that, although this is Kochanski's body in front of him, Rimmer has tampered with the hologram disk so that his own mind is in there. Lister continues with the exam, the attempt at distraction having failed, and Rimmer looks on worriedly as the computer delivers the results. With an ecstatic yell, Lister reveals that he has passed.

- BBC executives were hardly the biggest fans of science fiction in 1988, and Rob Grant and Doug Naylor had sold *Red Dwarf* to them as a 'sitcom in space', toning down the SF elements. 'Balance of Power', with its focus on the relationship between Lister and Rimmer, is perhaps the best example of what they originally intended the series to be like. It was only with the success of episodes such as 'Future Echoes' (recorded fourth but broadcast second) that *Red Dwarf* really began to spread its wings.
- This episode has an unusual 'cliffhanger' ending, as Lister claims to have passed a chef's exam which would make him Rimmer's superior and change the entire structure of the programme. However, Holly's introduction to the following episode makes it (belatedly) clear that he was lying.
- *Red Dwarf*'s most frequent guest star makes his first 'appearances' here, as Tony Hawks provides the voices of a dispensing machine and the bunk-room toilet (the latter uncredited). As the studio warm-up man at the time, Tony was always on hand for such roles: he reprised his dis-

pensing-machine part in 'Waiting for God' and recorded a voiceover for the cinema scenes in 'Me²' (both uncredited again), before appearing in the flesh as the guide to 'Better Than Life', a compère on 'Backwards' Earth and a waxdroid of Caligula ('Meltdown'). Perhaps most bizarrely, he also voiced a talking suitcase in 'Stasis Leak'. 'For the first series,' Tony recalls, 'the others referred to me as the "fifth Dwarfie", because of my many contributions.'

4: WAITING FOR GOD

Broadcast date: 7 March 1988.

Guest cast: Noel Coleman (Cat Priest), John Lenahan (Toaster).

Okay, so Lister was lying about passing the chef's exam, but any notions of a resit have now been driven from his mind. The Cat has been teaching him how to read the books of his people, their language being made up of a system of differing scents. Now, Lister is ready for the big challenge – the Cat Bible, which tells the full story of the Cat race. Lister is able to confirm what Cat originally told him. He is Cloister the Stupid, the Cat People's God – and he is appalled when he learns of the killing that has been done in his name. He discovers that thousands of Cats were slain during millennia of Holy Wars, simply over the colour of the cardboard hats in his proposed Hot Dog and Doughnut Diners on Fuchal. And what saddens Lister most of all is that both sides were wrong. Rimmer, meanwhile, is somewhat less than interested in Lister's problems. Holly has picked up an Unidentified Object, and Rimmer is convinced that it is the product of alien science. The Quagaars, as he calls his imaginary alien race, will doubtless extend the hand of friendship – and they'll probably give him a new body too. In reality, the pod is something quite different, as Lister has already surmised. Dismissing it from his thoughts, he delves more deeply into the history of the Cats, discovering that his every word to his pet cat Frankenstein has been corrupted through generations of the Cat race. He is particularly saddened when he learns of the deaths of half the Cat People, who left *Red Dwarf* to look for Fuchal, using one of his old laundry lists as a star chart. If only he owned more than one pair of underpants, a tragedy might have been averted. The rest of the Cats, apparently, have now also left the ship, leaving behind only the sick and the lame. The Cat that Lister is already familiar with is the son of two of these people, and as such is the last of his race to live on the ship. Well, almost. In fact, there is one other Cat on board – a blind old priest, dedicated to the service of Cloister, and now on his death-bed. Taking pity on him, Lister ensures that his lifetime of belief is finally rewarded. He enacts Cloister's 'second coming', even as the priest finally dies. With that drama over, Lister is able to turn his attention to the Unidentified Object – and just in time. He has the pleasure of being present as Rimmer finally realises that the object is, in fact, nothing more than one of *Red Dwarf*'s own garbage pods.

- Rimmer's voice interrupts the closing titles, with his realisation that the 'Quagaar ship' is in fact 'a smegging garbage pod'. This was a last-minute idea of Doug Naylor's, which was added to the show in post-production.
- For the first and only time, we see another Cat Person. Following the priest's death, it is suggested that our Cat is the sole survivor of his race, though the way is left open for more of his kin to appear in the future. Rob Grant and Doug Naylor once tackled the issue of what happened to the remaining felines in novel form, but decided to remove the chapter before publication. The idea is still on the shelf for possible future use on screen.
- This was the third episode recorded and it marked the first time that Norman Lovett, as Holly, actually appeared before the cameras. 'I was offered the part of Holly and I took it because I needed the work,' Norman tells us, 'but I was quite upset because it was only a voiceover, and I was complaining

every week. I said "I know how Holly can look on the screen." So, during the recording of the third episode, they went back and did my bits [from the first two episodes] again, and from then on it was a visual thing.' It wasn't until 'Me^2', however, that he was able to actually appear in the main bunk-room set.

5: CONFIDENCE AND PARANOIA

Broadcast date: 14 March 1988.

Guest cast: Lee Cornes (Paranoia), Craig Ferguson (Confidence).

Since coming out of stasis, Lister has been longing for the day when he could finally visit Kochanski's sleeping quarters. In particular, he wishes to view her dream recorder, just to check if she ever dreamt about him. Now, finally, that day has come. The radiation has been cleared from the officers' block and his journey of discovery may commence – or so he believes. In fact, Rimmer is a little behind schedule in that department, and by entering the still contaminated zone, Lister has subjected himself to forces unknown. Soon, for no apparent reason, it is raining herrings in the bunk room – something which delights the Cat no end – and when the Mayor of Warsaw spontaneously combusts in the corridor, Rimmer theorises that something must be wrong. Medical tests show that Lister has contracted a mutated strain of the pneumonia virus. The effect of this is that he is having hallucinations, which are being made startlingly real. And there is worse to come. Lister and his old friend Chen had always theorised that a person's mind is made up of two opposing forces – his Confidence, which urges him forward to achieve things, and his Paranoia, which holds him back and points out what could go wrong. The virus latches on to those images and makes them solid, manifesting Lister's Confidence and his Paranoia in human form. Quite naturally,

Confidence immediately wins Lister over with his incessant compliments, making him believe he can do anything he wants to. Meanwhile, Paranoia seems to have found an ally in Rimmer – after all, their opinions of Lister are very much the same. But Rimmer has seen both men for what they really are – germs created by the infection. He tries to persuade his companion to help him dispose of them but, spurred on by his Confidence, Lister refuses to listen to reason.

Rimmer's problems intensify when Confidence's support actually begins to have a positive effect upon Lister's mental processes. Not only is he able to work out how Holly can temporarily generate two holograms at once, he is also able to locate the personality disks hidden by Rimmer. At last, he will be able to bring back his lost love, Kristine Kochanski. Things take a nasty turn however, when Confidence murders Paranoia and is on the verge of persuading Lister that he can breathe in space without an oxygen mask. Coming to his senses, Lister refuses to give in without a struggle, and eventually it is Confidence himself who suffers the fate in store for anybody attempting such an action. Lister has to admit that Rimmer was right. But still, the episode has had its advantages. Lister attempts to restore Kochanski to hologramatic life – but Rimmer still has one more trick up his sleeve. He has shuffled the disks about in their boxes, so that when the second hologram forms, it is not Kochanski at all – but a second Arnold Rimmer!

- Kochanski's hologrammic projection box (presumably a forerunner of the more sophisticated light bee) is labelled 'Kochanski, C. Z.', suggesting that her first name should be spelt 'Christine'. However, although no evidence to the contrary is seen on screen, she is referred to as Kristine in all scripts, novels and spin-off publications, so it is perhaps easiest to assume that this is the correct variant.
- The Cat is seen 'marking his territory' with a perfume-like spray, for the first time (he later did the same thing in the alternative *Red Dwarf* of 'Parallel Universe'). The writers' intention was that the spray should contain urine, but they

decided not to make any specific reference to this.

- Originally the final episode of the first series, 'Confidence and Paranoia', would have concluded with the return of Kochanski in hologramatic form. However, an earlier script – in which Rimmer went insane and stole body parts from Lister in the hope of building a new body for himself – was deemed unworkable. Rob and Doug took advantage of the delay in filming to rework the ending of this episode so that it led into the newly scripted 'Me²'.

- Lee Cornes didn't need to audition for the part of Paranoia. Having worked with Ed Bye before on *The Young Ones*, he had been under serious consideration to play Rimmer and was asked to do this instead when that part went to Chris Barrie. 'I remember being pretty horrible to Craig Ferguson at the time,' he confesses, 'and I would like to apologise in print!'

6: ME²

Broadcast date: 21 March 1988.

Guest cast: Mac McDonald (The Captain).

There are two Rimmers on board – and life is now doubly hell for poor Lister. There are some advantages, though. He certainly doesn't complain when Rimmer leaves their shared bunk room to move in with his counterpart. Indeed, the move has its definite pluses, particularly when it unearths a certain video tape that Rimmer has been keeping hidden. A tribute to Arnold Rimmer, the video features Holly's recording of his death, preceded by an over-long eulogy (including poetry readings) narrated by the man himself. Lister's curiosity is aroused when he learns that Rimmer's dying words were 'Gazpacho Soup!' but the man's personal diary fails to shed any light on the subject. November 25 is marked as 'Gazpacho Soup Day', but no explanation is provided. Lister's curiosity has to be put to one side when Holly announces the arrival of a fighter ship belonging to the Norweb Federation. Apparently, Lister left a light on in his bathroom when he left Earth over three million years ago – and they want payment. In fact, the whole thing is a joke on Holly's part, but in the meantime, Rimmer's problems have become only too real. It seems that he is incapable of getting on even with himself, and the arguments between the two Arnolds soon reach ridiculous proportions. Lister decrees that one of them has to go, and both Rimmers agree. What they don't agree on is which it is to be. Lister makes a random selection – and it is the original Rimmer who loses out. With nothing to lose, and drunk from his final round of computer generated drinks, Rimmer is easily persuaded to tell Lister all about Gazpacho Soup Day. That day, he says, should have been the happiest of his life. He had been invited to dine at the Captain's table and, hoping to impress the officers, had sent back his first course – Gazpacho Soup – because it was cold. He had later discovered that it should have been served cold, and that the officers' laughter he had thought directed at the chef had in fact been targeted at him. He has never lived down the humiliation of that moment, and blames his subsequent lack of success upon it. For his part, Lister is almost sympathetic but the emotion doesn't last. He gleefully reveals that he has in fact already switched off Rimmer's double, and that the whole charade has just been a ruse to prise the secret of the soup from him. Still, Lister swears not to say a word on the subject again – but very soon discovers that the temptation to break that promise is just far too great.

- A few snippets of Lister's favourite cartoon – *Mugs Murphy* – were created especially for this episode. Lister wears a *Mugs Murphy* T-shirt, with the caption 'D-D-Don't Shoot!' (and continues to be seen in multicoloured variants of same throughout the second series). Rob Grant and Doug Naylor had intended the show to feature regularly, and had even considered a storyline in which its title character was brought to life. In the end, though, they realised that having the crew refer to more familiar icons (Wilma Flintstone,

Marilyn Monroe), while less realistic in a future setting, would be better for viewer identification.

- Rimmer's infamous gazpacho-soup incident was based on a real-life experience of the writers', who were served that very dish at a meeting in the boardroom of Thames Television and weren't sure why it was stone-cold. Unlike their creation, though, Rob and Doug didn't send the soup back.

- Mac McDonald appears in a brief flashback as Captain Hollister, but the actor didn't need to return to the studio as this was recorded alongside his scenes in 'The End'. 'I fit into that kind of role quite easily really,' Mac admits, 'that kind of scruffy, scabby starship captain.'

RED DWARF II

Although *Red Dwarf* had lost around 2 million viewers during the course of its first run of episodes, the BBC decided to continue with a further series. The reasons for their faith in the project were twofold: first, they had received many letters and calls praising the show, and secondly the Audience Appreciation Index (A1) was in the 80s (out of a possible 100). Reputedly only the Queen's Coronation in 1954 had fared better. Stylistically, the second series of *Red Dwarf* was much the same as its predecessor. Two of its episodes, however, provided something of a preview of the developments to follow. The series opener 'Kryten' featured the debut of the eponymous Series 4000 Mechanoid, played here by David Ross, while Hattie Hayridge appeared in the programme for the first time playing Holly's female counterpart Hilly in 'Parallel Universe'. This episode featured Norman Lovett's last appearance as the computer for nine years; having recently moved to Edinburgh he was unwilling to continue travelling to London for rehearsals and then to Manchester for filming. 'Parallel Universe' closed the season

on a cliffhanger of sorts in which Lister falls pregnant to his
own counterpart. Although *Red Dwarf III* would feature two
new regular cast members, they wouldn't be playing Lister's
twin sons Jim and Bexley.

Regulars: Rimmer – Chris Barrie. Lister – Craig Charles.
Cat – Danny John-Jules. Holly – Norman Lovett. Written by
Rob Grant and Doug Naylor. Produced and directed by Ed
Bye. Developed for television by Paul Jackson Productions.

1: KRYTEN

Broadcast date: 6 September 1988.

Guest cast: David Ross (Kryten), Johanna Hargreaves (The
Esperanto Woman), Tony Slattery (Android Actor).

Red Dwarf receives a distress call from Kryten, the service
android upon the *Nova 5*. His ship has crashed, and its three
crew members need help. For Lister, Rimmer and Cat, this is
the moment they have been waiting for. Not only is it their first
contact with life in three million years, but that life also
comprises three very eligible female humans. When Kryten
beams them ship's records – and photographs – of his charges,
it is confirmed that Jane, Tracey and Ann are just what everybody has been waiting for. As *Red Dwarf* rushes to the rescue,
its crew have their minds on first impressions and what they
might lead to later. Lister is wearing his least smeggy clothes
(including the T-shirt with only two curry stains) and Rimmer,
resplendent in his Admiral's uniform, implores the others to
refer to him as Ace. This was apparently his childhood nickname, although he bemoans the fact that no matter how much
he let them beat him up, the rest of his school would never use
it, preferring instead to refer to him as Bonehead. Even Holly
fits his computer image with a toupee as the rendezvous draws
closer, and the Cat, even more magnificent in his appearance
than normal, has severe problems of self-control whenever he

encounters a mirror. Unfortunately, the effort has been in vain. Upon arrival on *Nova 5*, it swiftly becomes obvious to everybody that the girls are all dead. In fact, it seems that they must have been dead for centuries, as they now have less meat on them than a Chicken McNugget. Programmed only to serve mankind, Kryten has been unable to accept this fact, and has continued to wait on the skeletons of his former owners. It doesn't prove easy persuading Kryten that he no longer has a purpose in life, but Rimmer eventually manages it, turning the situation to his own advantage at the same time.

Kryten returns to *Red Dwarf* with its crew and, within moments of his arrival, Rimmer has put him to work on a hundred and one menial tasks. For Lister, the mechanoid's constant desire to serve is nothing more than an irritation. All of a sudden, he can bend his boxer shorts, and, to make matters worse, Kryten has destroyed Albert, his pet mould, which he was growing specifically to annoy Rimmer. Things have to change, he decides, but how can he alter the attitudes of a mechanoid whose only joy in life is watching the soap opera *Androids*? Still, Lister perseveres in his chosen task and, using the film *The Wild One* for inspiration, he begins to programme a few new ideas into Kryten's head. It isn't long before his tuition pays off. Inspecting a painting of himself that he has ordered Kryten to create, Rimmer is furious to discover a major deviation from the specification. He confronts the android about his disobedience, and Kryten announces that he is rebelling. He tells Rimmer to 'swivel on it' and, borrowing Lister's space bike, heads off into space, leaving *Red Dwarf* behind forever – or at least until the next series.

- Kryten's name and personality were based on Kenneth More's eponymous butler in the film *The Admirable Crichton*.
- Although this was the mechanoid's first appearance, he wasn't yet destined to become a regular (a fact that confused even the BBC's continuity announcer for the 1995 repeat run, who promised Kryten's return next week). Rob Grant was reluctant to add an android to the cast, feeling it to

be unoriginal; however, Doug Naylor saw it as a way of facilitating storylines given that neither Rimmer nor Holly could touch anything and the Cat, at this point, was not inclined to help out his shipmates. Rob finally relented and Kryten came aboard for *Red Dwarf III*.

- Kryten's favourite soap opera, *Androids* (starring a not-quite-famous-yet Tony Slattery), is a Groovy Channel 27 production. The channel – apparently the only one to employ hologramatic newsreaders – was first mentioned in 'Future Echoes', and we see its output once more in 'Better Than Life' (complete with hologramatic newsreader). A psiren impersonates the channel's weather girl in 'Psirens', but she is not seen.

- David Ross became the first actor to suffer the discomfort of the Kryten costume. 'The most difficult thing for me was having that head mask made and having to be totally immersed in plaster. I'd had it done once before, when I was playing a cat in a commercial, and I was terribly, terribly claustrophobic. It didn't take very long to set – ten minutes or so – but it seems a long time when you're totally blacked out. I felt like tearing it off! Then, on the day of the actual filming, I was there at seven in the morning and I think altogether it took about nine hours to put [the mask] on. It's like having plaster on any part of you: it is terribly uncomfortable and, I suppose, wearing, due to just the strain of sitting there in a chair for that length of time. Then of course, come six o'clock, your audience are coming in and you've got to start doing your actual job!' Nowadays, it takes a little over two hours to get Robert Llewellyn into costume.

2: BETTER THAN LIFE

Broadcast date: 13 September 1988.

Guest cast: John Abineri (Rimmer's Dad), Debbie Ash (Marilyn Monroe), Jeremy Austin (Rathbone), Nigel Carrivick (The Captain), Tony Hawks (The Guide), Judy Hawkins

(McGruder), Tina Jenkins (The Newsreader), Ron Pember (The Taxman), Gordon Salkilld (Gordon).

For the last three million years, a post pod has been following *Red Dwarf* as it headed away from Earth, and now that the ship has turned around, it has finally been able to reach it. Naturally, most of the post is made up of bills and junk mail, although the Skutters are pleased to receive their latest package from the John Wayne Fan Club. Rimmer is less happy when a letter from his mother (addressed to 'Dear Rimmer') informs him that his father is dead. Well, he knew that of course, but seeing it in black and white like that upsets him. He confides in Lister, telling him some of the details of his unhappy childhood and of his memories of a father that he spent his whole life failing to impress. Obviously Rimmer needs a diversion, and thanks to another item in the post pod, Lister is able to provide one. Together with the Cat, the two of them plug their minds into Better Than Life – the total immersion video game in which everybody's dreams come true. As they wander around a mental landscape made from their dreams, Lister becomes incredibly rich and successful, whilst Cat twotimes Marilyn Monroe for a beautiful mermaid with the top half of a fish and the bottom half of a woman. Well, the other way round would be stupid, wouldn't it? For Rimmer, a swift promotion to Admiral and the undying admiration of his father prove to be short-lived fantasies, as Cat's desires intrude upon his own. His worst enemy, however, turns out to be himself – and before long he finds himself married to a pregnant Yvonne McGruder, with seven children, a mortgage, and the taxman in pursuit. Deep down, it seems that Rimmer really hates himself – and when his self-loathing gets out of hand, everybody else is caught up in the consequences. When all three players find themselves buried in sand and about to be eaten alive by an army of ants, their combined wills end the game, returning them to *Red Dwarf*. Rimmer is more unhappy than ever, but a previously unnoticed letter looks like it could solve his problems once and for all. His last exam result was wrongly computed, it says. He really did pass, and is now a fully fledged officer. Rimmer's jubilation is cut short, however, by the sudden arrival of the taxman and the jarring realisation that he is actually still playing Better Than Life. Even as his fingers fall victim to the taxman's hammer, the game finally ends for real.

- Much discussion was generated among *Red Dwarf* and *Star Trek* fans by the similarities between this episode and the 1992 *Next Generation* adventure 'The Game'. In fact, the addictive properties of the game in question were more reminiscent of the *Better Than Life* novel.
- Marilyn Monroe makes her first *Red Dwarf* appearance, in the Cat's computer-generated fantasy. She would later return (played by different actresses) as a mechanoid in 'The Last Day' and a wax-droid in 'Meltdown'.
- Guest actor John Abineri's time on *Red Dwarf* was about as brief as it could be. 'I was met at Manchester Station and driven to a hotel and went straight to wardrobe and then make-up,' he recalls. 'I was called on to the set, which was a long table at which sat eight or nine young fellows. I knew none of them. The director said to me: "Johnny boy, these are your marks and there is the camera. This chap is playing Rimmer and you're his dad." "Hi fellas," I said. "That's enough chat," said the director, "we've work to do." I said my three or four words – maybe it was five – the director seemed pleased. I said them again in exactly the same way (for Lloyds, as we say). Then I gave one different version, and ... "Cut it. Goodbye John and thanks," said the director. Twenty minutes later I was in the train heading back to London.'

3: THANKS FOR THE MEMORY

Broadcast date: 20 September 1988.

Guest cast: Sabra Williams (Lise Yates).

It's Rimmer's deathday, and Lister, Cat and Holly get together to organise a party for him on a nearby planet. The festivities continue into the small hours of the morning and Rimmer finds himself becoming more than a little intoxicated. Back on *Red Dwarf*, a fit of drunken melancholy prompts him to reveal the details of his sex life to Lister. Lister tries in vain to convince him that he will regret any such disclosures the following morning, and is dismayed when even so, Rimmer admits to only ever having had sex once in his entire life. That, he reveals, was with Yvonne McGruder, the ship's female boxing champion. It took place on 16 March, and lasted from 7:31 until 7:43. And that included the time it took to eat the pizza. Rimmer's despair at never having shared a real relationship with anybody arouses sympathy within Lister, who determines to do something about it. The following morning, however, the crew find a number of other things to worry about. *Red Dwarf* has been visited by aliens – or so Rimmer theorises. Four days have apparently gone missing, none of which are present either in Holly's data banks or in Lister's diary. Coupled with that is the mystery of why Lister and Cat suddenly have a broken foot each; but most amazing of all is the fact that Lister's jigsaw puzzle has somehow been completed.

In an effort to learn what happened during the missing days, Holly manages to track down the ship's black box recorder, which has been buried in a grave marked 'To the Memory of the Memory of Lise Yates'. This confuses Lister even more, as Lise was one of his old girlfriends. Still, the recording should shed some light on what has happened – except that it begins with a warning from Holly that, should it ever be discovered, Lister and Rimmer should not under any circumstances view it. Of course, they ignore the warning and watch on. To Rimmer's embarrassment, they see once again his admissions of sexual inadequacy, but this time, they see what happens next. Lister heads for the Hologram Projection Suite, where he is determined to give Rimmer the best present he has ever had. He lifts the memories of an old girlfriend from his own mind and copies them into Rimmer's, giving him the illusion that he has had an affair with Lise Yates. The transference has its problems, of course. Rimmer is confused about his total change of life-style during the affair, but puts it down to the love with which he was besotted. He is more concerned about the fact that he seems to have had his appendix out twice. But after all, he now cherishes the memory of a girlfriend that he never really had, and he is far happier for it. Things turn sour though, when Rimmer discovers the letters that Lise sent to Lister. She refers to having sex with Lister six times in one night – the same night that she had sex six times with Rimmer as well. Convinced that his only true love was a two-timing nymphomaniac, Rimmer becomes more unhappy than ever, and Lister is forced to admit the truth. Brutally disappointed, Rimmer insists that the memories of Lise Yates are purged from his mind. Moreover, he wants all records of the whole unhappy event to be destroyed. Lister and Cat bury the black box recorder, breaking their feet as they drop the gravestone they are carrying to mark its resting place. Lister removes the pages from his diary, and all concerned – including Holly – voluntarily undergo a memory wipe. As Lister climbs into bed, he slots the last piece into his jigsaw puzzle.

- Craig Charles was called away from filming to attend the birth of his son, Jack. Fortunately, as Dave Lister was wearing a spacesuit at the time, the production manager, Mike Agnew, was able to double for him. The substitution isn't quite seamless, though: if you watch carefully, you'll see that Lister's plaster cast vanishes when his replacement takes over.
- A clip from this episode – in which Lister and the Cat drop a gravestone intended to mark the burial place of *Red Dwarf*'s black box – made its way into the title sequence of *Red Dwarf III*.
- More uncanny similarities with *Star Trek: The Next Generation* (see 'Better Than Life'). The American show's 1991 episode 'Clues' has the cast waking up to find that time has passed of which they have no memory. Despite the insist-

ence of their mechanical crew member, they attempt to find out what has happened, but learn that they were better off not knowing. One of them even has a broken limb . . .

- After a false start in 'Better Than Life', this episode marks a turning point in the Lister/Rimmer relationship, as Rimmer in particular becomes a character to be pitied rather than loathed. Chris Barrie wholeheartedly approved of the development. 'Although he doesn't look it, I think he is, in many ways, probably the saddest person amongst them all – and possibly also the nicest. It's really weird to say that, but he probably is – and he's become more like that. His vulnerabilities are being brought out a lot more.'

4: STASIS LEAK

Broadcast date: 27 September 1988.

Guest cast: Morwenna Banks (The Lift Hostess), Sophie Doherty (Kochanski's Room Mate), C. P. Grogan (Kochanski), Richard Hainsworth (The Medical Orderly), Tony Hawks (The Suitcase), Mac McDonald (Captain Hollister), Mark Williams (Petersen).

Whilst going through Kristine Kochanski's personal possessions, Lister discovers a photograph which clearly shows the two of them getting married. Startled but ecstatic, he realises that the only explanation is a future excursion back through time. His quest for the source of the journey leads him to Rimmer's diary, in which he intends to investigate the truth about a certain event of three million years before. Bingo! Rimmer reports seeing a ghost of himself in his bunk room: one which attributed its sudden appearance to 'a stasis leak on Level 16'. At the time, he put the experience down to an overdose of Titan Mushrooms – or Freaky Fungus – accidentally fed to him by Lister, but now, of course, both know better. A harrowing lift journey takes Lister, Rimmer and Cat to Level 16, where they do indeed discover a stasis leak – that is, a 'magic door' to the past, as Cat puts it. Emerging rather embarrassingly in the shower room, they find themselves on the *Red Dwarf* of three million years before. Although anything they try to take back with them crumbles to dust, Lister realises that by persuading Kochanski to step into the spare stasis booth, he can ensure her survival right up to the present day. Rimmer, however, has other ideas. After all, there's only one spare booth – and it's got his name on it.

While Lister tracks Kochanski down to the Ganymede Holiday Inn and Cat leaps into ferocious battle against a deadly fox fur, Rimmer reaches his living self and tries to reason with him. But things happen exactly as he remembers, and the Rimmer of the past doesn't believe a word he says. When Captain Hollister arrives, dressed in a chicken suit for the evening's fancy dress party, the younger Rimmer is absolutely convinced that he is hallucinating and manages to talk himself into rather a lot of trouble. Meanwhile, Lister is deeply upset when he finally locates Kochanski – in the honeymoon suite. Another look at his photograph convinces him that he is, in fact, not the groom, but rather an onlooker. However, he is wrong. Kochanski appears at the door and introduces him to her husband . . . himself. Apparently, in five years' time, he will find another way to travel back in time, and it is then that the two will marry. In the meantime, he has to content himself with the bottle of champagne he manages to steal from her room. Meanwhile, things are going from bad to worse for Rimmer, and the appearance of his older self – the one who is destined to travel back in time with the Lister of five years hence – doesn't help matters. When all three Listers and all three Rimmers congregate in one room, along with Kochanski and Cat, the contemporary Rimmer's sanity reaches breaking point.

- The Ganymede Holiday Inn is, in reality, its less exotic Manchester equivalent (the Crowne Plaza Midland Holiday Inn), just down the road from the studios of BBC North. The *Red Dwarf* team had already travelled to nearby Sacha's Hotel for the restaurant scene in 'Better Than Life', and next year would see an excursion to the Hotel Piccadilly for 'Body Swap'.

- Continuity watchers will notice that the bunk room of three million years ago is, unfortunately, identical to the present one – right down to the inflatable banana and Marilyn Monroe pictures that were added only for the second series.

- C. P. Grogan was accidentally sent home early, when someone overlooked the fact that she was needed to appear alongside the future version of Lister in the episode's final scene. The Assistant Floor Manager, Dona DiStefano, was called upon to double as Kochanski, keeping very much in the background and obscuring her face with a large hat.

5: QUEEG

Broadcast date: 4 October 1988.

Guest cast: Charles Augins (Queeg).

A meteor crashes into *Red Dwarf*, damaging the Hologram Projection Suite. Rimmer goes to pieces, literally, as the bottom half of his body becomes independent of its top half, and his personality is upstaged by that of Brannigan, the ship's psychiatrist. It is left to Lister to repair the damage, with some help from Holly, whose less than sound advice almost leads to his untimely death. The incident, only the latest in a long series of foul-ups by the senile computer, precipitates the unexpected arrival of his replacement, Queeg 500. *Red Dwarf*'s back-up computer is scornful of Holly, claiming that he gets all of his information from the Junior Colour Encyclopedia of Space. He accuses Holly of gross negligence leading to the endangerment of personnel, and in accordance with Article 5, he immediately replaces him. Lister, Rimmer and Cat put up little objection, expecting that Queeg will perform better than Holly ever did, but they are in for a shock. A fierce enforcer of Space Corps policy, Queeg soon makes life hell for all aboard. Lister and Cat are forced to work for their food, whilst Rimmer's hologramatic body is put through the regulation 500 jerks and a gruelling three mile run every day – whether he is conscious or not. In their misery the crew turn to Holly, now the ship's night watchman, for support. Forgiving their earlier lack of support, he challenges Queeg to a game to decide who will run *Red Dwarf* in future. For the loser: erasure. Queeg accepts, but despite Holly's numerous other suggestions, chooses chess as the deciding game. Needless to say, Holly loses and the others watch sadly as he says his last goodbyes and is erased forever. Queeg is now in control of the ship – or so it seems. In fact, Queeg never existed at all – the whole thing has simply been a joke on Holly's part. The moral of the story? 'Appreciate what you've got – because basically, I'm fantastic!'

- When the first draft of 'Queeg' was written, Rob Grant and Doug Naylor had no idea how it would finish. It was Rob who finally came up with the April Fool idea: Doug was so impressed that he bought him a pint! Rob was also responsible for naming Queeg after the captain in *The Caine Mutiny*, being a fan of Herman Wouk at the time. Indeed, the man himself is given a fleeting mention in 'Marooned'.
- Holly rolls into battle to the theme from *High Noon*, included at the request of Rob and Doug and sung by *Red Dwarf*'s musical supremo, Howard Goodall.
- Danny John-Jules suggested his old dance teacher, Charles Augins, for the part of Queeg – and Rob and Doug listened because, according to Doug, 'Danny's always right about things like that.' 'We had dinner,' explains Danny, 'with Paul [Jackson] and Ed [Bye] and I brought Charles along with me. I had been talking to Rob and Doug about Queeg, and when they actually met Charles that night at the table they said, "He's the one." A lot of Queeg's personality came from that night: the way he should be and the kinds of things he says.'
- Charles Augins had to get used to the constraints of appearing only as a head on a screen: 'I'd be moving and they'd say: "We can hear your arms moving." It was literally like

that. And there were times when I had to react to Norman [Lovett] or the Cat, and there was nobody there. So it was very different for me – but in a way it was easier, because I didn't have to think: Where have I got to be? I just sat there!' Charles made a speedy return to *Red Dwarf*, to choreograph the 'Tongue-Tied' routine for 'Parallel Universe'; he also linked the two jobs by appearing as Queeg in Danny's 'Tongue-Tied' video five years later.

6: PARALLEL UNIVERSE

Broadcast date: 11 October 1988.

Guest cast: Suzanne Bertish (Ms Rimmer), Angela Bruce (Ms Lister), Matthew Devitt (The Dog), Hattie Hayridge (Hilly).

For once, Holly has good news. He has perfected the Holly Hop Drive, a device capable of taking *Red Dwarf* instantaneously back to Earth. The crew are sceptical when they see his innovation as, basically, it is a large box with stop and start buttons. Nevertheless, they take the plunge and try the machine out. However, instead of taking them home, the Drive transports them into a parallel universe; one where history has run parallel to our own, but in which the positions of the sexes have been reversed. Dave and Arnold meet Deb and Arlene, their own equivalents in this dimension, and both are disgusted. Arnold feels insulted by Arlene's attempts to pick him up by hypnosis, even though she is acting towards him only in the same way that he has always acted towards women. Likewise, Dave is appalled by Deb's party piece of belching 'Yankee Doodle Dandy', despite the fact that it is his party piece too. However, it is Cat who is the most disappointed by his counterpart – as rather than being female, it turns out to be a humanoid Dog. The machines, conversely, fare very well, with one of the Skutters actually managing to mate with its female equivalent and producing a stream of baby Skutters. Holly too gets on exceedingly well with his female equivalent, Hilly, which rather delays the repair process on the Holly Hop Drive. Work continues into the night and, despite his reservations, a drunken Dave Lister finds himself sleeping with Deb. Arlene Rimmer is scornful, hoping the 'little slut' will become pregnant – and she's not talking about Deb. Dave is appalled to learn that in this universe, it is the men who have babies, and when *Red Dwarf* finally returns to its own dimension, he immediately undergoes a pregnancy test. It is positive.

- 'Parallel Universe' came about from a desire on the parts of Rob Grant and Doug Naylor to see what *Red Dwarf might* have been like. When creating Lister and Rimmer they had considered various male/female combinations, including the possibility of having both played by women. At one point, they even thought of asking French and Saunders – and Holly was still female in the pilot script. The only character who wasn't given a female equivalent in this episode was the Cat, because Rob and Doug wanted to play with viewers' expectations. But the 'set' was later completed by the inclusion of Terry Farrell as a decidedly different feline in the second American *Red Dwarf* pilot.

- This was the first episode not to have opening titles, and the only one not to have an on-screen name (though both were tacked on for the video release). It begins with a song-and-dance routine, 'Tongue-Tied', which turns out to be one of the Cat's dreams. Rimmer had already dreamt himself at the forefront of a less elaborate musical production in 'Thanks for the Memory'.

- Hattie Hayridge made her first appearance, as Holly's counterpart, with no idea that her association with *Red Dwarf* was just beginning. 'Paul Jackson had seen me on *Friday Night Live* and he thought: Oh yeah, she's similar to Norman. I don't know quite how to take that, really!' She hadn't seen much of the programme at the time, and she prepared for her role by studying Norman Lovett's video copies of the first series.

- Suzanne Bertish 'had a ball' creating a female Rimmer. 'Chris had a highly defined character – it was quite barky, wasn't it? He's brilliant at voices and he's a brilliant mimic; in *Red Dwarf* he had quite a defined rhythm of speaking, so one could just try and cotton on to that. I'm quite a good mimic myself, but I never practise it and it only works when something captures my imagination, then I'll open my mouth and do an impersonation of somebody.'

RED DWARF III

There were big changes in store for viewers when *Red Dwarf III* (as it was called in the *Radio Times* if not on screen) appeared in 1989. At the root of these developments was the increased involvement of Rob Grant and Doug Naylor in the production side of things. Although the budget had not significantly altered, careful spending made it look as if it had increased substantially. *Red Dwarf III* looked like a very different series indeed; a fast-paced instrumental version of Howard Goodall's theme song accompanied the opening credits, which now culminated in a specially designed *Red Dwarf* logo courtesy of DeWynters. The cotton uniforms and T-shirts were discarded in favour of distinctive Space Corps and plenty of leather. And Mel Bibby was brought in to redesign the sets, this being explained away by having the centre of operations relocated to the more elaborate Officers' Quarters.

As well as the look of the programme, the emphasis altered too: instead of concentrating on its own internal continuity, the scope of the show broadened and other science-fiction concepts and themes were parodied. Events necessitated cast changes too. Rob and Doug considered that, at this juncture, it may have been a wise move to completely reinvent Holly. As it turned out they elected for a return to Hattie

Hayridge's successful portrayal of a deadpan *Red Dwarf* computer from the previous season. Virtually a try-out episode, series II's 'Kryten' had convinced Rob and Doug that a robotic character would be a valuable addition to the line-up after all. Unfortunately, David Ross was tied up in the theatre appearing in *A Flea in Her Ear*, so the mechanoid was reintroduced, complete with Canadian accent in the shape of Robert Llewellyn. Llewellyn had been spotted by the producer Paul Jackson playing a distant relative of Kryten in a stage production of *Mamon, Robot born of Woman*. One further addition in the series was the *Starbug*, the shuttlecraft that was destined to play just as big a part in the series' future as the new cast members.

A speedy *Star Wars*-style caption informed viewers of the changes aboard *Red Dwarf*. Lister is no longer pregnant, having had his twin sons and sent them to the Parallel Universe to live with their 'father'. The increasingly eccentric Holly has had a head sex change operation and is now a woman, and the crew have met up once again with Kryten who, having been rebuilt by Lister after an almost fatal accident, now has a slightly different personality. The Saga Continuums . . .

Regulars: Rimmer – Chris Barrie. Lister – Craig Charles. Cat – Danny John-Jules. Holly – Hattie Hayridge. Kryten – Robert Llewellyn. Written by Rob Grant and Doug Naylor. Production by Ed Bye, Rob Grant and Doug Naylor. A Paul Jackson Production for BBC North West.

1: BACKWARDS

Broadcast date: 14 November 1989.

Guest cast: Maria Friedman (Waitress), Tony Hawks (Compère), Anna Palmer (Customer in Cafe), Arthur Smith (Pub Manager).

Whilst Lister and Cat are busy admiring the delectable form of Wilma Flintstone, Rimmer escorts Kryten on his driving test in *Starbug* 1. Kryten however is far from expert with the craft's controls, and manages to send them both spinning through a time hole. They emerge on what seems to be the planet Earth, although a few anomalies are immediately apparent. There is a theory that states that, once the universe has stopped expanding, it will contract, causing time itself to run backwards – and that is exactly what is happening here. Indeed, time has already retreated past Rimmer's era, reaching the latter end of the twentieth century. With *Starbug* destroyed, Rimmer and Kryten resign themselves to the fact that they could be stuck in the year 3991 for quite some time. They will obviously need some way of supporting themselves, but Rimmer bemoans the fact that there is nothing they can do. He can't even decipher the backwards speech of this world's inhabitants without Kryten's translation unit to help him. Kryten is quick to remind him, however, that on this world, everything they do is special.

Meanwhile, Holly has located the crashed *Starbug*, and Lister and Cat take one of the other vessels through the time hole after their crewmates. Lister is overjoyed to find that the trail leads back to Earth and, seeing a signpost for Nodnol, he is convinced that they have landed somewhere in Bulgaria. It isn't long before the whereabouts of Rimmer and Kryten becomes apparent. Their presence is advertised everywhere as a great new novelty act, The Sensational Reverse Brothers – or rather, Srehtorb Esrever Lanoitasnes Eht. Indeed, they are doing so well that Rimmer feels he has finally found his niche in life, and doesn't wish to leave. Unfortunately, he has little choice in the matter. He and Kryten are unexpectedly fired from their job for a fight that is about to happen. The skirmish, of course, is caused by Lister, and he delights in the sudden disappearance of the bruises he has had since landing on this strange planet. As the bar-room 'tidy' is concluded, the crew leave for *Starbug* and, eventually, *Red Dwarf*. Only the Cat lingers, first to take some money from the charity box, as is the custom, and secondly to make use of a nearby bush –

something which turns out to be a big mistake.

- The inclusion of reversed dialogue gave some of the cast a chance to utter expletives, secure in the knowledge that a cleaned-up version of their dialogue would appear in sub-titles. One printable example occurs when the bar manager apparently accuses the *Red Dwarf* crew of unstarting a fight. He actually says (while pointing at Kryten): 'You are a stupidly square-headed bald git, aren't you eh? You, I'm pointing at you, but I'm not actually addressing you. I'm addressing the one prat in the entire country who's actually bothered to get hold of this recording, turn it round and actually work out the rubbish that I'm saying. What a poor sad life he's got.'
- Rob Grant makes a brief cameo appearance: he can be seen on Manchester's Portland Street, wearing dark glasses and smoking a cigarette.
- Craig Charles had to record a scene in which he walked backwards out of a lake. He had weights in his pockets to keep him from floating upward, and he got his foot caught in mud while underwater. Nobody knew what had happened until the cameras started rolling and Craig failed to emerge – then a quick rescue operation had to be mounted.
- The outgoing Holly actor, Norman Lovett, wasn't pleased to find that his character was staying on without him. 'This isn't Hattie's fault, but I was upset when they got her in because I wanted it to remain my part and for them to get a very different type of Holly, but they didn't do that. There was one episode ['White Hole'] when she had slicked-back hair and was faster and belted [her lines] out, and I felt that was how they should have done it all along.'

2: MAROONED

Broadcast date: 21 November 1989.

Guest cast: None.

Holly is shocked to discover that *Red Dwarf* is suddenly heading towards no less than five black holes. Time to abandon ship. Holly will do her best to navigate around the dangers and pick the crew up again afterwards. Unfortunately, Lister and Rimmer may not be around to be picked up. Colliding with an asteroid, *Starbug* crashes on to an arctic planet, where the two find themselves marooned. There is precious little food although fortunately, the presence of a tin of dog food prevents Lister from having to eat a Pot Noodle. Worse still, there is no source of heat. Rimmer doesn't need either, but it seems that Lister's days are numbered. As they try to lift each other's spirits, it seems that the pair are finally becoming closer. Lister tells of his loss of virginity on the Bootle Municipal Golf Course, and Rimmer is horrified at his admission that he never paid any green fees. Rimmer in turn makes a disclosure of his own, waxing lyrical on his past life as Alexander the Great's Chief Eunuch. To this day, he can't look at a pair of nut-crackers without wincing. However, the conversation is curtailed as heating problems become paramount. Rimmer's money has already been burnt, as have all his books. That only leaves his nineteenth-century figures of Napoleon's Armies Du Nord and the priceless camphor-wood chest which is the only thing his disapproving father ever gave to him. Not surprisingly, Rimmer is less than happy with the situation, but he soon finds a solution. Why should any of his things be destroyed when Lister's guitar would make such good firewood? Lister agrees – or so it seems – and Rimmer is deeply impressed by his selfless sacrifice of his most prized possession. He consigns his own soldiers to the flames, seeking to prove himself as much a man of honour as his companion.

Finally, the ordeal ends. Cat and Kryten track down the crashed shuttle-craft, and Lister's life is saved. Rather ashamedly, Holly admits that the five black holes didn't actually exist at all – they were simply five specks of grit on the scanner scope. Well, they were black, weren't they? However, the trouble isn't over yet. The reappearance of Lister's guitar and the discovery of a guitar-shaped hole in his priceless trunk causes Rimmer to cry out for the hacksaw. He's going to do to Lister what Alexander the Great once did to him!

- The working title for this episode was 'Men of Honour', hence the fact that Rimmer uses the phrase twice.
- A small logistical error creeps in as the supposedly intangible Rimmer is seen operating a console to send out a distress signal.
- An opening scene was filmed in which the crew played strip poker and Kryten was forced to remove his armoured casing, only to reveal that the body underneath it was identical. Continuing to lose badly, he then detached various body parts ('throwing his hand in', for one), ending with his head. However, it was felt that the whole effect was not convincing, and the scene was replaced in post-production by an establishing shot of *Red Dwarf* over which Holly's evacuation warning was dubbed.
- The dogfood eaten by Lister was real. 'I made sure I did that in one take!' Craig Charles assures us. It was at his insistence that the genuine article be used, though. 'I think if you're going to do it, do it. I try to be as "methody" as possible. I let myself go a bit when I'm playing Lister – I just try to tap into the Lister in me – because I'm getting increasingly less like him as I get older.' He didn't swallow the desperation meal, though; the camera wasn't watching as he spat it out into a handkerchief.

3: POLYMORPH

Broadcast date: 28 November 1989.

Guest cast: Frances Barber (Genny), Simon Gaffney (Young Rimmer), Kalli Greenwood (Mrs Rimmer).

Holly detects a non-human life-form aboard the ship, but Rimmer is sceptical. After all, the last one she alerted them to was simply one of Lister's socks. This time though, Holly is frighteningly correct. The ship has been invaded by a genetic mutant gone wrong – a Polymorph, which can alter its shape into that of anything, whether animal, vegetable or mineral. Arriving on *Red Dwarf* as a beachball, the creature focuses its first attack upon Lister. Its initial masquerades as a shami kebab and a pair of boxer shorts cause him enough problems, but the real trouble starts when it metamorphoses into an armour-plated killing machine and launches a vicious attack. Not surprisingly, Lister is frightened – and the true purpose of the Polymorph suddenly becomes obvious. It feeds off negative emotions, removing them from their originators for its own nourishment. Now it has taken Lister's fear away from him, he is determined to stage a suicidal re-match, and has to be sedated by the others. There's no point fighting it, they decide, so all are happy to follow Rimmer's suggestion that they run away instead. Unfortunately, the Polymorph is lurking in the cargo decks, ready to interrupt their packing. In the form of a beautiful woman, it arouses the Cat's vanity before stealing that emotion from him. Posing as Rimmer himself, it steals Kryten's guilt, and the sight of his mother in bed with Dave Lister causes Rimmer enough anger to feed it further. Emotionally crippled, the *Red Dwarf* crew disagree over their next move. Rimmer wants to hit the creature with a major leaflet campaign – 'Chameleonic Life Forms, No Thanks' – whereas Kryten imagines that he can buy his own freedom by handing over the others. Cat feels he is too unimportant to have an opinion, but Lister wants to 'nut the smegger into oblivion', and eventually all agree that that is the best option. In the end, it is a complete accident that causes the Polymorph to die under heat-seeking bazookoid fire. Still, there's always time for a re-match. Apparently, they travel in pairs . . .

- The designers continued to utilise BBC North's lighting gantries to double as *Red Dwarf*'s corridors, as they had done since 'The End'. Also, from here on, some filming was done at Padiham Power Station near Burnley. Later,

Sunbury Pump House and Bankside Power Station in Waterloo proved to be adequate replacements when the show made its southward move to Shepperton.

- For the first and, so far, only time in the show's history, a warning to the faint-hearted was given before this episode. Some people have linked this fact with the 15 certificate given to the video release. However, the warning was only a publicity stunt; the unique certification was 'necessitated' by an exchange in the preceding episode, 'Marooned', in which Lister talks about losing his virginity at the age of twelve.

- Hattie Hayridge recalls two problems during filming. One was that the entire Polymorph model collapsed just before the last shot – but the other, more serious, one was that the rabbit into which the creature was to metamorphose wouldn't do as it was told! 'This little furry rabbit just refused to sit there,' she recalls, laughing. With mock indignation, she adds: 'And they get paid millions, them rabbits! It was a bit strange really, because they were getting more annoyed about the rabbit than they were about the Polymorph collapsing. I thought: That poor rabbit's had millions more years of evolution; it's entitled to be more of a drama queen than the Polymorph!'

4: BODY SWAP

Broadcast date: 5 December 1989.

Guest cast: None.

A malfunctioning Skutter has run amok on *Red Dwarf*, causing over two thousand wiring faults and turning the whole ship into an enormous booby-trap. Whilst Rimmer and Kryten try to repair the damage, Lister operates the food machine and is more than mildly surprised to find that he has accidentally activated the self-destruct system instead. The problem is further compounded by Holly's admission that only the Captain and the senior officers can avert the coming catastrophe. They're all dead of course, but she never quite got round to updating the system. As the countdown nears its conclusion, it is Kryten, as always, who has the solution. During his time on the *Nova 5*, he had been involved in a mind swap experiment. It had been a total failure, but at least he thinks he knows what went wrong. Lister is uncertain but, as Rimmer says, the worst that can happen to him is that he will have to spend the rest of his life as a mindless gibbering vegetable – and how long will that be? Thus, Lister's body is given the mind and voice of Executive Officer Carole Brown. She orders the cessation of the destruct sequence, but nothing happens. The countdown continues, and finally reaches zero . . . at which point Lister's meal arrives as ordered.

The excitement is over, but the mind swap has given Rimmer an idea. Now that Kryten has perfected this new science, why doesn't he swap bodies with Lister? He can enjoy the benefits of a living body for a fortnight in return for getting his companion fit again. Lister reluctantly agrees – but instantly regrets that decision. Rimmer has been denied the pleasures of the flesh for too long, and the sensual experience causes him to go overboard on eating, drinking and smoking. Lister demands his body back, upset at its growth of breasts and at the sudden addition of two stone to its already ample frame. But Rimmer hasn't had enough. Pressing Kryten into service, Rimmer anaesthetises Lister as he sleeps, and steals his body. He flees *Red Dwarf* in *Starbug*, and Lister's pursuit leads to disaster as the shuttle-craft crashes. Rimmer has lost one of Lister's arms for him – or so he claims. But Lister is not amused by his little joke. All he wants is his own body back – now! Rimmer has to concede, but he's not beaten yet. Once again, Kryten and his chloroform pad are pressed into service – and the Cat's in for a big surprise.

- Craig Charles and Chris Barrie had to record their own dialogue over each other's movements. To enable this, many scenes had to be recorded twice – once mute to allow dubbing, but once with an audio track so that background noises could be picked up. Because of this, 'Body Swap' was the first episode of *Red Dwarf* not to be filmed before a studio audience. It was screened in its finished form to a small gathering at the Paris Radio Studio in London (where 'Dave Hollins, Space Cadet' was recorded), so that a laughter track could be added.

- The Production Manager, Mike Agnew, provided the voice of the dispensing machine through which *Red Dwarf*'s auto-destruct sequence is routed.

- This episode features the show's only (accidental) mention of the unmade *White Midget*, although the craft is not seen. Peter Wragg explains: 'Rob and Doug felt that the *Blue Midget* didn't work very well in the studio, because it became too cramped and it was difficult to shoot. They wanted another spaceship and it was going to be called *White Midget*. My assistants did some designs, and one of them [Alan Marshall] came up with this bug-shaped thing. Rob and Doug liked it, and they changed what was in the script to suit the design of the spaceship itself.' *White Midget* became *Green Midget* and finally *Starbug*.

- Having worked on *Red Dwarf* for only two days, Robert Llewellyn was swathed in his now familiar rubber and taken to the sauna of Manchester's Hotel Piccadilly. 'The whole crew were in shorts,' he complains. 'The cameraman was pouring in sweat and it was boiling hot. Craig was in a bath with a cigar and I had to come in with a tray and push it on a floor that was deadly slippery. Then I had to light a candle with my finger, and they had this brilliant lighter contraption extended through the glove. But it had an electric starter and there was a bare bit of wire running down my sleeve. I was so wet that I conducted electricity, and I got this huge electric shock. I just couldn't believe what was going on!' And not only did the scene go, as Robert recalls, to 'about sixteen takes', it was also cut in editing, leaving only a brief shot of Lister relaxing before Kryten's arrival!

5: TIMESLIDES

Broadcast date: 12 December 1989.

Guest cast: Robert Addie (Gilbert), Rupert Bates and Richard Hainsworth (Bodyguards), Emile Charles (Young Lister), Simon Gaffney (Young Rimmer), Stephen McKintosh (Thicky Holden), Louisa Ruthven (Ski Woman), Koo Stark (Lady Sabrina Mulholland-Jjones), Mark Steel (Ski Man), Ruby Wax (American Presenter). With special guest star Adolf Hitler as Himself.

Kryten accidentally makes a miraculous discovery. A batch of developing fluid, strangely mutated over three million years' storage, is suddenly capable of bringing photographs to life. Better still, when the same fluid is used to create slides, it becomes possible for the *Red Dwarf* crew to step into the action. After trying out the effect with photos of Rimmer's brother's wedding and of Adolf Hitler, only one drawback is found – it is impossible to move out of the confines of the original photographs. Still for Lister's purposes he doesn't need to. Lister is bored with his existence on *Red Dwarf*. He longs to change the course of his life and to that end, he is determined to go back in time and ensure that his younger self never joins the Space Corps as he did. Thanks to a photograph of his teenage band, 'Smeg and the Heads', he is able to do so. Moreover, he gives to himself the secret of the Tension Sheet, an amazingly simple device based on bubbled packing sheets which was actually invented by Arnold Rimmer's boarding school room mate, Fred 'Thicky' Holden. The experiment is a total success. The timelines alter, and Lister vanishes from *Red Dwarf*. So do Cat and Kryten as, without Lister's influence, they never would have existed. Rimmer is left alone, and he considers it his duty as a complete and total bastard to restore things to the way they were. Delving into her newly altered memory banks, Holly is able to provide a picture reference of Lister's new life. A quick application of the fluid allows Rimmer to step into it, and he is alarmed to find his one-time companion a multi-millionaire, married to sex symbol Sabrina Mulholland-Jjones. Rimmer tries to talk Lister into going back to his past life but of course, in this timeline, Lister's never heard of him. So Rimmer decides to beat Lister at his own game. He uses a slide of himself in the school dormitory to go even further back in time and give the secret of the Tension Sheet to himself. As he does so, however, he fails to realise that 'Thicky' Holden is listening from the next bed, and it is he who beats Young Rimmer to the patent office. Credit for the Tension Sheet reverts to him, and the timelines are returned more or less to normal. Lister, Cat and Kryten are returned to *Red Dwarf* with no memory of what has happened, but still, Rimmer is miserable. He has lost his chance to become a millionaire and to endure constant sex with Sabrina. Why is it, he complains, that whenever anything good happens to him, it always goes wrong? His spirits are suddenly lifted as Holly announces that, for reasons she can't quite fathom, the alterations to the timelines have meant that he is now alive. But Rimmer's earlier pessimism seems to be proved correct when, in his enthusiasm, he sets off an explosion which kills him once again.

- Two early scenes were cut. The Cat was to sink a putt on a table-golf game, but neither magnetising the ball nor pulling it on a string achieved the desired effect. When it did finally come off, Danny John-Jules was so surprised he forgot his line! Also, Rimmer was to be seen using a hologram box – a glass case with gloves in each side, into which he could insert intangible hands – to assemble a model kit, but this didn't look convincing.
- The crew enter a slide of a couple on a skiing holiday, and Lister explains that he was once sent someone else's snaps by accident. The couple were to have recalled that they got photos of some guys being sick. But, during recording, Craig Charles pointed out that, having been captured before the mix-up, they should have no knowledge of it. The scene was rewritten; Mark Steel and Louisa Ruthven retained credits

despite no longer having any lines.

- Although he remained accidentally uncredited, Craig Charles wrote, performed and produced three tracks: the instrumental 'Bad News' (to which Kryten is seen dancing), 'Cash' and Smeg and the Heads' infamous 'Om Song'. Craig's brother Emile was joined by members of Napalm Death (with whom Craig had just finished recording *What's That Noise?*) to form Lister's teenage group.

- 'There was a lot of hi-tech pushing of the system to get "Timeslides" done,' says Ed Bye. He cites an early scene in which the camera pans across a series of animated photographs. 'That's technically a very difficult thing to do, and when you look at it you think: Oh, it doesn't look that impressive. But the fact that it doesn't look impressive means it's worked.' Also, having people walk into and out of slides entailed 'the most complicated set of electronic wipes we'd ever done. The difficulty was that the stuff in the photographs had to be shot in another place. So we'd have Craig jumping at a camera on location and then jumping the same way in the studio and trying to match the two up.' Ed admits that the casting of his wife Ruby Wax as a TV presenter was an 'inside job': she stepped into the breach after the death of Graham Chapman, who had originally accepted the role.

6: THE LAST DAY

Broadcast date: 19 December 1989.

Guest cast: Julie Higginson (Girl Android), Gordon Kennedy (Hudzen).

A message pod from Diva-Droid International finally locates Kryten, and delivers its message to his 'owners'. A video of sales executive Jim Reaper announces to a stunned Lister that Kryten's service contract has expired. It's shut-off time.

Kryten has twenty-four hours in which to prepare himself for his death, a fate which he accepts with disturbing equanimity. Well, after all, this isn't really the end for him – it's merely the beginning of a new life in Silicon Heaven. Lister is appalled. Silicon Heaven is obviously a fictional concept programmed into all androids by their makers. It is only their belief in it that ensures their loyalty to humankind. As Kryten says, why would mechanoids spend their entire lives in service, if they didn't know they were going to get their rewards in the afterlife? Okay, so Lister can't stop Kryten's shut-off disc from activating, but he can certainly make the mechanoid's last day one to remember. Kryten is invited to a party in the Officers' Club, and treated to a special mechanoid menu devised by Holly. He is also the grateful recipient of a number of farewell gifts, including an ear-ring which Cat always hated anyway, and a robotic Marilyn Monroe which, despite its obviously shoddy construction, he finds quite enchanting.

The following day though, Kryten finds himself faced with a dilemma. For the first time in his life, he has actually experienced 'fun' – and it wasn't enough. He wants some more. Overriding the shut-down disc is no real problem. What is a problem though, is the impending arrival of Kryten's replacement, Hudzen. If Kryten doesn't terminate himself, Hudzen has orders to help him do so. Lister isn't worried. All they have to do is meet the replacement on the landing gantry and tell him he's not wanted. Simple enough, yes? No. Having tracked Kryten for thousands of years, Hudzen has gone completely mad. Not only that, but he's a good deal stronger than any of them. Of course, androids aren't allowed to harm humans . . . but the only person who truly fits that description is Lister and what the hell?! The ensuing battle is very much a one-sided affair. Kryten is to be the first to die, and Hudzen grips him by the throat, ready to administer the killing stroke. Time to visit Silicon Heaven – except that Kryten knows it doesn't really exist. Holly sides with him in persuading Hudzen of that truth, and the newcomer is stricken by a metaphysical dichotomy and forced to shut down. Lister is confused. If Hudzen's android mind couldn't handle the concept of there being no Silicon Heaven, how could Kryten's? The answer, says Kryten, is simple. He knew something that Hudzen didn't. He knew he was lying.

- Robert Llewellyn makes a brief appearance – his first time out of the Kryten costume – as the Diva-Droid executive Jim Reaper.
- Rimmer is said to have spent a morning on the Samaritans' switchboard, driving all five of his callers – including one wrong number – to suicide. The anecdote is repeated in 'The Inquisitor' (although morning becomes afternoon and five is reduced to four) but, more interestingly, also in the BBC 1 sitcom *The Brittas Empire*. Chris Barrie's character, Gordon Brittas, suffered a similar experience right down to the wrong number.
- 'The Last Day' replaced what would have been the season opener, 'Dad'. This would have taken up the story of Lister's pregnancy, ending with a reprise of the birth scene from 'Future Echoes'. However, Rob and Doug felt that the script wasn't working out – and, indeed, that it was in danger of becoming sexist and homophobic. Despite his experiences in 'Future Echoes', Craig Charles had been looking forward to becoming an on-screen 'mother': 'I would have liked to have played a pregnant man. That would have been a first. I've done a lot of firsts in *Red Dwarf* – I even ate a Pot Noodle! But I'm glad I didn't have to go through the epidurals and the breathing exercises . . .'
- As *Red Dwarf III* concluded, the series was making the transition from relatively unregarded BBC 2 show to cult phenomenon. Doug Naylor recalls: 'That was when it really hit the news that *Red Dwarf* was a huge hit all over America and everywhere else.' Rob Grant jokes: 'We put those lies about!' What happened, apparently, was that a Seattle television executive had referred to *Red Dwarf* as 'the biggest thing since *Python* in America'. Rob and Doug jokingly passed his comment on to a journalist, who

exaggerated it out of all proportion. 'It was completely, totally untrue!' says Doug.

RED DWARF IV

BBC North's Oxford Road Studios in Manchester were in the process of being refurbished when the time came to begin work on *Red Dwarf*'s fourth season. Consequently, the programme's original home was abandoned and Grant Naylor Productions looked for new accommodation for their increasingly popular show, which they found at Shepperton Studios. The close proximity of the studios to such locations as Sunbury Pumphouse, plus the opportunity to utilise other sets on the lot, made the move south a successful one, so much so that the venue has been used ever since.

Despite the upheaval, *Red Dwarf IV* continued along the lines established by its immediate predecessor; and like *Red Dwarf III* it garnered Peter Wragg's team the World Television Society award for their visual effects.

Regulars: Rimmer – Chris Barrie. Lister – Craig Charles. Cat – Danny John-Jules. Holly – Hattie Hayridge. Kryten – Robert Llewellyn. Written and produced by Rob Grant and Doug Naylor. Produced and directed by Ed Bye. A Grant Naylor Production for BBC North West.

1: CAMILLE

Broadcast date: 14 February 1991.

Guest cast: Judy Pascoe (Mechanoid Camille), Francesca Folan (Hologram Camille), Suzanne Rhatigan (Kochanski Camille), Rupert Bates (Hector Blob).

Lister becomes frustrated with Kryten's inability to lie and to disobey orders, particularly as Rimmer so often uses that to his own advantage. Using a series of simple exercises, he is determined to force the android to deviate from his programming – but even as Kryten believes he is getting the hang of things, he finds he just can't lie in front of an audience. The lessons do seem to have some effect, however. Whilst out in *Starbug*, Kryten and Rimmer pick up a distress signal from another android, who is trapped on a planet about to explode. Against Rimmer's express orders, Kryten guides the craft into terrible danger and succeeds in rescuing Camille. For both mechanoids, it is advanced mutual compatibility on the basis of a primary initial ident – but as always, things aren't what they seem. When Kryten returns Camille to *Starbug*, he is baffled by Rimmer's references to her as a beautiful woman. In fact, to Rimmer, she looks like a hologramatic bombshell and as holograms can touch each other, he suddenly finds himself very glad that Kryten did see fit to disobey him. Lister sees Camille as a female cross between himself and his lost love, Kristine Kochanski. Time to start recreating the human race, he thinks. But even before he can get his Spider Man suit out of storage, he realises that something is wrong. When he compares notes with his shipmates, his suspicions are painfully confirmed. Eventually, Camille admits the truth. She is a Pleasure GELF – a Genetically Engineered Life Form, who is seen by everybody as the object of their own desire. Whilst coming as a disappointment to Lister, Rimmer and Kryten, the news causes only excitement for the Cat, who rushes to see what form Camille will take for him. Perhaps not surprisingly, the object of his own desire turns out to be . . . himself. Ashamed, Camille finally reveals her true form, and Lister, Rimmer and Cat are repulsed by her appearance. But Kryten, already infatuated with the GELF, doesn't seem to care. He feels sure that their romance can continue, despite the obstacles in their path, and despite the fact that he is an android and she is a huge, green blob with tentacles. At last, both seem to have found true happiness. But it is not to last. Their blissful relationship is all too soon shattered by the arrival of Hector, the blob who has the honour of being Camille's husband. Camille doesn't want to hurt Kryten by leaving, but it seems that the mechanoid has finally become versed in the use of lies and, borrowing his inspiration from Casablanca, he persuades Camille to accompany Hector, leaving his life forever.

- When the Gulf War necessitated a change in the running order of *Red Dwarf IV* (see 'Meltdown'), it was decided that this love story was an appropriate episode to go out first, on 14 February.
- Dave Lister's love for the film *Casablanca* was first revealed in 'Better Than Life', though at the time he considered a remake, which starred Peter Beardsley and Myra Binglebat, to be the definitive version. By now, he has obviously grown to appreciate the original, as it is with this that he tutors Kryten in the art of lying.
- The Valentine's Day theme continued behind the scenes: the Pleasure GELF's Kochanski-like form was played by Suzanne Rhatigan – Craig Charles's real-life girlfriend – while, not very coincidentally, Kryten's perfect Camille was played by Judy Pascoe – Robert Lewellyn's 'better half'. 'It was so weird, the first time she walked into the studio with the full mask on,' says Robert. 'It was such a strange experience to look at each other and think: God, I don't know who that is!'

2: DNA

Broadcast date: 21 February 1991.

Guest cast: Richard Ridings (DNA Computer Voice).

Red Dwarf encounters a spacecraft of unknown origin and Rimmer is convinced that they have discovered aliens. A three-headed skeleton seems to confirm this – but then, why does it have a video club card in its wallet? In fact, the ship is from Earth, where technology has obviously advanced since the twenty-third century. The skeleton is the product of a DNA modifier, a machine that can change any living thing into any other living thing by rearranging its molecular structure. When Cat accidentally triggers the machine, Lister is turned into a chicken, and Kryten, whose brain is part organic, achieves his fondest desire – to become a human. It is no surprise then that, even once a way of reversing the transformations is discovered, Kryten wishes to stay as he is. His new form does have a few problems, however. The eyes don't seem to have a zoom facility and his nipples no longer pick up Jazz FM. Worst of all, he is worried about the unfamiliar and very ugly thing which hangs between his legs – and the effect which the sight of a super-deluxe vacuum cleaner has upon it. Lister is worried too. It is obvious that Kryten still has the mind of a mechanoid, and Lister feels that his transformation may not have been for the best. Eventually, after an uncomfortable confrontation with his spare heads, Kryten agrees. However, before Kryten's transformation can be properly reversed, it is necessary for Holly to master the controls of the Modifier and in doing so, she makes a mistake so simple that any deranged, half-witted computer could have made it. The result is that Lister's mutton vindaloo suddenly becomes a rampaging beast, half man, half curry. It shrugs off bazookoid fire undamaged, and it seems that there is no way to stop it – unless Holly can get things right this time and use the Modifier to turn Lister into a super-human. She gives it a try, but the results aren't all they could have been, and a minuscule Lister is left at the mercy of the rampaging creature. Quite by accident, he hits upon the answer. Lager – the only thing that can kill a vindaloo.

- The script reveals that this episode's title stands for 'Do Not Alter'; however, this never made it on to the screen.
- Two separate lines suggest that Lister and Rimmer come from the twenty-third century, and not the twenty-first, as had been established in 'Stasis Leak'. However, 'Psirens'

and 'Ouroboros' would later place their origins in the twenty-second century instead.

- The vindaloo beast is destroyed by Leopard lager, appearing here for the first time. Rob Grant and Doug Naylor had always been disappointed that, in the first series, even the lager cans were a uniform grey. They had argued that this made them look too much as if they were ship-issue cans, which wouldn't be the case. Now, at last, they were able to put this right, albeit by using a substantial proportion of the show's graphics budget. Ironically, when the labels were redesigned for *Red Dwarf VII*, they included a Jupiter Mining Corporation logo.

- Kryten becomes human, complete with a bizarre costume which was intended as an amalgam of all that the mechanoid had observed about his crewmates' fashion sense. 'I found it a really strange experience,' says Robert Llewellyn, 'because I'm so used to working on the set with the [Kryten] costume on. When I was actually sitting in there without it on, I felt really exposed. There was a lot of my family in that week and I was thinking, like: Oh, they're all going to see me! Usually, [*Red Dwarf*] is the only show I do where I don't get nervous before I go on, 'cos somehow I'm one step removed from it behind the mask. I feel it isn't really me: it's somebody else out there.'

3: JUSTICE

Broadcast date: 28 February 1991.

Guest cast: Nicholas Ball (Simulant), James Smillie (Justice Computer Voice).

Even a bout of space mumps isn't enough to keep Lister in the medical unit when he learns that there might be a woman on board. Rushing to the scene, he discovers that *Red Dwarf* has picked up an escape pod from a prison ship which was transporting a bunch of psychopathic simulants to Justice

World. The ship's black box tells of a mutiny that resulted in the deaths of everybody on board. Everyone, that is, except for prison officer Barbra Bellini and one of the simulant prisoners. Obviously, one of them is cryogenically frozen in the pod – but which one? There is little time for debate, as Cat has already started the thawing process. In twenty-four hours, it's either death or a date. For once, Holly finds a solution. She suggests that they travel to the fully automated Justice World themselves and beg the use of its facilities. These should be adequate to handle the occupant of the pod, should it prove not to be Babs. The others take her advice, and Lister is relieved when he makes a sudden recovery from his disease during the journey. The Cat is less pleased; the main symptom of the recovery was the bursting of a large, pus-filled swelling on Lister's head – and guess who was in the vicinity? Soon enough though, all are presented with slightly more to worry about than the colour co-ordination of Cat's clothing. Although the Justice Computer grants them permission to land on Justice World, it fails to warn them of its foolproof security system. The Computer needs to ascertain whether or not its visitors are suitable to enter or whether they should be locked away for good, and they are frozen into position as their minds are probed for any evidence of past misdemeanours. Lister in particular is worried. He is sure that his teenage record of petty crimes will earn him a stay in prison. He is therefore extremely relieved when clearance is granted. Rimmer, however, fares rather less well. He is found guilty of 1,167 counts of second degree murder – the deaths of everybody on board *Red Dwarf*. He is sentenced to eight years for each of his crimes, and given his hologramatic status, these sentences are to be served consecutively. He is to go to prison for over nine thousand years. Rimmer is sent to Justice World's containment area, known as the Justice Zone. At first, he is surprised to see that there are no bars or doors to keep him in position, but he soon learns why. The entire zone is surrounded by an amazing development known as the Justice Field, which acts to ensure that no crime can be committed within its confines. Anybody attempting to do anything illegal will immediately have the consequences of the act turned back upon himself – as Lister discovers, when Rimmer encourages him to try a spot of arson.

Meanwhile, Kryten lodges an appeal, building up a case around the fact that his client is a complete dork. Somebody like Rimmer, he contends, could never have been given enough responsibility to cause the leak of radiation that killed the *Red Dwarf* crew. Kryten theorises that what the mind probe has detected is the guilt which Rimmer himself feels about the incident, and that his actual culpability is nil. Despite Rimmer's constant objections to the insulting words of his own counsel, the Justice Computer accepts the plea, and he is set free. That still leaves one problem, however. The escape pod has opened – and it wasn't Barbra Bellini on board. Everybody flees into the Justice Zone, but the simulant tricks Lister into confronting him, to 'talk'. Although Lister has broken his promise and brought along a weapon, the simulant has done likewise and brought two. But in the ensuing battle, Lister is the first to realise that the Justice Field is turning each participant's blows against their perpetrator. Encouraging his attacker to assault him in the most vicious ways possible, he is amused to see the simulant defeat itself. Lister is left to realise that, no matter how much technology humans build to create true justice, life will always be basically unfair and, bored by his moralising, the rest of the crew are pleased to see the point proven by a mis-step into a gaping hole.

- Taking their cue from *Blade Runner*, Rob Grant and Doug Naylor introduce *Red Dwarf*'s first Simulant. These man-made mechanoid variants appear more human and are far more vicious than their servile counterparts, and they enable the writers to circumvent the problem of having no alien threats in an increasingly action-orientated SF series (as do the various GELF tribes, a prototype for which was seen in 'Camille'). They appear in at least one episode of every season from this point on.
- *Red Dwarf IV*'s slight retooling of continuity continues.

The number of people on the pre-accident ship is increased by one thousand to 1,169 and Rimmer is now assumed to be not guilty of causing their deaths. He is also now said to have failed his astro-navigation exam thirteen times; 'Future Echoes' had placed the number at ten (including the one when he had his spasm) while 'Waiting for God' had revealed that it was the engineering exam he had failed, a total of eleven times.

- The artist Colin Howard's painting of a scene from this episode made it on to the front cover of *Red Dwarf Magazine* vol 1, issue 2, and was considered so impressive by BMS (now Network) that they immediately made a T-shirt out of it.

4: WHITE HOLE

Broadcast date: 7 March 1991.

Guest cast: David Ross (Talkie Toaster).

Lister is horrified to discover that Kryten has repaired Talkie Toaster. Horrified because it was he himself who was responsible for smashing it to bits. He insists that it is nothing more than a one-dimensional, bread-obsessed electrical appliance and, once fixed, Talkie proves him right with his non-stop offers of bread-related products. However, Kryten has good reason for his actions. He has pioneered a process which can restore the mechanical intelligence of a device at the cost of reducing its operational life-span, and Talkie is his guinea pig. When the experiment is proved to be a complete success, Kryten reasons that the process should also work on Holly, curing her advanced case of computer senility and restoring her IQ to six thousand. In fact, the operation seems more than successful. Her intelligence raised to double its original level, Holly's only problem is that she can't get an intelligent, non-toast-related conversation out of Talkie. Then, making a quick check of her systems, she discovers the worst – the experiment has had a disastrous side-effect. Although Holly's intelligence has increased to twice the desired level, there has been an exponential reduction in her life-span. She only has 3.45 minutes of run-time left. Taking the only logical choice available, Holly shuts herself down and as a consequence, all of the ship's power systems do the same. Left to fend for themselves, the crew are in danger of either freezing to death or starving. Rimmer refuses to conserve emergency power by switching himself off, and Kryten advises that the life support systems will cease to function in all too short a time. As if that weren't bad enough, there is another problem – without Holly to guide it, *Red Dwarf* has run straight into a white hole. The opposite of a black hole, this spews time and matter back into the universe, and in doing so, it creates chaos aboard the ship. Holly is switched back on for one quick computation, and Lister is amazed at the solution she comes up with. The answer, it seems, is to play planetary pool, knocking a nearby planet into the 'pocket' of the white hole and thereby sealing it up. But Holly has got the shot wrong, he is sure. If they do it her way, the planet will be off the table and straight into someone's beer. To the horror of the others, Lister decides to trust his own pool skills over Holly's computations. He takes aim – and misses! *Starbug* is trapped in the path of an oncoming planet, and all aboard are doomed – until the 'balls' ricochet and the pot is achieved. A trick shot, claims Lister, played for and got. The incident also has an unexpected side effect. Now that the white hole is gone, the time it spewed into the universe no longer exists, and as it was during this time that Holly and the Toaster were 'repaired', these events no longer occurred. As *Starbug* fades around them and the *Red Dwarf* crew are returned to their ship with no memory of what has happened, Kryten takes this golden opportunity to tell Rimmer exactly what he thinks of him.

- Holly's exponentially increased IQ is somewhat less than evident when both she and Talkie Toaster read the number 345 (her remaining run-time, as yet without the decimal point) as 341, immediately after the experiment.

- The timelines are rearranged so that the events of this episode never happened and none of the crew remember them – so quite how Lister recalls, in 'Demons and Angels', that he once played pool with planets is beyond us. Perhaps it happened twice.

- Director Ed Bye was taken ill on the day of the studio recording, so the producer Paul Jackson had to take his place. He was not credited for this.

- Although he missed out on playing Kryten full-time, David Ross was pleased to be asked back to take over John Lenahan's first-season role as (the newly renamed) Talkie Toaster for this episode. 'I didn't even have to learn the lines. I just went in and read it. It was wonderful. It was also nice to feel part of the team again, especially in such a zany, one-off role. It's great to be able to say that you've played a toaster at one point in your career.' David also has a few ideas for his next *Red Dwarf* appearance. 'I'd like to maybe play a poker next time. I love pokers!'

5: DIMENSION JUMP

Broadcast date: 14 March 1991.

Guest cast: Kalli Greenwood (Mrs Rimmer), Simon Gaffney (Young Rimmer), Hetty Baynes (Cockpit Computer).

A glimpse into a parallel universe shows us the dramatic effect upon Arnold Rimmer's life of one single event in his childhood. In one dimension, he was kept down a year at school; in another, he wasn't. In our universe, this led to young Arnold's growth into the pathetic character we already know. In another, he became instead a handsome, heroic test pilot in the Space Corps, known to all as Ace. Ace Rimmer is everything that Arnold Rimmer is not, and chief amongst his outstanding attributes is his unparalleled courage. It is this that spurs him into accepting the greatest challenge of his life.

He is to test-fly a prototype craft which will exceed the speed of reality and take him into another dimension. Naturally, that dimension is ours, and Ace Rimmer makes an unexpected arrival directly in front of *Starbug*, which is currently taking the *Red Dwarf* crew on a fishing trip to an ocean planet. Despite the best efforts of the others, Arnold Rimmer has accompanied them on the expedition, so when Ace rushes to the crashed vessel to offer his assistance, the two Rimmers meet. It is hate at first sight. Arnold despises Ace, who he sees as the living proof of what he could have been had he had the lucky breaks in life that his counterpart obviously had. Ace, on the other hand, takes a dislike to the cowardly and incompetent Arnold, disgusted that he himself could ever be reduced to such a state. Naturally, Lister, Cat and Kryten side with Ace on the subject, sick as they are of Arnold's endless tales of morris dancing and his recitals of Reggie Wilson Hammond Organ classics. Indeed, Ace and Lister become firm friends, and Lister is pleased to hear that his other-dimensional counterpart, known as Spanners, is doing just as well for himself as Ace as a Space Corps engineer. However, Ace soon realises that he and Arnold simply cannot live together. One of them has to go! Despite the objections of the others, Ace prepares to leave, revealing as he does that in fact he was the one who was kept down a year at the age of seven. By Arnold's standards, it was he who got the lucky break – but in Ace's case, the humiliation had forced him to pull himself together and make a life for himself. With that, Ace leaves *Red Dwarf* forever, his departure not in the least obstructed by his counterpart's clumsy attempt at envy-motivated retribution. His destiny, he decides, is to roam the dimensions, meeting other versions of himself. He can't go back, but maybe one day, he'll find a universe that approximates his own. And perhaps one day, he'll even find an Arnold Rimmer who is as sad and worthless as the one he met aboard *Red Dwarf*. His impossible quest continues . . .

- The story of two Rimmers – one a success and one a failure – inspired a student to write into the offices of Grant Naylor.

Having done badly in his mock exams, he was encouraged by this episode to try harder and he secured a university place as a result. Rob and Doug hung the letter on their office wall as a reminder of how rewarding their job can sometimes be.

- In the original edit, it was clearer that Rimmer intended to bring a pile of kippers down on Ace's head. When his trap failed to operate, he wandered beneath the suspended fish to see what went wrong – and the episode concluded with a freeze frame of his horrified face as they came tumbling down. However, the sequence didn't come across well on tape, and it was replaced by a caption which told us of Ace's continuation of his mission, followed by the skutters' rendition of a Hammond organ version of the *Red Dwarf* theme: the first, but not the last, alternative closing theme to be used.

- We get to see Hattie Hayridge's whole body for the only time. But she was disappointed to see that her Holly persona never came into contact with Ace. 'I said: "There needs to be a reason why I don't have anything to do with him – why don't I just faint?" So they went for that.' She is quick to point out, however, that she didn't supply the flattering comment that induced the swoon. 'They probably wrote that to shut me up!'

- 'I remember there was a furore,' says Rob Grant, 'about who the other characters would play in Ace's dimension. Originally, we'd written Danny as a really slobby cleaner, which we thought was funny – but then there was a big argument about positive, black role models, which I found infuriating. I mean, *Red Dwarf* does have two black characters in it, and we never make a mention of it, and I think that's the way it should be. We didn't hire them for their colour and we don't make any play of it at all – so it annoyed me, really, that we had this thing about negative role models when we felt we'd been presenting positive role models for so long.'

6: MELTDOWN

Broadcast date: 21 March 1991.

Guest cast: Clayton Mark (Elvis), Kenneth Hadley (Hitler), Martin Friend (Einstein), Stephen Tiller (Pythagoras), Jack Klaff (Abraham Lincoln), Tony Hawks (Caligula), Michael Burrell (Pope Gregory), Forbes Masson (Stan Laurel), Roger Blake (Noel Coward), Pauline Bailey (Marilyn Monroe).

Kryten unearths a prototype matter transporter in the research labs, and Holly is pleased to report that it is capable of homing in on any atmosphere-bearing planets within 500,000 light years. When activated, it takes the *Red Dwarf* crew only a modest 200,000 light years away, to Wax-World, a Wax-Droid theme park. Unfortunately, this particular park has been left unattended for millions of years. The Wax-Droids have broken their programming, and a terrible war has begun between the exhibits in Hero World and those in Villain World. Rimmer and Kryten, arriving first to check the atmosphere, find themselves in the middle of Prehistoric World, where they are chased by a number of unconvincing dinosaurs into neighbouring Hero World. Lister and Cat, meanwhile, arrive in Villain World, falling right into the hands of a wax Adolf Hitler. Whilst Rimmer is busy assembling such luminaries as Einstein, Pythagoras and Mother Theresa to form an army, aided by Sergeant Elvis Presley, Lister and Cat witness the execution of Winnie the Pooh and find themselves being interrogated by Caligula. Lister is threatened with soapy frogs, but Cat is more worried that he might be forced into unfashionable clothing. Fortunately, neither of those dire fates comes to pass as, with the help of Abraham Lincoln, they manage to escape from their prison and flee to the camp of the good guys. There, Lister is horrified by Rimmer's behaviour. His battle strategy of a charge across a minefield under cover of daylight is an obviously suicidal one. Rimmer, it seems, is going mad – and Holly theorises that Lister is the cause. Well, perhaps he shouldn't have popped Rimmer's hologram-projecting light bee into his mouth like that. However, there is some method to Rimmer's madness. Whilst the forces of evil are occupied by their enemies' charge, Kryten and Queen Victoria stage a sneak attack from behind, and Kryten is able to ensure victory with one twist of a handy thermostat. With the heroes blown up and the villains melted down, Rimmer's tactics have succeeded in killing every single Wax-Droid on the planet. Lister is further disgusted by his companion's insistence that the sacrifice was well worth it for the 'grand victory' he has won. This time, he doesn't just put the light bee in his mouth, he swallows it whole, deciding to let Rimmer experience a complete trip through his digestive system. Does anyone fancy a curry?

- This should have been the first episode of *Red Dwarf IV*, but the BBC refused to screen it during the Gulf War because of its anti-war message ('Dimension Jump', with its 'war hero' character, was also pushed back in the schedule). Fortunately, hostilities ceased in time for 'Meltdown' to be tagged on to the end of the season.

- Hot on the heels of 'Dimension Jump' comes Howard Goodall's second alternative version of the closing theme, this one an Elvis-style rendition by Clayton Mark. Everyone concerned was impressed with Clayton, and Rob Grant and Doug Naylor considered writing an episode in which the 'real' Elvis was found adrift in space, so that they could ask him back on to the show. It never happened, but Danny John-Jules later snapped him up for an appearance on his 'Tongue-Tied' video.

- Problems were encountered on location, as the actor hired to play Gandhi was too frail to do press-ups as the script demanded. He was sent home and a replacement had to be hastily arranged.

- 'We completely misjudged "Meltdown",' confesses Doug Naylor. 'If it hadn't been for the Gulf War, it would almost certainly have gone out first – but, as we now know, it's one of the least liked of all the *Red Dwarf*s.' Rob Grant finds the episode's poor showing in fan polls curious: 'I thought Clayton Mark as Elvis was just sensational, and the battle looks great and it's weird and funny. I don't know what people have got against it. I've a feeling it's the way we told the story.'

RED DWARF V

Having directed every episode of *Red Dwarf* since its inception, Ed Bye was unavailable to continue working on the series. Juliet May stepped in as a temporary replacement but was in turn replaced by Rob Grant and Doug Naylor themselves. Also, Hilary Bevan Jones joined the team as producer. However, apart from the addition of a new serif-typeface logo, the only really discernible differences to the show were the result of Rob and Doug's conscious decision to change their approach to the narrative: the balance between comedy and science fiction was tipped somewhat towards the latter.

Regulars: Rimmer – Chris Barrie. Lister – Craig Charles. Cat – Danny John-Jules. Holly – Hattie Hayridge. Kryten – Robert Llewellyn. Written by Rob Grant and Doug Naylor. Produced by Hilary Bevan Jones. Directed by Juliet May (all except 'Quarantine') and Grant Naylor (all except 'Holoship' and 'Terrorform'). A Grant Naylor Production for BBC TV/BBC North.

1: HOLOSHIP

Broadcast date: 20 February 1992.

Guest cast: Jane Horrocks (Nirvanah Crane), Matthew Marsh (Captain Platini), Don Warrington (Commander Binks), Lucy Briers (Harrison), Simon Day (Number Two), Jane Montgomery (Number One).

Rimmer is repelled by Lister's choice of films: he has just been forced to sit through a love story, and he isn't convinced. Why on earth, he wonders, would somebody sacrifice his career for the sake of the woman he loves, knowing that he will never see her again? It just doesn't make sense. The rest of the crew are spared Rimmer's further comments as he is suddenly teleported away from *Starbug*. The Cat is all for getting away while they've got the chance, but of course, they have to find out what's going on first. Rimmer has, in fact, been teleported to a holoship – a hologramatic spaceship, inaccessible to living people, but a godsend to the dead. On *Enlightenment*, holograms can touch, feel and taste, and even have sex – something which ship's regulations require them to do at least twice a day for their own health. Rimmer is alarmed – that's more than some people manage in a lifetime! However, after his first act of sexual congress with Nirvanah, he begins to realise that he likes this place very much indeed. Moreover, though both deny it, the experience has affected them deeply. The two are falling in love. Naturally Rimmer wants to stay, but *Enlightenment* is a pioneering vessel crewed by the hologramatic cream of the Space Corps, and he, as a Class One hologram of a 'Tosspot by Royal Appointment', doesn't come up to scratch.

Desperate now, Rimmer applies – much to the amusement of the Holoship crew – to undergo the rigorous intelligence test which, if he passes it, will allow him to replace one of their number. *Enlightenment*'s computer, Stocky, runs his data through its systems and selects the crew member against whom he has the most chance of success. Unknown to Rimmer, that turns out to be Nirvanah. Faced with a projected 96 per cent chance of failure, Rimmer decides that, as always, he will have to cheat. He persuades Kryten to give him a mind patch and, with his own rather minimal intelligence augmented by the brains of two of the most intelligent people who ever worked on *Red Dwarf*, it is a very different Rimmer who sits down at a console and gets to work. Just when he is succeeding brilliantly, however, his mind rejects the patch and he is left floundering. He returns to *Red Dwarf*, where he finds the others interviewing replacements for the post of ship's hologram, and he is mortified to learn that Kryten is unable to perform a second operation. Rimmer returns to the holoship dejectedly, seeing no alternative but to withdraw from the contest. However, touched by his misery, Nirvanah not only persuades him to carry on, but withdraws herself, ensuring his victory. Nirvanah is deactivated and Rimmer takes her place as Navigation Officer on board the ship. Finally, his dreams have all come true until he is shown to his new quarters. Recognising them as Nirvanah's old ones, he realises the dreadful truth. Hardly believing his own actions, Rimmer resigns his commission and leaving behind a note for Nirvanah, returns forever to *Red Dwarf*, throwing away everything he has ever dreamt of for the sake of the woman he loves, even though he'll never see her again. He can't quite believe he just did that!

- 'Holoship' overran by an unprecedented eight minutes and, sadly, much of its effects footage was trimmed. Also falling victim to the editor's scissors was a character-building scene between Rimmer and Holly, as the hologram seeks urgent assistance in reversing the failure of his mind patch and the computer takes much delight in winding him up instead.
- 'I based my character on Joanna Lumley,' reveals Jane Horrocks, who is now perhaps best known for starring alongside the said Ms Lumley in *Absolutely Fabulous*. She enjoyed playing Rimmer's first true love, but for one thing: 'Chris Barrie was second only to Stephanie Beacham as a working partner – but I found the lines *very* difficult to learn!'
- The holoship itself was one of the visual-effects department's most spectacular creations. 'It was Paul McGuinness, one of my assistants, who made that,' Peter Wragg reveals. 'He designed it himself and made it. It's all made out of perspex, because what we wanted to do was try and create this idea of a hologramatic ship, by making it partially transparent. I think the effect that we got was great. Unfortunately, I don't think we did justice to Paul's model. We

really should have done some more shots to show it off a bit better.'

2: THE INQUISITOR

Broadcast date: 27 February 1992.

Guest cast: John Docherty (Inquisitor), Jake Abraham (Second Lister), James Cormack (Thomas Allman).

Starbug is taken over by a being called the Inquisitor, and returned to *Red Dwarf*. The Inquisitor, it seems, is a self repairing simulant who survived to the end of time and, realising that there is no God and no afterlife, decided that the only point of life is to make something of yourself. With that in mind, he built himself a time machine, and now roams all of history, visiting every living being in turn and judging their worthiness to hold on to the gift of life. Anyone who has wasted their time alive is exterminated and retrospectively erased from history, being replaced by a version of themselves that might have been, had a different sperm reached a different egg. Now, it is the turn of the *Red Dwarf* crew to be judged and needless to say, all are somewhat worried. The four trials take place on *Red Dwarf* itself. The Inquisitor takes on the appearance and the personality of the person he is judging, ensuring that they get the fairest trial possible, as they are tried by themselves. As it turns out, Rimmer and the Cat are acquitted. They are both shallow and selfish people, the Inquisitor proclaims, but having started with nothing in life, they have certainly lived up to their own extremely low expectations. Lister and Kryten, however, are not so fortunate. Kryten manages to talk himself into an early grave, whilst Lister's refusal to answer the charges against him seals his death warrant as well. Both are eradicated from history so that only their bodies remain to be disposed of. Death looks certain – until the Kryten of a few hours hence pops into existence, taking the Inquisitor from behind. The future Kryten is killed, but not before he has ripped off the Inquisitor's time gauntlet and thrown it to an astonished Lister. Lister and Kryten make a run for it, but find that they can't get very far. The Inquisitor has altered the timelines so that they never existed, and Holly will not let them through any of the security doors. Worse, she summons the crew of *Red Dwarf* to deal with the 'intruders', and Lister and Kryten are confronted by their ex-crewmates – who no longer recognise them – and two very different versions of their own selves. They are escorted to the brig but, as they proceed, the Inquisitor attacks, his mad assault causing the deaths of the new Lister and Kryten. The original Lister appropriates the hand of his dead 'sperm-in-law' and uses it, much to Kryten's total disgust, to get him through the ship's palm-operated doors.

They retreat to the hold, where Cat and Rimmer find them. Forming an uneasy alliance, the four head towards the storage bay where, according to Kryten's future self, the final confrontation with the Inquisitor is to take place. The Inquisitor is indeed there, and Rimmer and the Cat are gunned down mercilessly. However, the simulant chooses to toy with Lister, first regressing him to youth and then aging him enormously. His mistake! Kryten provides a distraction, enabling Lister to use the time gauntlet on the Inquisitor himself. He is frozen for just under ten minutes, during which time Kryten takes the gauntlet and travels to the past to carry out the act of self sacrifice which will get them into this mess in the first place. Lister is now alone, but he has a plan in mind. When the Inquisitor awakens, he is suspended over an abyss by a rope – a rope which Lister suddenly burns through. At the last possible instant, he hauls the simulant to safety, proudly proclaiming that since he has saved the Inquisitor's life, any attempt to eradicate him totally from history will cause the creature's own death too. Having nothing to fear now, he returns the Inquisitor's gauntlet to him. However, it seems that Lister has miscalculated. After all, if he is erased from time, he will never be around to threaten the Inquisitor's life in the first place. The Inquisitor can erase him with no problem whatsoever. Lister hadn't thought of that. Or had he? Before his untimely death, Kryten had re-rigged the time gauntlet. When the Inquisitor tries to use it, it backfires, and it is he who is himself erased from the time continuum. All of his past works are thus undone, and Rimmer, Cat and Kryten are restored to life, unharmed. An appropriate time, says Kryten, for Lister to 'give him five'. But Lister can do better than that – he can give him fifteen!

- Although uncredited, Duane Cox and Carl Chase play younger and older versions respectively of Dave Lister.
- Extensive use was made of the (plastic) *Red Dwarf* corridor set. To make this sound metallic, the sound supervisor, Keith Mayes, had to rerecord every footstep by walking on a metal grate in time to the actors on screen, then adding an echo. The overlaid sound of dripping water also helped to match the atmosphere of scenes filmed in Sunbury Pump House.
- *Red Dwarf V* introduced more than its fair share of popular characters, and the Inquisitor was just the first of them. Owing to the tremendous fan reaction, he went on to appear in comic-strip form in the *Red Dwarf Smegazine*, as did Mr Flibble ('Quarantine'), Duane Dibbley ('Back to Reality') and Jake Bullet ('Back to Reality' again). Well, we *assume* it was due to the fan reaction – they might just have been desperate for ideas.

3: TERRORFORM

Broadcast date: 5 March 1992.

Guest cast: Sara Stockbridge and Francine Walker-Lee (Handmaidens).

Rimmer and Kryten have met with a rather nasty accident whilst out moon-hopping. Kryten lies crushed and broken in the wreckage of *Starbug*, and Rimmer has gone missing altogether. With only sixty-seven minutes to live, Kryten is able to disconnect his own hand and send it back to *Red Dwarf* to fetch help. At first, the already arachnophobic Lister is alarmed by Holly's description of a tarantula-like intruder on the ship – and his fear grows when he finds it crawling up his leg. Eventually though, a VDU keyboard gives the hand the medium it needs to communicate its message, and Lister and Cat rush to the rescue of their crewmates. Repairing Kryten is a simple enough task, thanks to Lister's DIY skills, although as always, there are a few bits left over. Rimmer, however, is still missing, and it seems that he could be in deadly danger. The moon on which he and Kryten crashed is apparently a Psy-Moon, one of those rare planetoids that terra-form themselves in the pattern of the psyche of anybody landing upon them. That means that the whole moon has now grown into the shape of Rimmer's subconscious mind – and that's not a very nice place to be. As the others search for him, their journey takes them through the Swamp of Despair (where the frogs cry out 'Useless!' and huge, blood-sucking leeches bear the face of Rimmer's mother) and past the numerous gravestones of those qualities in Rimmer which have been long dead – amongst them Honour and Generosity, and a minute stone which marks the resting place of his Charm. A freshly dug pit looms open, awaiting the arrival of his Hope, and Kryten realises that Rimmer is in very grave danger indeed. In fact, the entire landscape is dominated by Rimmer's strongest emotion, as he is about to discover. His cries for a solicitor ignored, he has been captured and tied to a stake, the British Embassy nowhere in sight. The brief appearance of two skimpily clad, oil-bearing handmaidens gives him cause for hope, but it seems that their job is only to anoint him in preparation for the main event. Much to his dismay, it seems that this is to be his torture and sacrifice, at the hands of a hideous creature formed by his own Self-Loathing.

The rest of the crew arrive just in time to put their bazookoids to good use, but all watch on in horror as the weapons seem to have no effect. Rimmer, however, is touched by the very fact that they have risked their lives for him, and the momentary rekindling of his Self-Respect weakens the creature and forces it to retreat, at least long enough for him and the others to make a run for it. Rimmer's Self-Loathing isn't dormant for long though, and even as Holly tries to lift *Starbug* off the Psy Moon's surface, she finds it dragged back down again. The creature demands that Rimmer be handed over, otherwise it will never let the shuttlecraft leave. Things look bleak – until Kryten has an idea. In order to defeat the Self-Loathing creature, the others have to eliminate that emotion in Rimmer himself, by making him feel that he is loved. The words come harder to some than to others, and the Cat in particular has great difficulty, but the plan seems to work. On the surface of the moon, the change in Rimmer's psyche is mirrored in physical terms by the resurrection of his Self-Confidence and Self-Respect, which leap into battle against his Self-Loathing. The creature is weakened just enough for *Starbug* to break free, and Holly guides the craft back towards *Red Dwarf*. By now, of course, Rimmer has realised that there was only one reason for the words of friendship he has been hearing, and now that freedom has been achieved, the others decide that there is no need to keep up the pretence any longer.

- Lister and Rimmer have more in common than they might think. It was revealed in 'Better Than Life' that Rimmer's all-time greatest fear is to have a tarantula crawl up his leg; here, it is shown to be Lister's greatest fear too.
- *Red Dwarf Smegazine* received several letters of a dubious (and explicit) nature after Rimmer's clothes were torn off and he was oiled by handmaidens. Far from enjoying his newfound sex-symbol status, Chris Barrie's only comment is an embarrassed: 'I don't know where they come up with these notions.'
- Although two models of the Self-Loathing creature were built, it was barely seen. The Videotape Editor, Graham Hutchings, explains why: 'We purposely cut the amount of the model you saw down to a minimum, because it didn't

work if you saw it for a long time; just snatches of it were much better. With a lot of these things, if you have the chance to look at them for any length of time, you start looking at the flaws. That's the technique with editing: creating an atmosphere without giving too much away. It's a psychological game of what you can get away with without destroying the illusion.' Another casualty of Graham's scissors was the Cat's reluctant expression of love for Rimmer, which was removed to tighten up the scene as a whole.

- The Lighting Director, John Pomphrey, recalls an uncomfortable incident during filming in a swampy area behind Shepperton Studios. 'We were getting ready for a night shoot and, as we were setting up, two electricians and myself fell in the water. The lamps went in as well and all the scripts were soaking wet. It was awful, but it caused a lot of hilarity.' Filming for 'Emohawk – Polymorph II', the following season, necessitated a return to the area . . . 'and when the generator turned up, there was a life jacket on the side especially for me!'

4: QUARANTINE

Broadcast date: 12 March 1992.

Guest cast: Maggie Steed (Dr Hildegarde Lanstrom).

Answering a distress call from a hologramatic doctor, the *Red Dwarf* crew realise that they will have to commandeer Rimmer's remote projection unit to get her back to the ship. Furthermore, with Holly being capable of projecting only one hologram at a time, there are going to be problems when she gets there. Rimmer objects strenuously, but he is undone by Kryten's knowledge of Space Corps Directives. He is left to return to *Red Dwarf*, while the others go in search of Doctor Hildegarde Lanstrom.

They finally find her in a Viral Research Department,

where she is preserved in a stasis pod. Their arrival triggers her release and all are alarmed to see that she is, in fact, completely mad. Worse still, Lanstrom has developed amazing powers of telepathy, telekinesis and, most worrying of all, hex vision, with which she attempts to fry her would-be rescuers. Kryten theorises that she has caught a mutated holo-virus, which has stimulated the normally unused areas of her brain, at the same time taking so much energy from her that she will shortly expire. Lister tries to contact Rimmer, who is still sulking on *Starbug*, for back-up, but Rimmer delights in the opportunity to take his revenge. While he is still pretending not to hear Lister's frantic transmission, Lanstrom seizes the communicator and screams a death threat to him. Time, thinks Rimmer, to return to *Red Dwarf* after all. Fortunately for the others, they manage to avoid Lanstrom's deadly blasts until the virus finally strikes her down. They return to *Starbug* and make the journey back to *Red Dwarf*. En route, Kryten reveals a fantastic discovery. Lanstrom, it seems, had been working on a theory that viruses can be both negative and positive. To this end, she had synthesised viruses that cause positive effects. The Cat is worried that, if sexual magnetism is a virus, then he has a terminal case, but Kryten and Lister are more interested in Lanstrom's goodluck virus, which Lister tries out to great effect. However, none of the three are lucky for very much longer. Rimmer has been using his time alone to study the Space Corps Directives with which he was previously foiled, and as *Starbug* returns to the ship, it is diverted to Bay 47 – Quarantine. Lister, Cat and Kryten are to remain there, in accordance with Space Corps Directive 595, for three months. In the event, it takes only five days before arguments and fights break out between the captive trio. However, worse is yet to come, as Rimmer makes an unexpected appearance in a red and white checked gingham dress and army boots, carrying a ventriloquist's puppet that he calls Mister Flibble. The holo-virus, it seems, can be carried by radio waves, and Rimmer contracted it when he spoke to Lanstrom.

Completely insane, Rimmer orders that his shipmates

should spend two hours W. O. O. as punishment for their behaviour. W. O. O. means WithOut Oxygen but fortunately for all concerned, another dose of the good-luck virus gives Lister the fortune he needs to provide an escape route. Pursued through the corridors of *Red Dwarf* by the fanatical Rimmer – who has now, like Lanstrom, developed hex vision, telepathy and telekinesis – Lister, Cat and Kryten are cut off from the hologram projection unit with which Kryten feels he can do something about Rimmer's current problem. However, Lister's luck comes into play again as the equipment necessary to set up a remote link just happens to be found lying beside them. Not a moment too soon, Kryten is able to reverse the effects of the holo-virus, although Lister believes his good luck must have worn off when he discovers that Rimmer is, in fact, perfectly okay. Finally, a startled Rimmer wakes to find himself confined to quarantine, and supervised by his three crewmates, who have clothed themselves in a matching set of red and white checked gingham dresses . . .

- Rimmer gets his first look at a (hologramatic) copy of the Space Corps Directives manual. His misquoting of the directives was to become a running joke throughout *Red Dwarf VI*, but it was dropped thereafter when fans complained that it had gone too far.
- Maggie Steed had to wear latex make-up to portray Dr Lanstrom . . . 'as, playing a dying hologram, my face was supposed to be melting. This meant that I gave myself a heart attack whenever I passed a mirror, and had to get used to people wincing in the corridor when they saw me. I decided not to go to the canteen! The relief was enormous when I finally peeled it off.'
- 'We had one of the most horrific studio sessions ever,' Doug Naylor remembers. Rob Grant agrees: 'Nobody could remember their names: we had to have idiot cards when they were signing autographs at the end!' Doug: 'It happens sometimes. It's kind of infectious, like a disease – one of them starts forgetting and it just spreads between them.'

Rob: 'It took us fifty-seven minutes to record the three-minute scene between them and the ginghamed Rimmer. Fifty-seven minutes! I mean, we only get two and a half hours for the entire show.' Doug: 'I remember sitting in the van, and I was looking down at my knuckles and they were white, and someone was saying: "Oh, you're very good – you're not losing your temper or your patience." And it was just 'cos I was in shock – it was horrible!'

5: DEMONS AND ANGELS

Broadcast date: 19 March 1992.

Guest cast: None.

Kryten has developed another incredible device – a triplicator, which can create two extra copies of anything that is placed within its field. There are only three drawbacks. Firstly, the copies have a lifespan of one hour only. Secondly, whilst one is infinitely superior to the original, the other is infinitely worse. And finally, when Kryten attempts to reverse the procedure, *Red Dwarf* explodes – which is a bit of a problem for all concerned. Although the crew escape in *Starbug*, they soon realise that they don't have long to live. Even if they had enough fuel to reach a habitable planet, it would do them little good, as they only have enough oxygen for seven minutes. Rimmer and Kryten don't need oxygen of course, and Rimmer wonders if the jettisoning of Lister and Cat's corpses would lighten their load enough to reach safety. However, his plans are abruptly curtailed when Kryten points out that, as a hologram relying on emergency power only, he himself has less than four minutes of run-time left. Lister takes charge of the situation, and suggests a search of the wreckage for any oxygen or fuel tanks. What they find instead is something quite remarkable. Where once there was one *Red Dwarf*, there are now two – products, obviously, of the triplicator. Kryten surmises that instead of reversing the triplicating process, the machine actually reversed its field, thus re-creating *Red Dwarf* and everything on it. It was obviously the tremendous power drain required by this that caused the original to explode. Of course, these two new ships will be 'high' and 'low' versions of the original, and they will both fade away in one hour's time, but as each ship should have a triplicator of its own, Kryten feels that it should be no problem to reverse the procedure and merge the two vessels back into a perfect copy of the original. Of course, things don't go quite that smoothly. The two *Red Dwarf*s come complete with their own crews, and on the first ship, Lister, Rimmer, Cat and Kryten encounter spiritually enlightened versions of their own selves. The real difficulties begin, however, when the originals and their 'high' copies fly over to the 'low' ship, and instantly come under fire from the homicidal maniacs who have been formed from the dark sides of their own natures. Pacifists to the end, the 'high' Cat and Kryten attempt to reason with their counterparts, and are mercilessly slain. Lister is captured, and a spinal implant allows his 'low' self to dictate his every movement by remote control. He is forced to knife the 'high' Lister to death, and likewise to kill the 'high' Rimmer by crushing his light bee. Meanwhile, Rimmer, Cat and Kryten have made their way to the cargo bay with both triplicators, but they only have two minutes to evacuate the 'low' ship before it disappears.

Lister arrives at the last instant, but rather delays things by trying to murder the Cat. Kryten's chloroform pads put him out of action, a little less painfully than the Cat's attempt, which consisted of a knee to the groin. With only seconds to spare, the four originals pilot *Starbug* out into space, and watch as both the 'high' and 'low' ships vanish, to be replaced as planned by their own vessel, back in full working order. However, there is still the problem, of the spinal implant to contend with. With Lister still acting like a homicidal maniac, it becomes obvious that, despite the disappearance of the 'low' ship, the remote control unit and its operator have survived – and a quick blast of bazookoid fire brings the 'low' Lister out of hiding. Still smarting at the damage the controlled Lister did to his neckline, the Cat is delighted when he gains possession of the control unit. Kryten can remove the implant easily enough, but the Cat pleads with him to leave it in situ – just for one more week.

- The working title for this episode was 'High and Low'.
- Several uncredited 'doubles' of the cast were required to allow the characters to meet their alternative selves. Jake Abraham and Tim Yeates had already played 'more worthwhile' versions of Lister and Kryten respectively in 'The Inquisitor', and Yeates also stood in for Chris Barrie here. Helping out Danny John-Jules with his multiple roles was Johnny Orlando.
- This was the first episode of *Red Dwarf V* recorded, and the new Director, Juliet May, was not used to the unique conventions of the series. Hattie Hayridge in particular was disappointed that, after the make-up department had gone to the trouble of making her look different, she appeared only in the background of a few shots. Normally, a separate tape of her would have been recorded to drop into the episode at key moments. Juliet eventually decided that *Red Dwarf* was not for her, and Rob Grant and Doug Naylor stepped in to direct the remainder of the series. They refilmed several scenes from 'Demons and Angels', in a great hurry, on the day after the end-of-season party.
- The visual-effects department blew up their only model of *Red Dwarf* for this episode. Peter Wragg recalls: 'We had to make sure we'd got all the shots we needed with it, and then we loaded it up with pyrotechnics, turned the cameras on, crossed our fingers and hoped for the best. We had one camera that was running at three thousand frames a second, which is an incredibly high speed. The explosion probably took about two seconds – I mean it was literally bang-bang-bang-bang-bang-bang-bang-bang; we just fired them all off – but because we were running so fast, we got twenty seconds' worth of film.'

6: BACK TO REALITY

Broadcast date: 26 March 1992.

Guest cast: Timothy Spall (Andy), Lenny Von Dohlen (Cop), Anastasia Hille (New Kochanski), Marie McCarthy (Nurse), Jake Sharian (New Lister).

On a recon mission to an ocean planet, the *Red Dwarf* crew discover the wreckage of the SSS *Esperanto*, from which a marine seeding experiment once took place. Quite remarkably, it seems that the entire crew have committed suicide, even down to a haddock, which closed its own gills and suffocated itself. The reason soon becomes obvious, as Lister, Kryten and the Cat begin to suffer bouts of depression, caused by the presence of a substance which, Kryten theorises, is some kind of ink, such as might be squirted from a particularly large and dangerous version of a squid. From his safe haven back in *Starbug*, Rimmer is able not only to confirm Kryten's conjecture, but also to pinpoint the monstrous creature itself – no hard task, as it is frighteningly close, and getting nearer. One hurried return to the '*Bug* later, Holly lifts off for an immediate retreat, but the squid is too quick, and its deadly ink surrounds the fleeing vessel. Even as it does, *Starbug* veers out of control and into a quite spectacular crash. The vessel is completely destroyed and, needless to say, everyone on board suffers an immediate death. That means only one thing of course. Game Over. Lister, Rimmer, Cat and Kryten suddenly find themselves alive and awake, and plugged into '*Red Dwarf* – the Total Immersion Video Game' in which, after playing for four years, they have accumulated the phenomenal score of 4 per cent. Leisure World attendant Andy gleefully points out the areas they missed. Had they found the Captain's message, hidden in microdot form in the letter 'i' on one of Rimmer's swimming certificates, they would have discovered that Rimmer was in fact a hand-picked special agent for the Space Corps, on a secret mission to destroy *Red Dwarf* and guide Lister to his destiny as the creator of the Second Universe.

Andy is quite amused that, having missed that blatant clue, the group had been stuck with the prat version of Rimmer for four years. And how could Lister not have got Kochanski – the whole object of the game for him? Dejected, the foursome head for the recuperation lounge, passing on the way the group who are to replace them as Lister and company in the next game. The question on everybody's addled minds is now – who are they really? The Cat, for one, is not very pleased with the answer. He is Duane Dibbley, a 'no-style gimbo with teeth that druids could use as a place of worship'. Kryten, however, is quite happy with his new half-human form and his identity as Jake Bullet, an agent for the Cybernautic Division of the Police Department. Of course, says Rimmer, the Cybernautic Division could be traffic control . . . Most ironic of all, Lister and Rimmer turn out to be half-brothers. The twist is, Lister's new persona of Sebastian Doyle is a wealthy man, whilst brother Billy is a homeless tramp. Dispirited by this information, Dibbley, Bullet and the Doyles set out to reacclimatise themselves to the fascist world in which they apparently live. However, they barely manage to get to the car park, and Sebastian's limousine, before they find themselves on the wrong end of a policeman's gun. Oh, and the Cybernautic Division does turn out to be traffic control. Big trouble! Only the sight of Sebastian Doyle saves the group from a fate exactly the same as death. The old Lister learns with horror that he is really the Head of this totalitarian state's Ministry of Alteration – where people are altered from being alive to being dead. The news doesn't sit well with him. Nor is Kryten particularly pleased when, to save a young child from becoming the next victim of the fascist system, he is forced to shoot the cop down in cold blood. The group flee, but they realise they won't get far. In fact, none of them have gone very far at all. Back on *Starbug*, Holly watches with concern as Lister, Rimmer, Cat and Kryten veer madly around the cockpit, trapped in a shared hallucination caused by the Despair Squid's ink. Inevitably, the events they are 'witnessing' take their toll, and the four huddle together, ready to bid goodbye to life in the same way as the crew of the *Esperanto*. Finally, and in the nick of time, Holly is able to communicate with Kryten by broadcasting on a higher frequency, persuading him to make the moves which, in real life, will release a dose of lithium carbonate – a mood stabiliser – into the cockpit. A confused crew come back to reality, where Holly assures them that her limpet mines have seen off their attacker. All that is left then is for all to thank their good fortune, and to make their weary way back to *Red Dwarf*.

- The uncredited 'replacements' for Rimmer, Cat and Kryten were portrayed by Julian Lyon, David Lemkin and Scott Charles-Bennett respectively.
- Although 'Back to Reality' was the first *Red Dwarf V* script to be completed, it was one of the last handed to the Production Designer, Mel Bibby. He saved time and costs by stripping down and repainting the holoship set from an earlier episode, to be used as the arcade in which the *Red Dwarf* crew 'awoke'.
- A multi-tentacled model of the Despair Squid was put together by Peter Wragg and his special-effects team, and filmed thrashing about in a tank. During editing, however, it was decided that a subtle, electronically created shadow would be more effective and the model was never seen on screen.
- Rob Grant recalls that some of the regulars hadn't yet signed up for *Red Dwarf VI*: 'We'd written in the new Rimmer and the new Lister coming into the Virtual Reality suite, and in the stage directions we wrote "Are you worried yet, guys?" ' He was also particularly pleased with the casting of Lenny Von Dohlen, fresh from his role as the disturbed Mr Smith in *Twin Peaks*. 'I'm a major *Twin Peaks* fan – I think it's the best piece of television ever – so it was very exciting to have someone who'd touched David Lynch on set! I was a bit intimidated.' Von Dohlen was persuaded to do the show by Frances Barber, with whom he was staying while in England. She evidently thought highly of *Red Dwarf*, having enjoyed her own guest spot in 'Polymorph'.

RED DWARF VI

There was quite a gap between *Red Dwarf V* and *Red Dwarf VI*, mainly due to Grant Naylor Productions branching out into other projects. Because *Red Dwarf V* had seen a large increase in viewers the BBC asked Rob Grant and Doug Naylor to script a special 'introductory' episode for new viewers. The writers weren't keen on this idea, but it did partially prompt them into reintroducing the concept of the series via Lister's amnesia sequence in 'Psirens'.

With Andy de Emonny at the directorial helm *Red Dwarf* was completed and available in time for a spring 1993 broadcast. However, in order to maximise the potential audience, the BBC held it back until the autumn schedule. When it eventually reached the screen, 200 years were said to have elapsed.

Thanks to the publication of news revelations in the *Red Dwarf Smegazine*, the fact that *Red Dwarf VI* didn't feature Holly or indeed *Red Dwarf* didn't come as much of a shock to the series' hard-core followers. Nevertheless, these changes were rather drastic – especially the dropping of Hattie Hayridge. Rob and Doug realised that, as far as Holly and Kryten were concerned, there just wasn't enough dialogue to go around. This factor, coupled with their desire to make life more of a survival challenge for Lister and company, led them to devise the theft and subsequent tracking of *Red Dwarf*, which would provide the underlying theme of *Red Dwarf VI*. Not only would this subplot provide a convenient excuse to lose Holly but their favoured *Starbug* could logically be promoted to main ship of the series. In Rob Grant's opinion *Red Dwarf VI* was the best series so far, and indeed 'Gunmen of the Apocalypse' earned the series a prestigious Emmy award.

Despite the fight-for-survival angle, the remaining characters became subtly more capable than previously, most notably with Rimmer's acquisition of a hard-light drive and Cat's heightened sensory capabilities. Even so this didn't prevent the season's shock ending with the destruction of *Starbug* and the death of its crew, and the promise that the story was to be continued . . .

Regulars: Rimmer – Chris Barrie. Lister – Craig Charles. Cat – Danny John-Jules. Kryten – Robert Llewellyn. Written by Rob Grant and Doug Naylor. Produced by Justin Judd. Directed by Andy de Emmony. A Grant Naylor production for BBC North.

1: PSIRENS

Broadcast date: 7 October 1993.

Guest cast: Jenny Agutter (Professor Mamet), Samantha Robson (Pete Tranter's Sister), Anita Dobson (Captain Tau), Richard Ridings (Crazed Astro), C. P. Grogan (Kochanski), Zoe Hilson and Elizabeth Anson (Temptresses). Featuring the hands of Phil Manzanera.

Lister wakes from deep-sleep on *Starbug*, to find he has amnesia. Kryten fills in some details, and Lister is appalled to learn that he's a curry-eating slob. He also discovers that he can't play the guitar, although Kryten assures him that, once he regains his memory, he'll believe he can. A synaptic enhancer helps restore his mind, whilst Rimmer's hologram is rebooted. The crew have been out of action for two hundred years, ever since *Red Dwarf* was apparently stolen. Kryten has woken them because they finally have a chance of recovering it. The ship has taken a detour round an asteroid belt, but the smaller *Starbug* can slip through unharmed, thus closing the gap between them.

They head into the belt, but find themselves navigating through a spaceship graveyard. A message written with intestines and blood warns them of psirens, shape-changing

GELFs which lure unwary travellers to them and suck their brains out through straws. Two temptresses appear on the screen, begging for someone to fertilise their planet of three thousand women. Cat volunteers and only the common sense of the others saves him. The psirens then try their charms on Lister, presenting an image of his lost love Kochanski. He too resists, and Kryten also exposes a giant flaming meteorite as a similar illusion. A second such hazard is all too real though, and *Starbug* plummets down onto an asteroid. The landing stanchion is buried, so Lister goes out to repair it – to be confronted by the image of Pete Tranter's sister, whom he lusted after through puberty. A second GELF arrives, in the form of Kryten and a battle breaks out over his brains. He escapes, but unfortunately two Listers return to *Starbug* and the others have to work out which is which. The guitar test eventually separates them: having copied Lister's mind perfectly, the GELF believes it can play well and thus does so. Cat and Kryten shoot the creature without hesitation, and it flees into the ship's depths. When Kryten finds it, it emulates Professor Mamet, his creator, whom he is programmed to obey. It orders him into the waste compactor.

Meanwhile, Rimmer's power-pack runs down and he fades away. Then Lister and Cat discover a brand-new drinks machine, realising too late that it's a less than cunning psiren disguise. Producing a straw, the creature prepares to feast. But it has reckoned without Kryten's versatility. Emerging from the compactor as a cubic mass of trash, he drops onto the intruder from a great height.

- The postponement of *Red Dwarf VI* meant that the script for 'Psirens' was accidentally released in the Penguin book *Primordial Soup* long before the episode itself was broadcast.

- Captain Tau was named after *Red Dwarf*'s own commanding officer in the first American pilot. Rob and Doug never expected Anita Dobson to accept such a minor part: they asked her only because they were already approaching her partner, Brian May, to provide Lister's hands for his guitar solo. To their surprise, May couldn't make it (they got Roxy Music's Phil Manzanera instead) but Dobson could. Their one regret was that, had they anticipated this, they could have written something more substantial for her.

- 'Psirens' was omitted from the BBC's 1995 repeat run of *Red Dwarf*'s first six seasons. Craig Charles had been remanded in custody on a rape charge (later proved to be totally unfounded) and the Powers That Be felt that some of his more lustful scenes (Kochanski, Pete Tranter's sister) were inappropriate. They also cut references in 'Gunmen of the Apocalypse' to Lister's enjoying under-age sex in Artificial Reality.

- Mel Bibby had to redesign *Starbug* for its increased usage, not least because its cockpit now had to seat four. 'The cockpit looks the same,' he explains, 'but it's actually much bigger than it was before. [The ship] still has the same basic shape, but there are others sections built in.' An airlock, a kitchen and a whole upper floor had to be added. 'It wasn't as easy as it sounds. Certain things in the script required an airlock, for instance, where previously there had been no airlock. Well you can't hide that: the viewing public will know it's not the same *'Bug*. I discussed it with Rob and Doug and their argument was that, by the first episode, the crew have been in suspended animation and Kryten has spent two thousand years converting the ship.'

2: LEGION

Broadcast date: 14 October 1993.

Guest cast: Nigel Williams (Legion).

Twenty-four hours behind *Red Dwarf*, and *Starbug* is losing ground. Worse, space weevils have invaded the food stores and the only meat left is ... space weevil. Lister's 'crunchy king prawn' meal is fortunately interrupted, when an imminent threat sets Cat's nostril hairs vibrating. A heat-seeking missile has locked onto the ship and neither the blue alert bulb nor Rimmer's surrender seem likely to stop it. When the 'missile' hits, it forms an energy globe round *Starbug*, guiding it to a space station where the exploring crew are confronted by a being called Legion. Legion proves both his skills and his good intentions by removing Lister's appendix (which was on the verge of peritonitis) and converting Rimmer's soft-light drive into a hard-light one. The visitors are then guided into a hall filled with the finest pieces of art created. Legion is clearly a remarkable being, and Rimmer sees the value in signing him up to join the crew. Unfortunately, this means showing him that they aren't the uncouth morons Lister seems to be, and a skirmish with Mamosian anti-matter chopsticks does nothing to help. In the event, Legion has other plans anyway. The Dwarfers, he states, must remain with him until they die.

Legion shows his captives to their luxurious 'cells'. Features of Lister's room include eight-packs of lager, sugar puff sandwiches and a spare pair of sneakers in the ice box, whilst Rimmer's is perfect down to the over-starched pyjamas and nocturnal boxing gloves. Likewise Kryten, faced with dirty floors and a mop, is in hog heaven. However, despite the opulence of their surroundings, they are still prisoners – and Lister's cunning escape plan, culled from the film *Revenge of the Surf-Boarding Killer Bikini Vampire Girls*, does nothing to change that. In fighting off Lister, Legion loses his face-plate and the truth becomes obvious. His features are an amalgam of the *Red Dwarf* crew's own; Legion is a gestalt entity, a being made up of the essences of others. The various scientific and artistic triumphs around him were achieved during his previous incarnation, composed of five of the most brilliant minds of the twenty-third century. Since their deaths, Legion has been unable to live and he is now forced to maintain his existence through his present guests. However, Kryten knocks out Lister and Cat, removing their personalities from Legion's mix. Rimmer, with his new invulnerable form, is more problematic: even smashing him over the head with a vase doesn't help, and the hologram finally has to reach inside himself and remove his own light bee. Left with only Kryten to draw on, Legion becomes the android's double, sharing his regard for human life and thus compelled to carry the *Starbug* crew to safety. He even leaves them with a star-drive, which could make the journey to *Red Dwarf* in nanoseconds. Despite a healthy scepticism from the crew, it actually works. But due to a faulty connection, it doesn't take *Starbug* with it.

- The working title for this episode was 'Call Me Legion'.
- Only when Nigel Williams turned up to film the 'citadel' scenes in Marco Polo House (the former headquarters of the late, lamented satellite channel BSB) was it discovered that his Legion costume didn't actually fit. He squeezed into it in the end, but there was no persuading the zip to close, and the back of the garment had to be sewn up instead. Nigel was trapped inside it for the duration of the recording.
- This episode has the dubious honour of featuring *Red Dwarf*'s most celebrated continuity error, as Dave Lister is seen to have his appendix removed by Legion, although we know from 'Thanks for the Memory' that he'd already had it taken out several million years before (as did Rimmer). In his novel, *Last Human*, Doug Naylor attempted to explain this by suggesting that a unique medical condition had caused Lister to be born with two appendixes.

3: GUNMEN OF THE APOCALYPSE

Broadcast date: 21 October 1993.

Guest cast: Jennifer Calvert (Loretta), Denis Lill (Simulant Captain/Death), Liz Hickling (Simulant Lieutenant), Imogen Bain (Lola), Steve Devereaux (Jimmy), Robert Inch (War), Jeremy Peters (Pestilence), Dinny Powell (Famine), Stephen Marcus (Bear Strangler McGee).

Starbug has strayed into a rogue simulant hunting zone. The crew switch to silent running, to avoid detection; however, this means prying Lister away from the Artificial Reality machine in which he acts out his sexual fantasies. Shutdown comes too late: the ship is detected by a battle-class cruiser and hailed by its xenophobic occupants. Knowing that simulants loathe humans, Lister and Cat concoct a ruse involving Kryten's detachable eyeballs, their own chins and the act of lying upside down beneath a camera. The simulants are not impressed, and when their captain teleports onto *Starbug*, he discovers the truth of the so-called Vindalooan people. These four pathetic specimens, he decides, will prove no sport at all. He guns them down, and they wake three weeks later in a *Starbug* which has been upgraded and fitted with laser cannons. The simulants are expecting a game of cat and mouse, and as the Cat states, the only way to win that is by not being the mouse. To their enemies' surprise, *Starbug* attacks, and a fluke hit brings the simulant ship down. However, the captain transmits an Armageddon Virus into *Starbug*'s navi-comp. Locked onto a suicide course and only thirty-eight minutes from a large moon, the Dwarfers have one chance of survival. Kryten contracts the virus himself and, inside his own mind, struggles to create a dove program to eradicate the infection. The others patch into his dreams and view his misadventures as a sheriff in the Old West, where the virus is represented by the 'Four Apocalypse Boys'. However, it is stronger than Kryten predicted. His systems can't cope, and his dream persona turns to drink. For once, one of Cat's suggestions proves good: using the Artificial Reality console, the crew beam themselves into Kryten's dreams, as characters from an AR game. Lister is Brett Riverboat, knife thrower; Rimmer is Dangerous Dan McGrew, barefist fighter; and Cat is the gun-slinging Riviera Kid. The trio's newfound skills stand them in good stead when Rimmer precipitates a bar-room brawl, and they are able to drag Kryten to safety.

Time runs out quickly. The Apocalypse Boys – War, Famine, Pestilence and Death – ride into town, determined to rid themselves of Kryten. When the sheriff's new protectors face them, Death decides to even the odds. The virus spreads to the AR machine, and their special skills are erased . . . as Rimmer discovers during his all too physical confrontation with War. Outnumbered and outgunned, Lister, Rimmer and Cat leave the game. Everything is up to Kryten now, but the others have bought him the time he needs. He tells the Apocalypse Boys to go for their guns, then brings them down with his own dove program and 'spreads peace through the system'. Returning to the real world, Kryten only has to feed this antidote into the navi-comp. He does so, even as *Starbug* disappears beneath the molten surface of the moon. Tense seconds later, it explodes back into the atmosphere, and heads for the hills to a quartet of triumphant cries: 'Yeeee-haaaa!'

- Rimmer's change of costume (in 'Legion') caused a minor continuity problem. Chris Barrie had accidentally been filmed in his old red/intangible guise, so when he appeared in blue/solid for the main studio recording, a line was hastily added to the effect that he can use both forms. However, he was seen only once more in red, when the crew visited their past selves (just prior to this episode) in 'Out of Time'.
- The replica Wild West town of Laredo helped to give an authentic air to this spoof western; Howard Goodall enhanced the atmosphere with his third variation on the closing theme (and a bonus version, which played as the crew arrived in Existence).
- Denis Lill had just appeared in the pilot episode of Grant Naylor's *The 10%ers*, and it was at the press showing of this that a *Red Dwarf* appearance was mooted. 'I collared Rob and Doug during the showing and they just happened to let drop that they were doing a western episode. I said I would kill to do a western, so that was it!' At the time, he had never even seen *Red Dwarf*. 'When I knew I was doing it, I thought I'd better find out what it's all about. Of course I'm hooked now, I think it's absolutely wonderful.'
- 'Danny turned into Gloria Swanson when we did "Gunmen of the Apocalypse",' Craig Charles recalls. 'He was right

into his element, riding on horses. Robert came up with the best story about that: he said Chris was inexperienced and very, very nervous; Danny was excellent on a horse and very, very cocky; Robert had ridden horses before but was very cautious; and I'd never been on a horse but I was completely bulletproof and hence very, very dangerous. Not a hint of fear, just go for it! I loved that episode. It was like being a real actor, out on set, playing cowboys, kissing girls and firing guns.'

4: EMOHAWK – POLYMORPH II

Broadcast date: 28 October 1993.

Guest cast: Hugh Quarshie (Computer), Martin Sims (GELF), Ainsley Harriott (GELF Chief), Steven Wickham (GELF Bride).

Rimmer's petty-minded enforcement of Space Corps drills is halted by a real-life emergency. A computer-operated Space Corps External Enforcement Vessel charges the *Starbug* crew with looting derelicts. Frontier law decrees that the penalty is death – and, being totally guilty, the Dwarfers can't persuade their accuser otherwise. They flee towards a GELF zone, gambling that the vessel will not follow them. Struck by pulse bolts, they nevertheless make the trip successfully, and land safe but not sound on a GELF moon. *Starbug*'s auto-repair systems can handle most of the damage, but the oxy-generation (O/G) unit is a charred mess. The crew set out towards the nearest GELF settlement, and Kryten is pleased when they are afforded the creatures' warmest welcome: not being skinned alive. Presentation of a cornucopia of gifts, from Swiss watches to Levi jeans, buys the Dwarfers entry to the *watunga* – or hut – of the Kinitawowi tribe. There, the real negotiations begin. The tribe have an O/G unit ... but the price for it is Lister.

She may be the looker of the family, but Lister is not pleased at the thought of marrying the tribal chief's daughter: a warty yeti lookalike whose name sounds like a footballer clearing his nose. After some persuasion though, he agrees to walk down the aisle. The plan is a simple one: leaving with the O/G unit, Kryten and the others will repair *Starbug* and come back for their colleague. However, when his new bride demands her conjugal rights, Lister brings his planned escape forward. Pursued by outraged GELFs, the crew return to *Starbug* and make a hasty departure. However, the chief's pet emohawk – a domesticated polymorph – has sneaked on board. Like its larger cousin, it steals emotions: it takes Cat's cool and Rimmer's bitterness, turning the pair into Duane Dibbley and Ace Rimmer respectively. Ace seals Lister and Kryten in the engine room and prepares to sacrifice himself and Duane by opening the airlock, expelling the emohawk from the ship. However, his captives break free in time to prevent his foolish sacrifice. Armed with liquid dilinium, the quartet pursue their quarry on the engine decks, where Dibbley is the first to encounter the monster, disguised as his thermos flask. The emohawk metamorphoses into a grenade and Ace saves everyone by using his hard-light body to cushion the explosion. Lister freezes the creature with dilinium. By extracting DNA strands from the emohawk and reinjecting them into his colleagues, Kryten can return them to normal. However, Ace requests a twenty-four hour stay before his return to negativity and snidiness. Duane can't wait to get back to being the stylish Cat since, as Duane Dibbley, he never knows when the next klutzy thing is going to happen. His accidental triggering of the dilinium and the consequent freezing of his crewmates proves the point.

- The working title for this episode was 'Polymorph II – Emohawk'. It was altered in the hope that it would look slightly less like a football score! Bizarrely, however, the original version appears on the sleeve of the video release.
- The GELF settlement was a re-dressed medieval village set, which had been left behind in the grounds of Shepperton

Studios by a drama series called *Covington Cross*.

- Look carefully as the newly heroic Rimmer opens the air-lock door in preparation for his suicide attempt: it starts to slide open before he has operated the controls. A less visible on-screen mistake is the rather-too-vicious explosion that knocked Craig Charles out of his seat and pelted Danny John-Jules with polystyrene, so hard that he ended up with welts on his cheek.

- The spectacular reaction to buck-toothed geek Duane Dibbley in 'Back to Reality' guaranteed an early return; something that pleased Danny John-Jules. 'No one's ever written a black nerd before,' he enthuses. 'You see, with most writers, stereotyping is confusing them: they can't think beyond what they've read in the *Sun* or what they've seen on the telly. So [with Dibbley] half the job was done, just because it had never been seen before !' 'I adore him,' Rob Grant admits. 'It was one of our intentions at the start of writing Series VI to have the Cat encounter some kind of space problem where he constantly becomes his alter ego Duane Dibbley in times of stress and trouble, so they were all trying to keep him calm so that Duane wouldn't go around screwing things up – pulling the steering wheel off and things. But we found it got in the way of stories. We were desperate to bring Duane back, and we finally found a way.'

5: RIMMERWORLD

Broadcast date: 4 November 1993.

Guest cast: Liz Hickling (Rogue Simulant).

Despite cheating at his medical examination, Rimmer doesn't get the results he'd hoped for. Kryten advises a program of relaxation and the regular grinding of Chinese worry balls to stave off a stress-related electronic aneurism. Unfortunately, rest doesn't seem to be on the cards. *Starbug*'s refrigeration unit has packed in, and unless the crew wish to survive indefinitely on Kryten's fungus scrapings, they have to steal fresh supplies from the Simulant ship they shot down a few weeks ago. Rimmer argues that the expedition beggars logic. Not only might one of the xenophobic killers still be functioning, but the ship's superstructure has been weakened and the whole thing will soon disintegrate. Lister, however, breaks more bad news: the reserve fuel tank has been punctured and fuel is urgently needed. The crew board the Simulant ship and, using its teleporter, transport goods onto *Starbug*. But, true to form, one Simulant Lieutenant has survived the crash. She confronts Lister, Kryten and Cat, and even Lister's request for a date isn't enough to save them from death. Undetected, Rimmer might be their key to survival – but he's more interested in saving his own neck. Diving into an escape pod, he unwittingly sets off a shipquake and, taking advantage of the distraction, his colleagues teleport back to their ship. Unfortunately, they also jump a timeline, and find themselves a few days back into their own past. Kryten corrects the fault, and *Starbug* jets out of the ship even as it falls to pieces. Retrieving Rimmer is not so simple. His pod was looted by the Simulants from a seeding ship, and it's heading for the nearest S3 planet. That turns out to be on the other side of a nearby wormhole, which creates a rather interesting time dilation effect. Although it will take only an hour or so for *Starbug* to follow the pod's path, almost six hundred years will pass for Rimmer.

Rimmer arrives on the barren planet which he christens Rimmerworld. Thanks to a pair of eco-accelerator rockets in the pod, he is able to transform it into a lush paradise in seven days. His attempts at genetic cloning start off less successfully; his perfect female mate turns out to be an exact copy of himself. He resolves to try again – and six hundred years later, *Starbug* lands on a planet which, according to Kryten, displays thousands of life-signs. Almost immediately after arriving, they are set upon by armoured Rimmer clones. They take the captives to their leader, who wears the letter 'H' as a holy sign but, as Cat detects, is not the real Rimmer. The trio are accused of displaying un-Rimmerlike behaviour such as bravery, charm and compassion. They will be executed at dawn, and in the meantime, they are taken to a cell which they share with a certain cloaked figure who has been there long enough to wear a pair of Chinese worry balls down to the size of ball bearings. Rimmer has been in prison for five hundred and fifty-seven years, having been overthrown by his own snidy, double-dealing clones. Lister decides it's time they left, and formulates a daring escape plan involving knotted sheets and cunning disguises. Kryten suggests they use the teleporter instead, but another calibration fault takes them temporarily into their own future . . . where, apparently, the crew are bemoaning the fate which awaits Dave Lister!

- 'Rimmerworld' was filmed back to back with 'Gunmen of the Apocalypse' and was to have been broadcast immediately after that episode, hence the return to the Simulant ship and the reappearance of Liz Hickling as one of its occupants.

- A shot of *Starbug* leaving a doomed *Red Dwarf* in 'Demons and Angels' is reused here, as *Starbug* leaves the doomed Simulant craft instead. It is reversed, though: if you look carefully, you can make out the backward lettering on the side of the ship.

- The episode concludes with a visit to the future, during which it is hinted that Lister has suffered a terrible fate. Originally, this was to have been revealed as a cruel joke played by the future crew on their past selves: the future Lister would have entered the room immediately after their visit, oblivious to what had gone on. However, given the new order of the episodes, this was altered in favour of a cliffhanger leading into 'Out of Time', in which a future Lister did indeed suffer a terrible fate (although there is no point during 'Out of Time' at which this scene could have occurred).

6: OUT OF TIME

Broadcast date: 11 November 1993.

Guest cast: None.

Starbug has lost *Red Dwarf*, and relations are becoming strained. Even Rimmer's weekly morale meetings offer no help. Then the ship runs into a storm front and a nasty jolt wounds Lister and reveals a startling fact: he's a 3000 series android, made to look realistically human and technically of a lower rank than Kryten. Kryten takes the news badly. All these years he's been looking up to Lister – worse, scrubbing his gussets. Taking command of the ship, he ensures that his former idol goes about his new cooking and cleaning chores diligently. However, Kryten soon realises that *Starbug* is passing through pockets of unreality and distorting the perceptions of its crew. Restored to the helm and waited on by a mortified android, Lister guides the ship through the reality minefield, which first causes the Cat to disappear then fits the entire crew out with animal heads before stealing *Starbug* from around them. Kryten theorises that this is a defensive device fitted to a Space Corps test ship, something with a prototype drive so powerful that no one must get their hands on it. The test ship will be at the epicentre of the field, so to prevent the crew from being distracted by more hallucinations, he places Lister and Cat in suspended animation and guides *Starbug* in himself. One quick looting mission later, the Dwarfers have their own time-drive – as a quick trip to take in the heady medieval atmosphere of deep space proves.

Returning to their own time, the crew receive an SOS message from what appears to be another *Starbug*. It transpires that on board the ship are their own future selves. Their time-drive has malfunctioned, and they need to copy components from the newer machine. Kryten is wary of communicating with them, worried about the crew seeing their own future. However, they can't ignore a plea for help.

Kryten volunteers to meet the future versions himself, as he can wipe his brain of what he learns. However, the discovery that something horrible has happened to Lister proves more than he can cope with. The future crew board the ship, and Lister, Rimmer and Cat are sealed on the obs deck to avoid meeting them. However, Lister patches the medi-scan through to the monitors and watches delightedly as a balding Cat, an obese Rimmer and a wig-wearing Kryten arrive on board. Then he sees himself: merely a brain floating in a tank!

Kryten learns that, having found the long-sought star-drive, the future crew are now epicures, travelling through time and enjoying the best that mankind has to offer. Unfortunately, most of the best is in the hands of ruthless dictators, and Kryten is startled to learn that they consort with the likes of Louis XVI and Adolf Hitler. Lister, too, has heard enough. He shoots his way off the ops deck and demands that the visitors leave. They are forced to agree, but upon returning to their ship, they broadcast this warning: if they can't have the time-drive, then no one can. They will fight for it to the death. Lister is prepared to engage them, as is Cat – and Kryten would rather die than wear that toupee. To everyone's astonishment, even Rimmer announces that he's 'Better dead than smeg!' They go in hard, but the fight is decidedly one-sided. Lister drops first, then Cat, then Kryten, whose last words indicate that there might yet be a way out. Seizing upon this hope, Rimmer grabs a bazookoid, heads for the time-drive and fires, just as *Starbug* explodes . . .

- The working title for this episode was 'Present from the Future'.
- Rimmer was to have saved the day by destroying *Starbug*'s time drive so that the crew's future selves couldn't use it. However, the BBC had already asked for a seventh series, so Rob Grant and Doug Naylor decided to go out on a cliffhanger: they replaced this sequence with a shot of *Starbug* exploding, over which the words 'To Be Continued . . .' were superimposed. The original conclusion appeared on the *Red Dwarf Smeg-Ups* tape – but, although

a more than adequate amount of the preceding action was included, the original final scene was inexplicably not. This would have seen the crew relaxing after their close call, with 'Margueritas' – only to find that Kryten had given them urine re-cyc instead. Real Margueritas were provided for the actors as a sort of end-of-season celebration – but, recalling the scene ruefully, Danny John-Jules comments: 'At one point, I actually thought urine might have tasted a bit better!'

- Because *Starbug*'s destruction was an afterthought, there was neither the time nor the money left to actually blow up the model (as they did *Red Dwarf* the season before). Instead, video trickery was used to overlay an explosion on top of stock footage of the craft in space.
- The script was completed only days before recording began, forcing Rob Grant and Doug Naylor to come up with something that required only the four regulars and the *Starbug* set. Inadequate rehearsal time also necessitated the use of an autocue, not for the first time this series. 'I found it harder because I'd never done it before,' confesses Danny John-Jules. 'I mean, I used autocue when I did things like *Jackanory*, but with *Red Dwarf*, because you have to look away from it, it tends to break the natural look of the piece. If you're not careful, it can look like you're reading idiot boards. For me, anyway, it was a distraction – but there was nothing we could do about it: it was that or nothing basically.'

RED DWARF VII

Heralded by a *Radio Times* cover (the programme's first), the seventh series of *Red Dwarf* finally appeared on our screens in 1997, over three years after the previous season ended.

Much had happened during those three-plus years. In 1994 Craig Charles was falsely accused of rape and spent three months on remand. In the same year Rob Grant decided to end his long-term writing partnership with Doug Naylor. Not surprisingly, rumours concerning the return of *Red Dwarf* abounded – everything from the possibility of a fifty-minute Christmas special to Chris Barrie's reluctance to be involved in a further series. To the distress of many of the show's fans when *Red Dwarf VII* got the official go-ahead, it was announced, as feared, that Chris would not be appearing throughout. On the plus side the season was to get an extra two episodes – the eight episodes of *Red Dwarf VII* plus a similar number for *Red Dwarf VIII*, will bring the series total to fifty-two, enough to comprise a syndication package for US television.

With Rob Grant out of the picture, Doug Naylor became the guiding light behind the extended seventh season, which incidentally he subtitled 'Back from the Dead'. To replace the outgoing Rimmer he chose a character who, although she had appeared only sporadically in the series, was still a significant part of the *Red Dwarf* mythos: Kristine Kochanski. However, he chose to re-create – and recast – Lister's old flame, to fit more easily into her new, expanded role. A Parallel Universe scenario presented an opportunity for recasting without causing too much fuss; the actress Chloe Annett slipped effortlessly into the role.

Doug Naylor wasn't left entirely to his own devices, however. For the first time in the programme's history other writers would contribute to *Red Dwarf*'s scripts. These included Paul Alexander, who would also double as the script editor, and Robert Llewellyn, who took the opportunity to elaborate on Kryten's origins and to write himself another role.

Red Dwarf VII (which, ironically, was numbered on screen for the first time but not in the *Radio Times*) saw the timely return of Ed Bye to the director's chair. His return coincided with the decision to film the series without a live studio audience present, allowing for greater flexibility in the use of sets and the structure of scenes. These innovations, along with increased use of computer-generated effects and specially treated video tape, gave the long-awaited seventh series of *Red Dwarf* a look distinctively different from that of its forerunners. With or without the new production techniques, there was little doubt that this long-awaited season would be a success; as expected *Red Dwarf* regained its position at the top of BBC 2's chart.

Regulars: Rimmer – Chris Barrie (episodes 1–3, 5). Lister – Craig Charles. Cat – Danny John-Jules. Kryten – Robert Llewellyn. Kochanski – Chloe Annett (episodes 3–8). Scripts edited by Paul Alexander. Produced and directed by Ed Bye. A Grant Naylor Production for BBC North.

1: TIKKA TO RIDE

Broadcast date: 17 January 1997.

Written by Doug Naylor. **Guest cast:** Michael J. Shannon (John F. Kennedy), Toby Aspin (Lee Harvey Oswald), Peter Gaitens (FBI Agent), Robert Ashe (Cop).

Lister begins a video log by explaining how the destruction of *Starbug* – and, therefore, of the time drive – prevented its crew's future selves from travelling back in time to destroy *Starbug*. The camera can't cope with his explanation and chooses an honourable death instead. In the meantime, anomalies have merged from both realities to cope with the paradox – the upshot of which is that the future crew have been wiped out and their present-day selves returned to life at a moment before they found the time drive, albeit with a battle-damaged ship. A freak side effect of this is that *Starbug*'s cargo deck has been vastly expanded. This is no consolation to Lister, however, when he learns that a breached water tank has flooded Supply Deck B and wiped out his entire supply of curries and lager. He wants to retrieve the time drive and use it to find a good takeaway, but Kryten advises against this, citing the laws of causality. Desperate for a good vindaloo, Lister takes the mechanoid by surprise as he is downloading his surplus memories, and fits him with a spare head in which he overrides the guilt chip. The others suspect something amiss when their normally polite crewmate takes up smoking and stirs their drinks with his groinal attachment, but they accept his assurances that a journey to the past will be safe.

Kryten mishandles the controls of the time drive and transports the crew to the offices of the Texas Book Depository, Dallas, on 22 November 1963. Lister stumbles into one Lee Harvey Oswald and knocks him out of an open window. When the Cat discovers Oswald's gun, it becomes clear that the *Starbug* crew have saved President Kennedy's life and catastrophically altered their history. They are arrested for Oswald's murder, but use the time drive to escape to 1966. Here, they encounter a different world from the one that should be: Kennedy has been arrested and removed from office, and his successor – J. Edgar Hoover – is in the pocket of the Mafia. The Russians have been allowed to build a nuclear base in Cuba and the streets of Dallas are all but deserted as its citizens have fled from the possibility of nuclear warfare. Worse still, *Starbug* no longer exists in the future, so its crew are unable to return to it. As they tuck into a meal prepared by Kryten – only to discover that, thanks to the absence of his behavioural protocols, he has prepared them roast human – they discuss how they can put history back on to the right tracks.

They return to 1963 and ensure that Oswald takes his shots from a different window, a floor above, where he will not be interrupted. However, his aim restricted in this new location, he only wounds the President. Lister realises that they'll have to organise Kennedy's death themselves, and he sees a convenient grassy knoll from behind which they can fire the fatal shot. But the question remains: who will do it? Lister has an idea that will drive the conspiracy nuts crazy. He travels to 1965 and, approaching Kennedy just after his arrest, tells him of the world he has come from, in which the President died but became a liberal icon. Kennedy agrees to his plan, and goes back in time to shoot his younger self even as Oswald's bullets fail to do the job. He fades away as the timelines return to normal, and Lister only regrets that he forgot to ask him where the nearest curry house was.

- This episode features *Red Dwarf*'s first flashback to 'old' material, as the ending of the previous season is reprised.
- The Space Corps test ship from 'Out of Time' is belatedly given a name – the *Gemini 12* – and is seen for the first time, thanks to *Red Dwarf*'s first ever computer-generated sequence.
- Continuity errors aplenty ... Lister tells us he has recently passed his twenty-eighth birthday. He was twenty-five in 'Future Echoes', which places the first six seasons into a time frame of about three years (of Lister's life). However, this is contradicted by dialogue in 'Stasis Leak', 'Holoship', 'Back to Reality', 'Out of Time' and, later, 'Epideme'. Perhaps he is just lying about his age! On a similar note, fans complained that the time drive was incapable of travelling through space as it does here (indeed, 'Out of Time' made great play of this fact). Also, when the future *Starbug* crew kill their past selves, the resulting paradox restores the victims' lives – and yet when JFK does it, his younger self remains dead. If we wanted to be very pedantic, we could also mention that the existence of a second gunman behind the grassy knoll becomes a part of history in this episode – and yet it was referred to by Kryten in both 'Emohawk – Polymorph II' and 'Timeslides' (when he jokingly suggested travelling back in time to save JFK's life!).

2: STOKE ME A CLIPPER

Broadcast date: 24 January 1997.

Written by Paul Alexander and Doug Naylor. **Guest cast:** Brian Cox (King), Ken Morley (Captain Voorhese – also spelt Vorhese), Sarah Alexander (Queen), John Thompson (Good

Red Dwarf's crew before the accident.
C P Grogan appears as Kochanski.

Kryten (Robert Llewellyn) strides fearlessly into battle.

Craig Charles stars as Dave Lister, the last human alive (well, unless you count those from other dimensions).

Rimmer (Chris Barrie) in smug mode – probably quoting some Space Corps Directive, we shouldn't wonder.

Norman Lovett recently returned to *Red Dwarf* as Holly, which meant sadly that the limbs and body had to go.

Hattie Hayridge as Holly,
showing how black clothes can
reduce the need for full bodily
amputation.

A new face aboard *Red Dwarf* – in fact, a new face on Kochanski's shoulders. Chloe Annett takes over as the object of Lister's desire.

Knight), Alison Senior (Princess Bonjella), Mark Carlisle (Lieutenant), Mark Lingwood (Gestapo Officer), Kai Maurer, Stephen Grothgar, Andy Gell (Soldiers). With special thanks to London Zoo for . . . Alison (Voorhese's crocodile).

Ace Rimmer is in the midst of a typically heroic exploit. Captured by the evil Voorhese, he manages to slip his bonds by dislocating both shoulders and popping them behind his ears. Voorhese abandons his plane, leaving his crocodile to fight Ace – but the interdimensional adventurer overcomes his attacker, steals the captain's parachute in free fall, rescues Princess Bonjella from a firing squad and still has time for sex if it's on the menu. Lister, conversely, is so desperate for sex that he's in danger of exhausting *Starbug*'s water supplies with his cold showers. His answer is to enter an Artificial Reality game with a book of cheats designed to help him bed the Queen of Camelot. But his quick fumble is interrupted by a power failure.

Ace Rimmer's dimension-spanning vessel – its computer distracted by the crush it has on its pilot – has materialised too close to *Starbug*. Rimmer is not pleased to see his braver, more handsome, more able counterpart, but Ace has a special mission in mind for him. He reveals that he is not the original Ace, but rather a hard-light hologram from yet another dimension, to whom the baton has been passed. He has taken a shot and is dying – electromagnetic radiation is bleeding from his light bee – but the universe needs someone to look up to. Rimmer must take his place. But Rimmer isn't interested: he dismisses the request as fevered ranting, and Ace confides in Lister in the hope that he can help. Lister's loudly expressed amusement at the situation provokes Rimmer into proving he is as good as his other self. Taking Ace up on his offer, he begins training in the Artificial Reality suite.

Ace hopes to unleash the cougar in Rimmer, but all Rimmer can find is a hamster. He wants to give up, but Ace prepares him for the ultimate test instead. He reconfigures Rimmer's light bee so that he appears as Ace: if he can fool his crewmates, he is ready for the job. A knight breaks out of

Lister's AR game, and only Rimmer is around to stop it. His swordfighting isn't up to scratch, but a bazookoid blast does the trick. Astonished by his own success, he never finds out that the knight in question is Lister in disguise, nor that the bazookoid fired blanks. He rushes to tell Ace of his achievement, only to watch as Ace passes on to that great airfield in the sky. When Cat and Kryten discover his defunct light bee, they assume it is their own crewmate's, and Lister encourages the misconception.

Rimmer, in the Ace persona that now belongs to him, is present at his own funeral. The previous Ace left a beacon with Lister, and this guides the coffin into orbit around a world alongside millions of similar caskets. Each of them holds a Rimmer who went on to become Ace, and our Rimmer now knows that he can do it too – so long as he can sort out the takeoff controls from the ejector seat. The new Ace leaves *Starbug*, with the immortal words: 'Stoke me a clipper, I'll be back for Christmas!'

- The working title for this episode was 'Natural Born Rimmers'.
- Howard Goodall provides his fourth variation on the closing theme: this time, the newly promoted Ace Rimmer is given a stirring hero's farewell.
- The opening sequence, featuring Ace Rimmer's heroic rescue of the Princess Bonjella, was filmed at the RAF base in Northolt. The *Red Dwarf* team had made a deal with the Ministry of Defence, which also allowed them to use RAF Farnborough as a stand-in for Idlewild Airport in 'Tikka to Ride' and to create Pride and Prejudice World (for 'Beyond a Joke') around a training lake in Hampshire. However, aircraft noises were sometimes a problem.
- 'My overwhelming memory of *Red Dwarf* is that we had to do it all again,' says Brian Cox of his scenes in an AR simulated field, 'as, the first time, we filmed in the pouring rain with the canopy above me full of water, which kept dripping on my beard, and with poor Ed Bye struggling to be heard above the noise of the rain. It was a completely

ludicrous experience. But it was great fun, and the nice thing was – I got paid twice!'

3: OUROBOROS

Broadcast date: 31 January 1997.

Written by Doug Naylor. **Guest cast:** Gary Bleasdale (Frank), Juliet Griffiths (Barmaid), Adrienne Posta (Flight Announcer), Alexander John-Jules (Baby Lister).

26 November 2155: a baby is found in a cardboard box beneath the grav-pool table of the Aigburth Arms. On the box is scrawled the word 'Ouroboros', which is taken by the barmaid as an attempt to spell 'Our Rob or Ross'. She prophesies a terrible fate for the child. Three million (and a bit) years later, the adult Dave Lister sneezes out a tooth cap and makes the mistake of putting it back in with wood glue and then flossing. He has no time to deal with the problem, however, as the Cat detects a tear in the fabric of time and space. Kryten suggests aiming *Starbug* at the eye of the storm, and they get through the worst of it. But there is a disturbance on the engineering deck, where the membrane between two realities has temporarily collapsed and a linkway has been formed through non-space into a parallel universe. The *Starbug* crew explore, as do their counterparts from the opposite side. Lister is astonished to come face to face with a hologramatic version of himself and mortified when, dressed in a fluffy dressing gown provided by Kryten and with a box of floss attached to his face, he meets a very solid alternative version of Kochanski. In her reality, it seems, she discovered Lister's pet cat and, unable to condemn it to death, hid it herself. She was caught and sentenced to six months in stasis, waking three million years later and choosing to bring back Lister as a hologram.

The couple apparently have a good life, but Kochanski regrets that her Lister can't give her a baby. She wonders if our version will oblige – but, to Lister's disappointment, she has an in-vitro fertilisation in mind. Suddenly, a GELF ship penetrates non-space and fires on the linkway, rupturing it. Lister's facial floss comes in handy as a lifeline for an endangered Kochanski, but she is appalled to find herself in the wrong reality as the linkway shatters. Nonetheless, she quickly takes command of a *Starbug* crew less efficient than her own, and shakes off the pursuit of the GELF ship, in which Lister's erstwhile bride is pursuing her unfortunate husband. Kryten, fearing that Kochanski's presence will drive a wedge between him and his beloved master, helps her to re-establish the linkway and, after the two crews have swapped supplies, Kochanski takes her in-vitro tube and bids farewell. It is only as he inspects a crate from the other ship that Lister sees the word 'Ouroboros' inscribed upon it. Kryten explains that Ouroboros is the worm that devours its own tail, the symbol of infinity (the box contained Ouroboros batteries), and Lister realises that his previously unknown father is ... himself! He can't let Kochanski take the in-vitro tube back to her own dimension, and he rushes to stop her. In the confusion, the GELF ship attacks again, and Kochanski is caught on the wrong side of the rift as the linkway is broken once more. She makes a jump for her own universe, but plunges into non-space. Lister finds a crossbow (obtained by Kryten from the other ship in case his bride came back) and some rope, and improvises a lifeline – although his shot goes astray and spears Kochanski's leg. The linkway is broken for ever, and Kochanski is trapped in a dimension not her own. Eighteen months later, Lister uses the time drive to take his younger self to the Aigburth Arms. He tries to explain to the baby that he is here to create a paradox: so long as his life forms an unbreakable circle in time, humanity can never be truly extinct.

- For the first time since 'Parallel Universe', an episode of *Red Dwarf* is bereft of opening titles.
- The GELF ship in which Lister's jilted bride chases *Starbug* was a perfect example of recycling to fit within a budget: the visual-effects department made it from a garden vacuum and two water pistols. Their newly constructed

White Midget, however (see also 'Body Swap') was less cost-effective, as it wasn't needed after all. The same applied to a special model of *Starbug*, with a detaching front section, which was to have featured this season.

- Chris Barrie had intended to record only two episodes of *Red Dwarf VII*, but was persuaded to double his commitment. Doug Naylor chose to write him out in the second episode anyway, and to feature him in flashback and dream sequences thereafter. He appears here in our first look back at the pre-accident *Red Dwarf* since 'Stasis Leak'. Having never liked the look of the first series, Doug set this scene in an alternative dimension to explain the crew's new blue uniforms and, more importantly, the fact that another actress was playing Kochanski. Another slight 'tweaking' of continuity is the revelation that Kryten was responsible for the deaths of the *Nova 5* crew. This was the case in the *Red Dwarf* novels, but it had never been established on TV before.

- We finally get a good look at the Aigburth Arms, and learn that it was not just Dave Lister's local but also the pub in which he was discovered in a cardboard box. The real-life establishment of the same name was once a frequent haunt of Rob Grant and Doug Naylor. 'We used to go in there while we were at Liverpool University,' Rob confirms. 'One of the Rag Week stunts was to drink the Aigburth dry. I think we managed about eight pints each – we didn't get close!' 'It had an excellent pool table,' Doug recalls – hence its brief appearance in 'White Hole'.

4: DUCT SOUP

Broadcast date: 7 February 1997.

Written by Doug Naylor. **Guest cast:** None.

The heating system has gone bonkers. It's ninety-seven degrees and Lister can't sleep. Nor can Kochanski who, having been quartered in the room next to the sewage processor, finds the noises coming from its clapped-out pipes unbearable. She is not settling in to her new life well, and she complains to Kryten about the lack of a proper bath on *Starbug*, not to mention a pot of cottage cheese with pineapple chunks in. Lister whiles away the night with the Cat, watching Kochanski's knickers going round in the laundry room. He offers to swap rooms with Kochanski, even providing a makeshift bath in his quarters – but Kryten misunderstands the situation and believes that the pair intend to sleep together. He imagines a dreadful future, in which Lister no longer has any time for him and he is forced to pack his things and leave.

Presently, the ship's generators fail. All doors are automatically sealed and the crew are trapped in Lister's room. With the autopilot down, they fear that *Starbug* will be heading for disaster – but the only way to reach the cockpit is through two miles of twisting service ducts, in a journey that Kryten estimates will take six hours. They get started, but Lister hampers progress by falling prey to claustrophobia. Kochanski's revelations about her own dimension take his mind off things for a while, even if they do turn out to be lies – but the Cat doesn't help matters in the slightest. At least his sharp hearing detects the roaring sound of water – and Lister remembers that the ducts are backwashed every four hours! The crew dive for – and reach – cover, but Lister and the Cat aren't quite prepared for the drying process. Finally, Kryten gets into a storeroom, finds a first-aid box and injects Lister with a tranquillising drug to calm his fears. But the situation becomes more urgent as things begin to heat up: *Starbug* is on a collision course with a nearby sun. Overcome by guilt, Kryten admits that he has caused the whole problem, as a jealousy motivated ploy to keep Lister and Kochanski apart. Fortunately, Lister has a plan. When water next courses through the ducts, the crew ride out the tidal wave on a pallet. They emerge, wet and battered – right back where they started! But Kryten now admits that the doors aren't sealed after all: he excluded them from his shutdown override in case of emergency. Lister and the Cat head for the cockpit to do some serious reversing, as Kochanski takes out her frustrations on the mechanoid's head.

- This was the last episode of *Red Dwarf VII* to be written. It replaced a script in which the Cat had to have sex or die, as money had become too tight to film this. By utilising only the regular actors and (for the most part) sets, Doug Naylor was able to make 'Duct Soup' far more cheaply.
- The opening titles are omitted again: they were felt to be expendable when the episode overran, though we did at least get a caption slide this time. Also cut was a scene in which Lister talked about his past, and in particular the nocturnal habits of an old schoolmate, 'Squeaky' Gibson. Craig Charles claims that this was his favourite scene in the whole season!
- The cast didn't particularly enjoy being pelted with cold water, and it proved to be an expensive business too. One of Robert Llewellyn's Kryten costumes was destroyed by the deluge.
- Fans of Craig Charles had nothing to complain about on Friday nights. Not only was *Red Dwarf VII* going out on BBC 2, but his new chat show *Funky Bunker* was on ITV, and Channel 4 had the alleged comedy series *Captain Butler*, in which he played the title role (and in which Robert Llewellyn once guest-starred as Admiral Nelson). Craig was unhappy about this scheduling, not only because months of work would quickly pass before the public, but because he felt it left him open to ridicule. Indeed, this was the week that *The Girlie Show* named him 'Wanker of the Week' for no better reason than that he had unintentionally monopolised the Friday night airwaves.

5: BLUE

Broadcast date: 14 February 1997.

Written by Kim Fuller and Doug Naylor. **Guest cast:** None.

Lister is making an effort to get closer to Kochanski: he even gives up spicy food to make his breath more pleasant. Kryten, however, wants her off the ship before she can move the salad cream again. Fortunately for him, she wants that too. She has detected another dimensional tear, and hopes to use it to return to her universe – and her Lister. However, our Lister takes *Starbug* through the tail of a comet, ruffling the Cat's hair and spilling the contents of the chocolate dispenser, among other things. By the time they've repaired the ship, the tear will have closed. In the meantime, Kryten tries to explain some of the house rules to his new crewmate, while Lister and the Cat clear out excess cargo in the hope of improving *Starbug*'s performance. This has an unexpected side effect on Lister: old keepsakes remind him of the pastimes he shared with Rimmer – specifically, golf and the locker-room game – and he finds that he actually misses him. His worries are compounded by a disturbing dream, in which he ends up snogging with a Rimmer who is witty and light-hearted. Lister seeks psychological help from Kryten, but it is Kochanski who suggests that perhaps Rimmer wasn't such a bad guy after all. Perhaps he sacrificed his own happiness and pretended to be something he wasn't, for the sake of following Holly's directive to keep Lister sane.

Not to be outdone, Kryten uses Rimmer's extensive diaries to create a fairground-type attraction which he calls 'The Rimmer Experience', in the Artificial Reality suite. This, he says, is the antidote to any feelings of loss. Subjected to excerpts from Rimmer's version of his life – in which he is a brave hero, forever rescuing the cowardly Lister and the hopeless Kryten from peril before passing on useful fashion tips to the Cat – Lister vows that he never wants to see that scum-sucking, lying, weasel-minded smeg-head again. Kryten considers his job well done.

- The working title for this episode was 'Heartache'.
- Rimmer is seen wearing the wrong uniform in another flashback to the pre-accident days on *Red Dwarf* (in our own dimension this time, although the locker-room set created for 'Ouroboros' remains the same).

- Lister and Rimmer share a passionate kiss in a dream sequence: the culmination of a behind-the-scenes joke that had run for several years. 'In Series V,' Rob Grant explains, 'Chris got oiled and got to go to bed with Jane Horrocks, and Craig was very upset that he was the only human being and he wasn't getting laid.' There followed a succession of kisses between Lister and various disgusting creatures in *Red Dwarf VI* – but, until now, Rob and Doug had only threatened to write the ultimate snog scene ... 'We were toying with the idea of an episode where they find a culture that's trapped in cyberspace; they go in to speak to them and two of the cyberspace inhabitants come out and kidnap Lister and Rimmer's bodies.' Doug Naylor takes up the story: 'We were trying to organise it so that you'd have a man and a woman who are lovers in their bodies, and there'd be a big snog scene between Chris and Craig. We were going to say to Craig, "Hey, you wanted snogs!" '

6: BEYOND A JOKE

Broadcast date: 21 February 1997.

Written by Robert Llewellyn and Doug Naylor. **Guest cast:** Don Henderson (Simulant), Vicky Ogden (Mrs Bennet), Alina Proctor (Jane Bennet), Catherine Harvey (Kitty Bennet), Sophia Thierens (Lydia Bennet), Rebecca Katz (Mary Bennet), Julia Lloyd (Elizabeth Bennet).

It is the anniversary of Kryten's rescue from the *Nova 5*, and the mechanoid has spent two days preparing a surprise celebration supper. To his delight, he has been able to procure lobsters from the stasis chamber of a derelict ship, the SS *Centauri*. He is dismayed, however, to learn that his ship-mates have other plans. The *Centauri* also yielded up a rare copy of *Jane Austen World* for the Artificial Reality machine, and Kochanski wants to show Lister and the Cat around Pride and Prejudice Land. She spent a lot of time there while in

Cyberschool and she finds it a fascinating cultural experience; the attraction for the Cat, however, is that the Bennet sisters are so hot they're steaming. But Kryten's resentment reaches boiling point, and he follows the others into their virtual game and picks off the girls one by one. When an elaborate trap involving ropes and an enormous log backfires, he decides on a more direct approach. He borrows a T72 tank from a World War II simulation, fires on Mrs Bennet's tea party, eradicates her gazebo and announces that supper is served. The others agree to eat, but the Cat is less than tactful about the quality of the meal. The final straw comes when Lister asks for ketchup, and Kryten's head literally explodes. Lister and Kochanski attempt to repair the mechanoid, but they go through all his spare heads just trying to find out what's wrong with him. Their only hope is to find more spares on the *Centauri*, and, fortunately, they do. Unfortunately, the heads are lacking their primers – which are in the hands of a rogue Simulant who has made the *Centauri* his home.

Simulants hate humans, so Kochanski and the Cat disguise themselves as GELFs to negotiate for the primers. Too late do they learn not to trust a Simulant: this one has stalled them while his colleague ransacked *Starbug* and took Kryten's headless body. The Simulant hands Kryten to the enslaved Able, another Series 4000 mechanoid, who repairs his 'brother'. Restored, Kryten is appalled to see that Able's circuit boards have been corrupted by his ultra-zone addiction. Meanwhile, the *Centauri* pulls away at a speed that *Starbug* can't match. Kochanski sets a course away from the *Centauri* instead: an action which would make sense only if she had set a large bomb on the ship. The Cat is confused, but the Simulant is convinced enough to turn around and teleport on to *Starbug* with Kryten and Able. He demands to know where the mythical bomb is, and Lister offers to exchange this information for Kryten. A deadlock is broken as Able takes off his own head and hurls it at his former master. Kryten sends the Simulant back to the *Centauri* and they flee. However, his erstwhile captor's parting gift was to unlock hidden files in his core programming.

Kryten now knows a terrible truth about himself: all Series 4000 mechanoids were created to be cruel caricatures of Professor Mamet's ex-fiancée. They were fitted with nega-drives, on which all feelings of anger and resentment were stored until the drive was full and the mechanoid blew its top – just as John Warburton used to do. It is this revelation that has driven Able to ultra-zone, but Lister assures Kryten that he has grown beyond Mamet's original programming. The *Centauri* comes after *Starbug*, but the smaller ship hides in an asteroid belt. So long as they maintain engine silence, they'll be okay – but Able secretly shoots up with ultra-zone in the cockpit, and knocks a control. *Starbug* is discovered and the *Centauri* opens fire. Able redeems himself by taking an escape pod and routing all the energy from Kryten's nega-drive through its thrusters to engulf the *Centauri* in a field of Kryten's negativity. The Simulant is driven to thoughts of suicide and the *Centauri* is destroyed. The escape pod crashes and Kryten sadly recovers his brother's corpse for a dignified burial before joining the rest of the crew for an AR curry with the Bennet family. Sadly, a computer glitch makes the vindaloo too hot for even Lister to handle.

- Kryten's destruction of Pride and Prejudice Land gave the co-writer Robert Llewellyn the chance to express his irritation at the plethora of unoriginal historical dramas on TV. Unfortunately, the tank in which he wreaked his carnage (a former 'star' of *Goldeneye*) was caught in traffic on the M25 and arrived late. As recording continued, the climactic explosion set off car alarms and attracted complaints from nearby residents.
- The GELF costumes worn by Kochanski and Cat are totally convincing – as they should be, having already been utilised by the 'real thing' in 'Emohawk – Polymorph II', 'Duct Soup' and this very episode. The SS *Centauri* also had a history: the visual-effects department built a GELF freighter for *Red Dwarf VI*, only to find it missing from the final scripts. It was brought out of mothballs to appear here.
- Sadly, this turned out to be one of the last TV appearances of

veteran actor Don Henderson. Don was no stranger to SF villains, having played one of Darth Vader's minions in *Star Wars* and the evil Gavrok, leader of the Bannermen, in *Doctor Who*. He cited *Red Dwarf* as one of the highlights of his long career, commenting: 'A great script, producer, director, crew, technicians, writers, unit and actors! Sheer bliss to be in.'

- 'Writing *Red Dwarf* was a truly terrifying experience,' confesses Robert Llewellyn, 'mainly because I used to talk to Doug Naylor and Ed Bye with my five terribly clever ideas of the week and Doug would say, "Yeah, funny, but it's a bit like . . .", and he would name one of the existing thirty-six episodes.' One idea was accepted, though . . . 'It's very difficult, when you're in something like *Red Dwarf*, to try and write it. Very hard to be objective. I wrote and wrote and rewrote, and then I'd read it through and realise I'd written for me, Craig, Danny and Chloë, not Kryten, Lister, Cat and Kochanski. Now, when I watch the finished programme, I can say to myself every now and then, "I wrote that," or "That was my bit," but to be honest Doug had a large hand in it and it was just as well! Especially once I have that head on, I turn from an erudite, witty, searingly observant commentator on contemporary ethics and morality into a brain-dead semi-moron with an insatiable hunger for Chinese takeaway food and pizza.'

7: EPIDEME

Broadcast date: 28 February 1997.

Written by Paul Alexander and Doug Naylor. **Guest cast:** Nicky Leatherbarrow (Caroline Carmen), Gary Martin (Epideme).

Starbug approaches a huge astro-glacier, and Kryten notes that it might be time to replenish water supplies. But the crew are surprised to detect a Jupiter Mining Corporation ship –

the *Leviathan* – buried in the iceberg. When they reach and board it, they are even more surprised to find one Caroline Carmen – a former supplies officer from *Red Dwarf*, who left before the accident – frozen in a block of ice. What's more, Kryten detects lifesigns. They take Caroline back to *Starbug*, but are unable to thaw her. But, as they sleep, she emerges from the ice of her own volition and makes her way into Lister's bed. Feeling her breath on his neck, Lister assumes that Kochanski has succumbed to his charms at last – but, before he can investigate further, Kryten knocks on the door and Lister bundles his bunkmate up in a duvet and hides her in the shower. Kryten reads Lister's guilty expression and is upset to think that Kochanski is here; that Lister prefers her to him after all. The pair argue, waking Kochanski in the process. Kryten is shamefaced when she arrives to see what is happening, but Lister assumes that she has climbed out of a vent shaft in the shower to fool the mechanoid. His attempt to proceed with their unfinished business earns him a punch – but, worse, his attempt to retrieve his duvet earns him a snog from the rotting, but animated, corpse of Caroline. She collapses, and Kryten detects that she has been dead for three million years. It seems the lifesign readings came not from her but from a virus that she was carrying.

The Epideme virus was manmade as a rival to the nicotine patch but, instead of merely blocking the body's need for nicotine, it blocked its need for blood and oxygen too. It kills its hosts in forty-eight hours, then takes their bodies in search of fresh victims – or freezes them to preserve itself if none are available. Now the virus has been passed to Lister, and there is no cure. The Epideme is intelligent, and Kryten is able to arrange for Lister to communicate with it. However, his pleas for clemency have no effect. He asks his shipmates to find a solution, no matter how radical, but he doesn't count on having to surrender a limb. Using antivirals, Kryten and Kochanski force the virus into Lister's right arm (although, at his request, they had been aiming for the left: he did all his favourite things with the right) and then they amputate. But not all of the Epideme is eradicated: they have bought Lister only fifty-eight more minutes of life. Determined to go out with a bang, and to take his killer with him, he heads for the *Leviathan* with forty pounds of Incinerex blasting plastic. But he changes his plans when the Epideme lets slip that the *Leviathan* had been heading towards Delta 7 in the hope of finding a cure.

Starbug isn't fast enough to reach the planet in time, but the Epideme absorbs knowledge from all its hosts and Kryten tricks it into telling him how to make their vessel faster. Ultimately, though, it is the *Starbug* crew who have been tricked! Delta 7 is a dead planet, having been flamed in an unsuccessful attempt to kill the Epideme. They have been sent on a wild-goose chase, to stop Lister from carrying out his threat. Finally, Kochanski has an idea. She stops Lister's heart and waits for the Epideme to animate his body and to bite her hand, transferring itself into her. But the hand – and the arm attached to it – was really Caroline Carmen's, injected with blood and adrenaline. Kochanski has tricked the virus out of the Epideme's body and she is able to revive Lister without lasting damage. Except, of course, that he still has one limb fewer than a full quota.

- This is the second – and, to date, last – episode to conclude with a 'To Be Continued' tag. The saga of Lister's lost arm is carried over to the following week as the writers play with fans' expectations that the prediction of a future Lister with an artificial replacement ('Future Echoes') will come to pass. Although he experiments with just such a prosthesis in 'Nanarchy', he is eventually able to grow a new flesh-and-blood limb, thanks to Kryten's nanites.
- A model sequence of *Starbug* landing on the glacier was filmed, but replaced by a computer-generated shot in the final edit.
- If you think you've heard the voice of the Epideme before, it's because Gary Martin is an old hand at putting words into the mouths of telefantasy heroes. He has voiced characters from Judge Dredd to the Mysterons to the Thing (of *Fantastic Four* fame) to Dennis the Menace's pal Pie-Face, in various radio and TV projects.

- Not surprising, perhaps, Chloë Annett's most vivid memory of 'Epideme' was 'trying to cut my own arm off. We must have done it at least eight times. I was of course reduced to hysterical giggles, a common occurrence whilst filming. My costume was so charred, red paint had to be sprayed on it, a lot of which ended up on me. Despite this and many other "incidents",' she adds, of her first series as a *Red Dwarf* regular, 'it remains the happiest shoot of my career.'

8: NANARCHY

Broadcast date: 7 March 1997.

Written by Paul Alexander, Jamies Hendrie and Doug Naylor. **Guest cast:** Holly (Norman Lovett).

Lister is finding one-armed life difficult, despite the help Kryten gives him to play the guitar, dunk biscuits, scratch his nose and operate doors. His shipmates try to cheer him up but, when pressed, they come up with a pretty inadequate list of historical figures who have lost an arm and yet achieved something. Kochanski also disagrees with Kryten's nannying attitude: she believes in tough love, to help Lister become independent, and she suggests that the mechanoid take time away from wipe alert (that's wiping crumbs from Lister's mouth, obviously) to build him an artificial arm. He does, but the replacement is hardly suitable. Lister would have to take the morning off each time he wanted to pick up a ball – and when Kryten adjusts the impulse valve to make the aid more sensitive, it responds to its owner's subconscious thoughts and takes to punching the mechanoid who left him in this predicament in the first place. There's no question of allowing him near Kochanski with it, of course. So it's back to square one – until Kochanski recalls that the Kryten of her universe had a self-repair system made up of subatomic nanobots. They are capable of breaking anything down into its component atoms and rebuilding it in a different form, so they could probably make Lister a new arm from his own excess body tissue. The only snag is, the nanobots deserted Kryten after the incident on the *Esperanto*. There is no chance of finding them – but Lister won't give up anyway.

The crew go into deep sleep while *Starbug* returns to the ocean world on which the *Esperanto* was found. But the computer wakes them early as, towards the end of the journey, it detects a strange planetoid straight ahead. Kryten can't believe the evidence of the scanners, which indicate that the planetoid is *Red Dwarf*. The Cat explores, happy to brave the electrical storm which whips sand all about the planetoid so long as he has a comb to hand. His particle analyser confirms the scanners' diagnosis and, what's more, he is able to salvage items that are undeniably from the lost ship. The hairnet requisition forms and inflatable sharks are unmistakable – as is the remote link with a surprisingly male Holly. Holly reveals that Kryten's nanobots mutineered and took over *Red Dwarf*, resculpting it into a size more appropriate for them. They turned the excess matter into a planetoid and dumped Holly who, once they'd repaired his core programming, turned out to be useless. Despite an inability to remember Kryten, though, he is pretty useful to the ship's displaced occupants. Hearing that they spent months following the vapour trail of the sub-atomic *Red Dwarf* before losing it, he theorises that the nanobots took their purloined ship to the one place where *Starbug*'s scanners wouldn't detect it: into *Starbug* itself. An internal scan finds them in Lister's laundry basket, where they have been exploring the strange micro-universes of his dirty clothes for years. Kryten nails the little blighters in a glass and communicates with them in machine code, telling them how unbelievably naughty they have been. They agree to his demands to restore both *Red Dwarf* and Lister to their original conditions. Lister isn't pleased, however, to find himself possessed of a rather oversized body – and the Cat is alarmed by another error of scale as he pilots *Starbug* into a *Red Dwarf* that is far, far too big for it.

- Kryten opens the episode with a recap of the salient points of 'Epideme', becoming the first character to directly address the viewers as viewers ('Last week on *Red Dwarf* . . .'). We don't count Holly's distress signal in seasons I and II, of course.

- As *Red Dwarf* finally appears in *Starbug*'s viewing portals and the Cat brings the shuttlecraft around, Howard Goodall reprises his original opening theme for the series, not heard since 'Queeg'.

- Although there has always been more than one *Starbug* (as dialogue in 'Backwards' and 'The Inquisitor' tells us), this is our first glimpse of two of the ships side by side. This was achieved by placing the *Starbug* model over a shot of the craft in its landing bay, from the fifth series (you can see that the supposedly stationary *'Bug* is actually about to take off). They both have the registration *Starbug 1*, though.

- 'I enjoyed the seventh series,' says Norman Lovett, 'especially the final episode where they meet up with Holly again. I love that guy!' More seriously, he tells us: 'It was nice to be asked back, and deep down inside it was something that I always thought would happen. Doing Holly again was easy and it was like I'd never been away. I can't believe it was eight years since I'd last played him. I hope to feature strongly in the eighth series, and of course the proposed feature film, but in the meantime I'm just pleased to have returned to the role.'

SECTION FOUR:

DATABASE

Capitals denote items which have their own entries elsewhere in the index.

A

A TO Z OF *RED DWARF*, THE: The book inside which RIMMER kept his diary hidden.

A TO Z OF THE UNIVERSE, THE: A comprehensive guide being compiled by HOLLY, including street names, post offices, steeples and everything.

ABLE: A green-hued Series 4000 Mechanoid. He was a zoney, addicted to ULTRA-ZONE. His addiction placed KRYTEN at risk, but Able redeemed himself by sacrificing himself to save his brother mech and the others.

ABORT SEQUENCE X1X: The AUTO-DESTRUCT system override, for which only Senior Officers have security clearance. Since all the Senior Officers are dead, HOLLY should really have thought to update this.

ACE: RIMMER's childhood nickname – which unfortunately, none of the other kids would use, no matter how much he let them beat him up. They preferred instead to refer to him as BONEHEAD.

ADVANCED MUTUAL COMPATIBILITY ON THE BASIS OF PRIMARY INITIAL IDENT: The state experienced by KRYTEN and CAMILLE upon their meeting each other for the first time. Humans would refer to the sensation as 'LOVE at first sight'.

AENEID, THE: After reading a comic book version of Virgil's epic poem, featuring the story of the Wooden Horse,

LISTER came to the conclusion that the adage 'Beware Greeks bearing gifts' should be amended to 'Beware Trojans, they're complete SMEGheads'.

AFTER-EIGHT MINTS: At the last count, there was only one of these left on board *RED DWARF* – and everyone is too polite to take it.

AGORAPHOBICS SOCIETY: LISTER claimed to belong to this group in order to explain his presence – along with RIMMER's and the CAT's – in a shower cubicle together. The real explanation, of course, is that they had just travelled back in time via a STASIS LEAK, and had found themselves there by accident.

AIGBURTH ARMS: The Liverpool drinking establishment where DAVE LISTER left himself as a baby. It would subsequently provide the setting for much of his misspent youth.

AIR BELGIUM: Notable only for their dull magazines.

AIR HOSTESSES: When *STARBUG*'s completely unreliable scanners detected a world populated entirely by these, its crew still thought it was worth searching the place for two weeks. In CAT's opinion they'd given up too soon and should have stayed an extra week.

AIR, JANE: A Mapping Officer on board the *NOVA 5*. The *RED DWARF* crew discovered her body when they answered a distress call from the ship's MECHANOID, KRYTEN. See also GILL, ANNE and JOHNS, TRACEY.

ALBANIAN STATE WASHING MACHINE COMPANY: An organisation which boasts technology in advance of *STARBUG*'s. Nothing unusual there.

ALBERT: LISTER's pet mould, which he intended to grow to a height of two feet. Albert was tragically killed when KRYTEN washed out the cup he was living in.

ALEXANDER THE GREAT: RIMMER believes that in a past life, he was in this Emperor's household as the CHIEF EUNUCH.

ALICE: RIMMER's cousin; daughter of his uncle FRANK, and twin sister of his cousin SARAH. RIMMER wasn't sure if she fancied him or not. Chances are she didn't!

ALIEN INVASION FLEET: Fortunately this turned out to be one of LISTER's old sneezes congealed on the radar screen.

ALIENS: Theoretical creatures from other worlds. Despite scientific evidence to the contrary, RIMMER believes in their existence fervently, and uses them to rationalise any phenomenon he cannot himself explain. His fondest hope is that he will run into the alien QUAGAARS and that they will use their advanced technology to provide him with a new body. Of course, both the race and the technology are products of his own imagination.

ALISON: A fictional sister, for whom RIMMER requested NAPOLEON's autograph when the two met in a BETTER THAN LIFE fantasy. Apparently, her name was shortened to Arnie!

ALL-GIRL CUSTARD WRESTLING FINALS: An Olympic event which caused a surge on the power grid during the commercial break.

ALLMAN, THOMAS: An unfortunate who was adjudged unworthy of having existed by the INQUISITOR and was consequently erased from history.

ALL-NATIONS AGREEMENT: That great preserver of democracy which, amongst other things, stipulates the right of POWs to non-violent constraint, and makes sure the Chinese don't take too many car park spaces.

ALPHABET SOUP: In between ACE RIMMER'S visits RIMMER had been busy alphabetising each individual letter with its fellows, not to mention researching the definitive history of pockets. And if not for the fact that he had his shoe collection to sort out he'd've been a sight keener to become the next Ace.

ALPHABETTI SPAGHETTI: Allegedly used as some form of SEX aid by LISTER and the POLYMORPH, when the latter was in the form of MRS RIMMER.

ALPHONSE: Talented hair stylist at ASTRO CUTS.

AMATEUR HAMMOND ORGAN RECITAL NIGHT: Wednesdays – the day on which RIMMER leads the SKUTTERS in playing his favourite instrument, much to the annoyance of the rest of the crew.

AMNESIA: This condition deserves a mention here; we just can't remember why.

ANEURISM, ELECTRONIC: The unpleasant fate awaiting RIMMER if he can't avoid stressful situations.

ANDROID HOME BREW: A sort of cross between Vimto and liquid nitrogen, this intoxicant was designed by HOLLY in order for KRYTEN to properly celebrate his last day party.

ANDROIDS: (1) Otherwise known as MECHANOIDS. These mechanical creatures were built by humans purely to serve. Each has been programmed to believe in the fictional notion of SILICON HEAVEN, as an encouragement for them to obey their masters.

ANDROIDS: (2) KRYTEN's favourite soap opera. This GROOVY CHANNEL 27 production featured Android 14762/E as KELLY, Android 97542/P as BROOK, Android 442153/2 as Simone, Android 72264/Y as Gary, Android 24/A as Brooke Jnr, Android 980612/L as Bruce and Android 791265/B as the Android in the Bus Queue. The show was produced and directed by KYLIE GWENLYN.

ANDY: A Brummie twonk who was actually the product of a group HALLUCINATION. He was the LEISURE WORLD staff member who greeted DUANE DIBBLEY's party as they emerged from the *RED DWARF* TOTAL IMMERSION VIDEO GAME, and happily ridiculed their performance.

ANGER: The emotion the POLYMORPH stole from RIMMER. It coaxed it from him by taking on the form of MRS

RIMMER and waxing lyrical on the tricks that LISTER could get up to with ALPHABETTI SPAGHETTI.

ANORAK: An essential component of DUANE DIBBLEY's tasteful attire – and the final nail in the CAT's coffin!

ANUS: LISTER's main talent seems to be his ability to open LAGER bottles with this.

APPENDIX: Of course, LISTER couldn't have had his appendix taken out twice, hence these four possible explanations:
1. When LEGION claimed to have removed said object to prevent PERITONITIS, he was really engaging LISTER's trust through an insidious illusion.
2. So confused was he by LISTER's pasting of eight months' memories into his mind, that RIMMER only thought those eight months included an appendectomy.
3. LISTER made a mistake whilst working on RIMMER's mind, so that someone else's recollection of the operation strayed into his mind.
4. Rob and Doug screwed up.

ARCHANGEL GABRIEL, THE: Fearful for his existence, when attempting to justify himself to THE INQUISITOR, RIMMER claimed to have had a vision of this heavenly apparition and to have become an instant convert.

ARGON 5: Planet where LISTER dreamt that his former bunkmate had as ACE RIMMER not actually fought in the BELLAGOSIAN WAR – just before they kissed!

ARIES: LISTER's star-sign. So now you know.

ARKS: The means by which the CAT PEOPLE left *RED DWARF*. There were two of these; one for the CAT faction which believed the CARDBOARD HATS on FUCHAL should be red, and one for those who believed they should be blue. Unfortunately, the Blue-Hats, who were in the first of the arks, used LISTER's LAUNDRY list as a star chart and crashed straight into an asteroid.

ARMAGEDDON VIRUS: A computer virus programmed into *STARBUG*'s navi-comp by the defeated SIMULANTS, who were obviously sore losers. *See* DOVE PROGRAM.

ARMIES DU NORD: Amongst RIMMER's most prized possessions were a full set of miniature replicas of this army, hand-carved by the legendary DUBOIS BROTHERS. However, when he and LISTER were marooned on an ICE PLANET, they had to be burnt to ensure LISTER's survival.

ARM, RIGHT: LISTER would have preferred to lose his left arm in order to be saved from the EPIDEME VIRUS. He did all his favourite things with his right arm and had grown very attached to it – he thought they were inseparable.

ARMSTRONG, NELLIE: The first woman on the moon in the female dominated PARALLEL UNIVERSE.

ARNOLD J. RIMMER – A TRIBUTE: The video RIMMER made of his own death, which featured an extensive eulogy and poetry readings – by himself.

ARROWS: Weapons from which CAT's sense of smell can glean a great deal of information. On the GELF moon of the KINITAWOWI, he was able to determine that one such projectile had been shot from a bow.

AR SIMULATION SUITE: Located aboard *STARBUG*, it was here that ACE RIMMER (2) attempted to train up his successor – in a setting that RIMMER considered more suited to Maria Von Trapp. Usually, however, it is used for playing Artificial Reality GAMES, such as CAMELOT, JANE AUSTEN WORLD, WWII, and CURRY WORLD. KRYTEN utilised its technology to create the Arnold RIMMER EXPERIENCE.

ART COLLEGE: Attended by LISTER . . . for ninety-seven minutes.

ARTICLES: Presumably working hand in hand with the SPACE CORPS DIRECTIVES, these are the guidelines by which QUEEG insisted *RED DWARF* be run. In particular, Article 5 states that in the event of the ship's computer being guilty of gross negligence leading to the endangerment of personnel, the back-up computer (QUEEG himself) should take over its position. When this happened, the crew initially saw the move as a good one – until QUEEG invoked Article 497, which required them to work in order to earn credits for their food. Of course, as QUEEG was really HOLLY all along, it is disputable how much of what you have just read is in fact true.

ARTIFICIAL ARMS: LISTER has had at least two of these, the first a clumsy-looking pink appendage copied by KRYTEN from a twenty-first-century example. The second he acquired in a future that may have been negated due to the effects the various time-hopping exploits of the *RED DWARF* crew have had on the time stream.

ARTIFICIAL REALITY MACHINE: Similar to TIV technology. Well, exactly the same really. The DWARFERS picked up an AR console from a derelict spacecraft, and LISTER used it to play such role-playing GAMES as GUM-SHOE and STREETS OF LAREDO. More precisely, he used it to simulate SEX, notably with LORETTA. And with the ball girl at Wimbledon. She might have been jail bait, but at least she had great pixels.

ASTEROID BELT: CAT hates going through these as all the tipping from side to side messes up his hair, and makes him look like TINA TURNER.

ASTEROID SPOTTING: A pastime enjoyed by RIMMER, who sometimes asks KRYTEN to take him out in *STARBUG* for this purpose.

ASTEROIDAL LICHEN STEW: Along with DAN-DELION SORBET and SPACE NETTLE SOUP, this culinary delight prompted LISTER to risk life and limb in pursuit of better food supplies.

ASTRO CUTS: The place to get a good hair cut if you're in Alpha Sector of Dimension 24.

ASTRO GLACIER: A big iceberg at the heart of which was discovered the *LEVIATHAN*.

ASTRO-NAVIGATION AND INVISIBLE NUMBERS IN ENGINEERING STRUCTURE MADE SIMPLE: A BOOK owned by ARNOLD RIMMER – for all the good it ever did him.

ATHLETES' FOOT: Suffered by LISTER and left untreated when RIMMER borrowed his body. The best treatment he has found for it so far has been RIMMER's abortive attempt at making a lemon meringue pie.

ATTACK OF THE KILLER GOOSEBERRIES: A film of which HOLLY was reminded when, his consciousness having been projected into a WRIST WATCH, he discovered a large hole in LISTER's pocket.

AUGUSTUS, **SS:** KRYTEN's ship before the *NOVA 5*. Its crew selfishly died of old age leaving the mechanoid all on his own.

AUNTIE MAGGIE: One of RIMMER's relatives, whose birthday fell on 17 July.

AUTO-DESTRUCT: All spaceships seem to include this facility, which must make most space travellers rather nervous. When a crazed SKUTTER wired *RED DWARF*'s destruct system to a food DISPENSER, it was fortunate that HOLLY had previously had the foresight to remove the bomb. It was just a pity that she neglected to mention the fact to anyone.

AUTO-PILOT: Well, in actual fact 'it's Muggins here that has to do it,' as HOLLY is quick to remind us.

AUTO-REPAIR: *See* SELF-REPAIR UNIT.

AWOOGA: The distinctive sound of *RED DWARF*'s klaxon alarm, or at least HOLLY's verbal equivalent. As the CAT says, when the Awooga waltz starts it's time to do a quick step to cover.

B

BACKLOG: *See* BLACK BOX.

BACKWARDS EARTH: EARTH after THE BIG CRUNCH, on which time was running backwards. It was visited by the *RED DWARF* crew in the year 3991.

BACO-FOIL: There is none of this left aboard *STARBUG*, so while RIMMER thought Ace's jacket made him look like a reject from a gay pride disco, KRYTEN believed he could put it to some practical use, such as roasting a CHICKEN.

'BAKED BEAN BOMBSHELLS, VOL 12': Nude wrestling video discovered by LISTER while playing the LOCKER-ROOM GAME.

BAKED POTATO TIMER: See HAZARD APPROACH LIGHTS.

BALD BLOKE: Amateur dramatics aficionado married to CASHIER NUMBER 4; he discovered his wife naked on a crate of tinned asparagus in the MEGAMART stockroom and refused to believe her claim that she was getting an all-over tan from the lightbulb. See BOOTLE PLAYERS.

BALL: What LISTER attempted to pick up with his twenty-first-century copy ARTIFICIAL ARM. His conscious mind was willing his arm to pick up the ball, but his subconscious was telling it to punch KRYTEN in the head.

BANANA AND CRISP SANDWICHES: LISTER found one of these in ADOLF HITLER's briefcase, after using the TIMESLIDES to steal it from him; having been temporarily restored to life, RIMMER ate it.

BANANA BOMB: A drink enjoyed by LISTER in his BETTER THAN LIFE fantasy.

BANANA, GIANT INFLATABLE: An essential component of the tasteful decorations in LISTER and RIMMER's original bunk room.

BANANA YOGHURT, FAMILY-SIZED TUB OF: A prominent feature of one of the CAT's more enjoyable dreams. He apparently shared the interior of the tub with three beautiful girls.

BANGALORE BELLY: The condition to which LISTER put down what was actually a near-fatal case of PERITONITIS.

BARMAID: AIGBURTH ARMS employee who was working on the day the baby LISTER was discovered there.

BARRINGTON, FIONA: A girl RIMMER got off with at the age of fifteen, in his father's greenhouse. RIMMER thought he'd got lucky, in fact he'd got his hand in warm compost.

BAR-ROOM TIDY: A non-violent reverse pub brawl, as indulged in by the *RED DWARF* crew on BACKWARDS EARTH.

BATEMAN, STINKY: An old school mate of RIMMER's. He had the misfortune to have his turn-ups set alight in an untypical act of bravery by RIMMER in third-form prep.

BATMAN OUTFIT: LISTER thought that getting into this outfit might turn KOCHANSKI on. It didn't. See also SPIDER-MAN COSTUME.

BATTERING RAM: A use to which KRYTEN was not too pleased at being put. His six foot long, fairly sturdy construction – and his flat head! – made him the ideal device to enable the others to move around the ship when the electric doors ceased to operate. The experience so damaged his brain that he temporarily took to referring to LISTER as Susan.

BAXTER, BING: An American quiz show host, who LISTER associated with CONFIDENCE. When his own CONFIDENCE took on physical form, it assumed Baxter's voice.

BAY 47: Not only was this the location of QUARANTINE, it was also the place where the car belonging to SEBASTIAN DOYLE was parked – an amazing coincidence or what?

BAY CITY ROLLERS' GREATEST HITS: As he no longer considered these a priority KRYTEN dumped the memory into his TRASH FILE. He was confident that retaining 'Bye Bye Baby' would prove sufficient for most cultural purposes.

BAZOOKOIDS: Heavy-duty weapons with a heat-seeking setting. These are standard issue on *RED DWARF*, and have been employed by the crew against creatures such as the POLYMORPH and RIMMER's SELF-LOATHING.

BEADLEBAUM, HARRY: A simple carpenter's son who went on to own the biggest chain of PIZZA stores in history.

BEANBAGS: Allegedly made by GELFS from the skins of their victims.

BEARDSLEY, PETER: An actor who starred in what LISTER considered to be the definitive remake of the film *CASABLANCA*. It is unknown whether or not he was in any way related to the twentieth-century footballer of the same name. *See also* BINGLEBAT, MYRA.

BEER MILKSHAKE: See MARIJUANA GIN.

BELLAGOSIAN WAR: A conflict mentioned only as part of a joke, and it was in a dream anyway. Don't know why we mentioned it really.

BELLINI, BARBRA: An officer aboard a prison ship, which was taking a group of SIMULANTS to JUSTICE WORLD. When a MUTINY led to the deaths of the entire crew, the one surviving SIMULANT abandoned ship in Barbra's personal ESCAPE POD. Needless to say, it was later picked up by the crew of *RED DWARF*, whose hopes for a date were rather thwarted.

BENNET, ELIZABETH: Perhaps the hottest of the BENNET SISTERS if Mr Darcy is any judge of such matters.

BENNET, MRS: Mother of the five BENNET SISTERS. She was advised by KOCHANSKI to have the omelette with the big chips but chose instead to go for the VINDALOO.

BENNET SISTERS, THE: Jane, Kitty, Lydia, Mary and ELIZABETH BENNET, the five hot chicks encountered by LISTER and co in PRIDE AND PREJUDICE LAND.

BENTLEY V8 CONVERTIBLE: The vehicle belonging to his brother, in which RIMMER claimed to have lost his virginity to a girl called SANDRA.

BERMUDA TRIANGLE: This is, of course, one of the great mysteries of the universe . . . how did that song ever get to be a hit?!

BERNI INN: One of the biggest advantages of being THREE MILLION YEARS into deep space is that the nearest example of this type of restaurant is sixty billion miles away.

BETTER DEAD THAN SMEG: Even RIMMER agrees!

BETTER THAN LIFE: A fantasy GAME that allows the players to enjoy a shared illusion, in which everything they desire comes true. This was experimented with by LISTER, RIMMER and CAT. See also TOTAL IMMERSION VIDEO.

BEXLEY: LISTER's second son; see JIM for more details. Currently living in a PARALLEL UNIVERSE, Bexley will – if we can believe the FUTURE ECHOES – return to his death in the *RED DWARF* drive-room in his mid-twenties.

BHINDI-BHAJI: The companion of TARKA-DAL . . . actually the CAT.

BIG BLACK TOM: The real culprit responsible for FRANKENSTEIN's so called VIRGIN BIRTH.

BIG CRUNCH, THE: When the universe finally stops expanding, this reverse Big Bang will occur and time will begin to flow backwards.

BINGLEBAT, MYRA: An actress who starred in what LISTER considered to be the definitive remake of the film *CASABLANCA. See also* BEARDSLEY, PETER.

BINGLEY, MR: Owner of the ill-fated gazebo in PRIDE AND PREJUDICE LAND.

BINKS: A Commander aboard *ENLIGHTENMENT* who was not greatly impressed by the crew of *RED DWARF*. He curtailed his insults, however, when LISTER threatened the use of a HOLOWHIP.

BIOLOGY CLASSES: One of the many lessons to which LISTER never paid any attention at school. In this one, he was more concerned with turning to page 47 of the text book and drawing little beards and moustaches on the sperms.

BIO-SUITS: The vitally important items of life-saving protective apparel which LISTER, CAT and KRYTEN did not wear in the VIRAL RESEARCH DEPARTMENT.

BIRTHDAY PRESENT: Surprisingly, RIMMER once gave LISTER a $£5 BOOK token, though he had already borrowed $£15 from LISTER to buy it with. He never paid it back, either.

BLACK BOX: *RED DWARF*'s indestructible FLIGHT RECORDER, which was buried temporarily on an unnamed planet. All space ships are required to have these and even KRYTEN possesses his own version, albeit smaller and considerably less useful.

BLACK CARD: An imaginary object called into existence by RIMMER when he wished to end a conversation with LISTER. *See also* WHITE CARD.

BLACK HOLE: A dangerous spacial phenomenon which sucks time and matter out of the universe. HOLLY evacuated *RED DWARF* when she thought it was about to run into five of these, but they turned out to be specks of GRIT on the monitor screen. She protested that black holes are actually quite difficult to spot in space, what with them being completely black.

BLACK-RIBBED KNOBBLER: LISTER's greatest ever catch when CONDOM FISHING was a magnificent two-pound specimen of this type.

BLOBS, HUGE GREEN: The best description we have of the race to which the PLEASURE GELF, CAMILLE and her husband HECTOR belonged.

BLOW PIPE: Used by KRYTEN to dispatch various BENNET SISTERS. He later opted for a more practical method – a T72 tank.

BLUE ALERT: Engaged primarily to keep RIMMER happy, this emergency state serves to ensure that all crew members remain on their toes. On *STARBUG* it consists of a blue light flashing the word 'alert' on and off, and its effectiveness is thus questionable. *See also* RED ALERT.

BLUE-GREEN PLANETOID: Where *RED DWARF* was parked when its crew carelessly lost it.

BLUE MIDGET: The smaller of the two types of shuttle-craft which the *RED DWARF* carries. *See also STARBUG* and *WHITE MIDGET*.

BLU-TACK: The means by which LISTER's posters are stuck to the wall of his bunk room. In fact, the Blu-Tack belongs to RIMMER, who attempted to take it with him when he moved out.

BOB: The name by which KRYTEN refers to one of the SKUTTERS.

BOB, BENT: An affectionate nickname for a catering officer aboard *RED DWARF*; obviously it was used only behind his back. Bob was one of LISTER's few gay friends, which isn't really surprising is it?

BODY SWAP: *See* MIND SWAP.

BOG-BOT FROM HELL: *See* KRYTEN.

BOG ROLL: When an entire roll was used up in one day, RIMMER was convinced that ALIENS were responsible.

BOMBAY ALOO: Having survived being eaten by LISTER, some of these evolved, eventually forming a folk group. Well, according to KRYTEN, and he never lies.

BONEHEAD: RIMMER's real childhood nickname. *See also* ACE.

BONGO: One of ACE RIMMER's friends in his own dimension. Bongo looked suspiciously like KRYTEN did when he attained human form – and both bore a startling resemblance to JIM REAPER. Amazing, eh?

BONJELLA, PRINCESS BERYL: Placed before a firing squad by the NAZIS for reasons unknown, she was extricated from her predicament by ACE RIMMER (2). Presumably the fatal injuries he sustained during the attempt ruled out any post-rescue sex. But knowing Ace . . .

BOOKS: According to RIMMER, LISTER has read the same number of books as Champion the Wonder Horse – zero. LISTER even admitted it on one occasion. Of course, neither were including any with lift-up flaps or where the main character is a DOG called Ben. His reading opportunities were further curtailed when he and RIMMER were marooned on an ICE PLANET, and LISTER had to burn many of their books to survive. These included *Biggles Learns to Fly*, *LOLITA*, *The Caretaker* by Harold Pinter and the complete works of WILLIAM SHAKESPEARE. Other books owned by RIMMER include *THE A TO Z OF RED DWARF* (actually a hollow shell in which his diary is kept), *HOW TO PICK UP GIRLS BY HYPNOSIS*, *1001 Fabulous Chat-up Lines* and *ASTRO NAVIGATION AND INVISIBLE NUMBERS IN ENGINEERING STRUCTURE MADE SIMPLE*. LISTER is also the proud owner of the *POP-UP KARMA SUTRA* – ZERO GRAVITY EDITION. Finally, HOLLY claims to have read every book ever written, particularly enjoying the works of AGATHA CHRISTIE and particularly disliking Kevin Keegan's book, *FOOTBALL – IT'S A FUNNY OLD GAME*. It was once alleged that his entire store of knowledge came from *THE JUNIOR COLOUR ENCYCLOPEDIA OF SPACE*. *See also* CAT BOOKS.

BOOTLE MUNICIPAL GOLF COURSE: LISTER lost his virginity at the age of twelve to MICHELLE FISHER, by the tenth hole of this course – and he wasn't even a member of the club.

BOOTLE PLAYERS: Although relieved to be let out of the crate, LISTER wasn't too happy to find himself bollock-naked in the middle of the stage during this group's performance of *The Importance of Being Earnest*. *See also* BALD BLOKE and CASHIER NUMBER FOUR.

BOXER SHORTS: LISTER was quite upset when KRYTEN laundered his boxer shorts, transforming them into the bendable variety, but not quite as upset as he later became when he discovered that the pair he was wearing was actually a POLYMORPH.

BOXING, FEMALE TOPLESS: A sport greatly enjoyed by LISTER – as a spectator, of course.

BOZO BROTHERS: KOCHANSKI's term for the culturally unsophisticated CAT and LISTER.

BRAINS: PSIREN snacks, best enjoyed with the aid of a straw.

BRANNIGAN: The ship's psychiatrist, whose personality RIMMER temporarily took on when the HOLOGRAM SIMULATION SUITE was damaged.

BRAS: Thanks to a unique ironing technique, KOCHANSKI's come back from the LAUNDRY shaped like KRYTEN's head.

BREAKFAST: LISTER shows a preference towards onion-covered cornflakes with tabasco sauce and chilled VINDALOO juice.

BREASTS: After messing around with KOCHANSKI's HOLOGRAM DISK, RIMMER was shocked to find himself left with one of these wobbly extremities. However, he was in no great hurry to be rid of it, unlike LISTER who developed a couple of large ones following RIMMER's misuse of his body during a MIND SWAP.

BROOK: A character in the *ANDROIDS* soap opera, presumably married to KELLY, who was shocked to discover that Brooke Jnr was not his ANDROID. He was played by ANDROID 97542/P.

BROWN, CAROLE: An executive officer, whose mind was brought temporarily back into service for a failed attempt to abort the AUTO-DESTRUCT sequence.

BSc, SSc: The qualifications which RIMMER likes to quote himself as having. In fact, they stand for Bronze Swimming Certificate and Silver Swimming Certificate. In *RED DWARF* – THE TOTAL IMMERSION VIDEO GAME a microscopic message which CAPTAIN HOLLISTER had hidden in the letter 'i' on one of the certificates provided a blatant clue to the GAME's solution.

BUCHAN: A science officer on *RED DWARF* whose scientific knowledge was given to RIMMER via the MIND-PATCHING process. *See also* McQUEEN.

BUGGY: A transport vehicle used on planets where *STAR-BUG*'s scanners have revealed a warm, sunny, hospitable climate, because that's the last thing you'll find there.

BULGARIA: A country not visited by any members of the *RED DWARF* crew whilst on BACKWARDS EARTH.

BULLET, JAKE: The macho-sounding detective from Cybernautics, who was actually responsible for traffic control – or would have been if the policeman hadn't been merely an imagined persona of KRYTEN.

BUTCH ACCOUNTANT AND THE YUPPIE KID: RIMMER's favourite type of Western, at least as far as LISTER can tell from his behaviour at the LAST CHANCE SALOON.

C

CADET SCHOOL: It is no surprise whatsoever to learn that RIMMER once attended such an establishment. The school in question was run by a Training Officer called CALDICOTT, and RIMMER's fondest memory of his time there was the occasion on which he beat him at RISK. Whilst there, he also enjoyed a brief liaison with a fellow cadet called SANDRA although, despite his claims, he never actually lost his virginity to her.

CADMIUM 2: The type of RADIATION that wiped out the entire crew of *RED DWARF*.

CALDICOTT: RIMMER's Training Officer at CADET SCHOOL.

CALLISTO: A moon of Jupiter, on which PETERSEN purchased a Build-It-Yourself MARILYN MONROE kit.

CAMELOT: AR simulation in which LISTER OF SMEG attempted to satisfy his sexual urges with the QUEEN OF CAMELOT, much to the annoyance of the KING. He achieved this by cheating. Cheat 1, 'Steed Cheat', allowed him to dispatch his opponent, the GOOD KNIGHT, while the second codeword, 'Chastity Cheat', got rid of the Queen's chastity belt.

CAMERON MACKINTOSH AIR-COOLED DIESEL: A rarity which RIMMER was delighted to discover during his ten-day vacation on the DIESEL DECKS. Apparently, the item in question was a 184 – almost identical to the 179!

CAMILLE: A PLEASURE GELF with whom KRYTEN fell in love – even when she revealed her true form as being that of a HUGE GREEN BLOB. However, when her husband HECTOR arrived on the scene, the ANDROID took inspiration from *CASABLANCA* in persuading her to leave with her spouse.

CANNIBALISM: Inadvertently indulged in by LISTER following a spot of guilt-free cooking by KRYTEN.

CAPTAIN A. J. RIMMER, SPACE ADVENTURER: How RIMMER wished to be referred to, in order to impress the crew of the *NOVA 5*. He also wouldn't have minded being called ACE or Big Man.

CAPTAIN'S TABLE: To RIMMER especially, the ultimate honour was to be invited to dine here. Unfortunately, he managed to ruin the occasion. *See* GAZPACHO SOUP.

CAP, TOOTH: LISTER's is made from a skeleton in the medi-bay; when it came out he fixed it with wood glue.

CARDBOARD HATS: An intrinsic part of the CAT PEOPLE's view of Heaven, based on LISTER's own ambitions as related to FRANKENSTEIN. The hats were to be worn in the HOT DOG AND DOUGHNUT DINERS on FUCHAL. Unfortunately, nobody could agree on whether they should be red or blue, and vicious HOLY WARS broke out. LISTER was particularly saddened by this, as the hats were supposed to be green anyway.

CARGO BAY: The site of one of LISTER's more unpleasant experiences, when his safety harness snapped and he cracked his spine in three places. RIMMER found the whole incident extremely amusing, and said so. LISTER perhaps got his own back by smashing one of the *STARBUG*s into the cargo bay doors, although KRYTEN did rather a better destruction job with *STARBUG 1* shortly before that. The cargo ramp here is also frequently used by LISTER and CAT when playing soap-sud slalom.

CARGO DECK: A good deal bigger in *STARBUG* following the reality-altering business with the TIME DRIVE.

CARGO DECKS: The storage areas of *RED DWARF*, in which the CAT PEOPLE evolved and lived. They are situated two thousand levels from LISTER and RIMMER's sleeping quarters in the officers' block, and take over two days to reach on foot.

CARMEN, CAROLINE: Former supply officer aboard *RED DWARF*. Her ostensibly still living body was discovered encased in ice aboard the *LEVIATHAN*. In an attempt to make KOCHANSKI jealous, LISTER claimed to have had an affair with her. His words became almost prophetic later on when the freshly-thawed, EPIDEME-infected Caroline got into his bed looking a lot like Tutankhamen's horny grandma.

CARMEN, KAREN: LISTER's attempt to make KOCHAN-SKI (2) jealous by mentioning his fling with CAROLINE CARMEN was doomed to failure when he got her name wrong.

CARTOONIVORE: Always a man of compassion, LISTER refuses to eat any animal that has been featured in cartoon form. Presumably he's never heard of Foghorn Leghorn then.

CASABLANCA: A FILM much admired by LISTER, who considered the definitive version to be that which starred PETER BEARDSLEY and MYRA BINGLEBAT. He used the FILM as an integral part of his teachings when he instructed KRYTEN in the art of LYING. KRYTEN obviously enjoyed it, for he shared it with CAMILLE, who decided that it would be 'their movie'. However, when her husband HECTOR turned up, KRYTEN borrowed a trick or two from the film to persuade his love to return to her husband.

CASHIER NUMBER 4: Twenty-two-year-old MEGAMART employee with come-to-behind-the-bacon-counter eyes. Some-thing about the way she held her pricing gun made LISTER crash his trolleys, so they had a bit in the stock room.

CAT: The only one of the CAT PEOPLE remaining aboard *RED DWARF*, and presumably the sole surviving member of the entire species.

CAT AND MOUSE: Despite cartoon propaganda, CAT maintains that the only way to win such a game is by not being the mouse.

CAT BOOKS: The literature of the CAT PEOPLE, made up of scents instead of words.

CAT-MARSHALLED: What LISTER joked he'd be for bringing an unquarantined animal aboard *RED DWARF*.

CAT PEOPLE: The race which evolved from LISTER's pet cat FRANKENSTEIN.

CAT PRIESTS: Keepers of the word of CLOISTER, these religious leaders wore the HOLY CUSTARD STAINS, the

SACRED GRAVY MARKS and the CARDBOARD HATS which were his icons. LISTER met one of the Priests on *RED DWARF* only moments before he died, and was able to convince him that his faith had been justified.

CAVALRY TWILL TROUSERS AND A PAISLEY SHIRT: The kind of thing CAT might wear if he ever took heed of RIMMER's fashion tips.

CENTAURI, **SS:** Ship plundered by our heroes, who failed to notice it was crewed by a rogue SIMULANT and a GELF. See CHRYSTALLINE TURBINE DRIVES for more information on this ship's origins.

CGI: No we don't know what it stands for, but see SEBASTIAN DOYLE anyway.

CHAMPAGNE: KRYTEN thought it was well worth cracking open a bottle to celebrate the fact that KOCHANSKI (2) was leaving; as it turned out he should have saved it for another time.

CHANNEL 72: TV station which ran the surprisingly unsurprising *Tales of the Unexpected*.

CHASM OF HOPELESSNESS: An area of the PSYMOON located not too far from the SWAMP OF DESPAIR and quite close to the WOOD OF HUMILIATION.

CHEAT BOOK: *See* CAMELOT.

CHEESE-SLICE SNAP: A GAME which, as you might expect, provided only limited entertainment value, but was played anyway.

CHEN: One of LISTER's friends and drinking partners aboard *RED DWARF*.

CHESS: The GAME chosen by QUEEG in the final showdown with HOLLY, despite HOLLY's alternative suggestions, which included draughts, Monopoly and snakes and ladders. HOLLY was not exactly a novice at chess, however. He and fellow computer GORDON had been involved in a tournament that spanned THREE MILLION YEARS, though only one move had ever actually been made.

CHICKEN: The disguise chosen by HOLLISTER for a FANCY DRESS PARTY, which earned RIMMER eight years' PD when he mistook his commanding officer for a drug-induced HALLUCINATION. Later LISTER was transmogrified into such a bird by the DNA MODIFIER, and learnt exactly why they cluck so much (see also HAMSTER). For no apparent reason the EMOHAWK transformed itself briefly into said fowl during its visit to *STARBUG*. Currently, there are no live chickens on board, thus precluding the enforcement of SPACE CORPS DIRECTIVE 68250. However, if you plan to travel by XPRESS LIFT in the future, it's worth mentioning that the chicken served up on board tastes slightly worse than its container.

CHICKEN MERENGO: The entry which some people argue should have been in the index last time. We disagree.

CHICKEN, ROAST: The form which RIMMER thought his fictional ALIEN race the QUAGAARS had taken, when one was discovered in what turned out to be one of *RED DWARF*'s GARBAGE PODs.

CHICKEN SOUP NOZZLE: An integral part of Z SHIFT's duty roster was to keep these items clear of blockages.

CHICKENS, REHYDRATABLE: When LISTER and RIMMER inventoried the ship's stores, they discovered that there were 140,000 of these on board.

CHIEF EUNUCH: RIMMER believes that, in a past life, he occupied this role in the court of ALEXANDER THE GREAT. LISTER believes it too. Even today, RIMMER claims that he can't look at a pair of nutcrackers without wincing.

CHILD PSYCHOLOGIST: LISTER had to see one of these at age six, in order to cope with the death of his stepfather. Having been told that his dad had gone to the same place as his dead goldfish, he spent hours with his head down the toilet bowl trying to communicate with him.

CHINESE WORRY BALLS: Given to RIMMER to aid him in stress management, they were more like Chinese Worry Marbles by the time he was rescued from RIMMERWORLD.

CHIPS: These items control certain aspects of ANDROID behaviour. We know, for instance, that KRYTEN has, amongst others, a guilt chip, an anxiety chip, a sanity chip and a good taste chip.

CHLOROFORM: A particular type of anaesthetic which KRYTEN is a dab hand at administering. On RIMMER's instructions, he chloroformed LISTER and CAT so that their bodies could be swapped with RIMMER's without their agreement. The technique came in more useful, however, as a painless way of halting LISTER when he became a remote controlled homicidal maniac.

CHOCOLATE DISPENSER: *STARBUG*'s auxiliary flight modulator was short-circuited, the internal trimmers were down, and the stabilisers were very unstable; but worst of all, the nutty fruit snack bars had been ejected on to the galley floor and were sliding around!

CHOCOLATE WRAPPER: The item used by LISTER to take notes whilst revising for the Chef's EXAM. RIMMER saw it as conclusive proof that he was not displaying quite the right attitude.

CHRISTIE, AGATHA: A novelist whose works were so enjoyed by HOLLY that he arranged for his memory banks to be erased so that he could read them all over again.

CIGARETTES: One of LISTER's many vices, which he indulges in despite RIMMER's objections and the No Smoking sign that he has deliberately placed in their bunk room. RIMMER has made use of the habit in the past, however, by hiding LISTER's supply and giving them back to him at the rate of one for every day that he obeyed orders. By the time

LISTER uncovered the hiding place, he had earned the grand total of four and three quarters.

CINEMA: An area of *RED DWARF* is allocated for this use. It is frequented by the SKUTTERS, in defiance of RIMMER's orders, by LISTER, who apparently visits it every Sunday afternoon, and it was also where KRYTEN took CAMILLE to see *CASABLANCA*.

CINZANO BIANCO: The nickname which LISTER claimed to have been given by his fellow POOL players at the AIGBURTH ARMS, so called because, once he was on the table, they couldn't get him off.

CLAUSTROPHOBIA: Suffered by LISTER. Cat wondered if he was born that way or just plain sissy, but apparently he's had it ever since his experience in a crate. See also BOOTLE PLAYERS.

CLEARANCE ZONE: The area of JUSTICE WORLD in which the honesty of visitors is assessed, before they are allowed to proceed any further.

CLIFTON, FIELD MARSHAL: The dignitary who invited RIMMER to dine with him during his BETTER THAN LIFE fantasy.

CLITORIS: Acronym for the Committee for the Liberation and Integration of Terrifying Organisms and their Rehabilitation Into Society. This was one of the names put forward by RIMMER in his anger-free campaign against the POLYMORPH. *See also* THE LEAGUE AGAINST SALIVATING MONSTERS.

CLOAK: A device fitted aboard *STARBUG*, with the ability to render the shuttle-craft invisible.

CLOISTER THE STUPID: According to legend, the CAT PEOPLE's deity, who will return to lead them to the Promised Land of FUCHAL. Unfortunately for the CATS, Cloister is really LISTER, and the whole thing's been a bit of a mistake.

COCKPIT COMPUTER: The mechanism which ran ACE RIMMER's dimension-spanning LIGHT SHIP. Possessed of Artificial Intelligence and a female personality, it was smitten with ACE's manly charm.

COFFEE: LISTER likes to take his double caffeinated with four sugars.

COFFINS: Those containing the remains of the many ACE RIMMERs made up the rings of a planet. Seeing these persuaded RIMMER to don the WIG and become the next ACE; though they ought to have shown that he was pretty likely to end up dead again before too long.

COLOSTOMY EXPLOSION: Rock band which LISTER may have liked, since he had the T-shirt.

COLUMBO: According to RIMMER, the man in the dirty mac who discovered America.

COME JIVING: Presumably a future version of *Come Dancing*; it has been commented that the CAT could have passed for a finalist in this competition.

COMPLAINTS: Rimmer filed 247 against Lister – including one of MUTINY.

COMPUTER RASH: A weak excuse used by HOLLY to explain the lipstick marks which covered his face while he was 'working' with HILLY.

COMPUTER SENILITY: The 'illness' with which HOLLY became stricken during his THREE MILLION YEARS alone. KRYTEN successfully cured this by raising the now female HOLLY's IQ to a staggering 12,000. Unfortunately, a side-effect of the experiment was that her operational life-span was drastically reduced. Fortunately the closure of a WHITE HOLE negated the 'repair' anyway, so it was back to square one for the loopy computer.

COMPUTER SLUG: A small item on which HOLLY can record information. The slug – and therefore the data – can then be plugged into any other computer.

CONDOM FISHING: An activity in which LISTER indulged in his younger days. As the local canal was devoid of FISH, condoms were all he and his friends could catch – although he is particularly proud of the 2lb BLACK-RIBBED KNOBBLER he was once able to land.

CONDOMS: RIMMER sewed name tags in his ship's-issue ones.

CONDOM, TRIPLE-THICK: DUANE DIBBLEY likes to keep one with him at all times. Well, you never know.

CONFIDENCE: One of the imaginary beings who LISTER and CHEN theorised lived inside their heads. He became frighteningly real when LISTER caught a mutated PNEUMONIA virus which allowed his HALLUCINATIONS to become solid. Confidence was modelled after all the things that LISTER associated with confidence – he looked like a player from the LONDON JETS, and sounded like BING BAXTER. He died when he took off his helmet in space, in an attempt to convince LISTER that he didn't need oxygen to breathe. *See also* PARANOIA.

CONFIDENTIAL REPORTS: CAPTAIN HOLLISTER kept one of these on each member of his crew, presumably on their PERSONAL DATA FILES. RIMMER, of course, took his death as an opportunity to review his own, and he wasn't too pleased by what he found!

CONTRACEPTIVE JELLY: The substance for which LISTER once swapped RIMMER's toothpaste as a practical joke.

'COPACABANA': A hit song of the 20th century, an instrumental version of which was selected by KRYTEN's CPU to keep him company when severe damage caused it to go temporarily off-line.

COTTAGE CHEESE WITH PINEAPPLE CHUNKS: Food enjoyed by KOCHANSKI (2). She denies she ever looks at LISTER as if he were a tub of this – the plain sort maybe, but never with pineapple chunks.

COUNTRY AND WESTERN CHANNEL: Sadly, some things never change.

COWS: One of the types of animal that LISTER wanted to breed when he got his farm on FIJI.

CRANE, NIRVANAH: A Flight Commander aboard the HOLOSHIP *ENLIGHTENMENT*, who fell in love with RIMMER. As crew member 4172 she was selected by STOCKY as RIMMER's opponent in a contest for a position aboard the HOLOSHIP. The computer's prediction that she would be RIMMER's best chance proved accurate, since she was prepared to sacrifice her own existence so that he might replace her in the crew and thus fulfil the potential she believed he possessed.

CRAPOLA, INC.: The company which, much to LISTER's regret, manufactured the TALKIE TOASTER.

CROCHETED HATS: The colourful items of head wear that, thanks to a handy knitting pattern magazine, thoughtfully provided by RIMMER, LISTER made during his five-day stint in QUARANTINE.

CROCODILE: Fierce pet of CAPTAIN VOORHESE. ACE RIMMER (2) used it to indulge in a little sky-surfing.

CROSSBOW: Brought over from the alternate *STARBUG*; KRYTEN thought it might be useful if LISTER's wife turned up again.

CROSSBOW: The means by which the hallucinating KRYTEN intended to kill himself and the others, believing it to be a handgun.

CROSSWORD BOOK: The means by which RIMMER hoped to 'kill a couple of centuries' when LISTER intended to go into STASIS, leaving him alone for THREE MILLION YEARS.

'CRUISE WITH ME FOR A WHILE': A sticker on LISTER's guitar. A bit sad, our noticing that don't you think?

CRUNCHIE BARS, FUN-SIZE: The most important task of Z SHIFT (as commanded by ARNOLD RIMMER) was to ensure that the VENDING MACHINES didn't run out of these objects.

CRYSTALLINE TURBINE DRIVES: These allowed CAT to narrow down the *CENTAURI*'s origins to the twenty-first, twenty-second, twenty-third, twenty-fourth, twenty-fifth, twenty-sixth or twenty-seventh centuries. But don't hold him to that because it may be the twenty-ninth.

CUFFLINKS: A fashion accessory favoured by the CAT – even on space suits.

CURRIED RICE KRISPIES: Another of LISTER's idiosyncratic breakfast selections.

CURRY: A type of food very much favoured by DAVE LISTER, who has diligently introduced the CAT to its wonders. Of course, he is always willing to sample other types of food too. One June, for instance, KRYTEN recalls him trying a PIZZA. Unfortunately the meal was missing that one certain something – curry sauce! See also VINDALOOS.

CURRY NIGHT: Friday, Saturday, Sunday, Tuesday, Wednesday and Thursday. What's on Monday then? Surely not pasta!

CURRY WORLD: AR simulation where the CURRY proved too hot even for LISTER. MRS BENNET enjoyed it though.

CUSTER, DEREK: The heroic figure who, along with companions Kit and Titan, rescued RIMMER from RIMMER-WORLD.

CYANIDE CAPSULES: These are provided as standard equipment in XPRESS LIFTS, due to the unlikeliness of escape in the event of an accident.

CYBER-PARK: The existence of one of these on LEGION's space station would have allowed his 'guests' to visit any time period and indulge in any fantasy with anyone they chose. Seems they escaped a bit too soon.

CYBERSCHOOL: Attended by KOCHANSKI for eleven years. Here she was taught by perfect computer-generated teachers and made perfect CG friends.

D

DAILY GOAL LIST: The list which RIMMER set himself every day – and always failed to complete.

DAMAGE REPORT MACHINE: The one on *RED DWARF* was last reported to be damaged. The one on *STARBUG* exploded.

DANDELION SORBET: The perfect dessert to follow ASTEROIDAL LICHEN STEW.

DANDRUFF: A flake of this was the only thing RIMMER could find that contained any of his cells and could therefore be used to form a clone body via the DNA MODIFIER. Unfortunately, one sneeze from CAT ruined his ambitions.

DARTBOARD: A vital piece of equipment contained aboard *STARBUG*.

DAVRO: *See* LEGION.

DAY-GLO ORANGE MOONBOOTS: The noxious and fetid items of footwear which once set off a chemical alarm. LISTER believed they would help him score with the crew of the *NOVA 5*; the girls never realised how lucky they were to be dead.

D DECK: A good place from which to urinate on RIMMER aboard *STARBUG*.

DEADIES: A derogatory slang term for dead people who have been re-incarnated as HOLOGRAMS.

DEATH: (1) A lot like being in Swindon, apparently.

DEATH: (2) Leader of the FOUR APOCALYPSE BOYS in KRYTEN's ARMAGEDDON VIRUS inspired dreamscape. He looked suspiciously similar to the SIMULANT captain responsible for said virus, and his motto was: 'Have infection, will travel.'

DECIMALISED MUSIC: HOLLY's notion for improving music. Innovations include replacing the octave with a decative, adding the notes H and J and incorporating woh and boh into the musical scale. He christened his invention HOL ROCK.

DECOYS: *STARBUG*'s way of confusing oncoming missiles; used once and unsuccessful.

DEEP-SLEEP: A form of suspended animation available on *STARBUG*. Unlike STASIS, which freezes time, deep-sleep merely reduces the ageing process, albeit dramatically.

DEFENSIVE SHIELDS: See DEFLECTOR SHIELDS.

DEFLECTOR SHIELDS: A rather useful defensive system, not possessed by *STARBUG*.

DEGANWY: The site of a school summer camp which LISTER once attended. This was run by his geography teacher, MISS FOSTER.

DELTA 7: The destination of the *LEVIATHAN* in a vain mission to seek a cure for the EPIDEME VIRUS.

DESCARTES: A French thinker whose philosophical astuteness is often confused with that of POPEYE the sailor man.

DESPAIR SQUID: The product of an experiment into accelerated evolution by planetary engineers. This enormous cephalopod emitted a venom which not only caused HALLUCINATIONS but induced a state of extreme melancholy. As a result of coming into contact with the squid's ink, the crew of the SSS *ESPERANTO* were compelled to commit SUICIDE, a fate also suffered by the other marine life on the unnamed world.

DEVELOPING FLUID: A batch of this substance mutated over THREE MILLION YEARS in storage, and KRYTEN discovered that it could make photographs apparently come to life. Using the fluid, he was able to develop TIME-SLIDES.

DEVIANCY, GROSS: On RIMMERWORLD, this meant displaying charm, bravery and honour, as opposed to double-dealing, and two-facedness. DEREK CUSTER and friends were charged on eight counts and CAT believed he must be Public Enemy No. 1.

DIARIES: Both LISTER and RIMMER possessed one, but only RIMMER had the good manners to read his bunkmates's diary behind his back. The diary belonging to RIMMER proved useful in locating the STASIS LEAK.

DIARRHOEA: The illness for which LISTER requested sick leave no less than five hundred times during his eight month stint with the JUPITER MINING CORPORATION.

DIBBLEY, DUANE: The styleless, buck-toothed geek who took a party into *RED DWARF* – THE TOTAL IMMERSION VIDEO GAME. In reality the person the CAT imagined himself to be when under the influence of the DESPAIR SQUID's ink. As a preference CAT chose death over a life spent in plastic sandals and an anorak. However, an encounter with an EMOHAWK and the subsequent theft of the CAT's cool and style resulted in a temporary return for the DUKE OF DORK.

DICE, FURRY: Optional extra found in *BLUE MIDGET* and in RIMMER's BETTER THAN LIFE fantasy JAGUAR. *STARBUG* used to have a set as well, but the elastic snapped when the shuttle-craft collided with ACE RIMMER's ship. HOLLY seemed quite pleased about the incident, and commented that the cockpit was now a lot more tasteful.

DICK: A fictional character who featured in the elementary books of the CAT PEOPLE.

DIESEL DECKS: The setting for a ten-day hiking vacation which RIMMER took, along with two SKUTTERS. The subsequent slide show presentation threatened to melt KRYTEN's intelligence circuits.

DIMENSION THEORY OF REALITY: The theory developed in ACE RIMMER's dimension that stated that a ship travelling at the theoretical SPEED OF REALITY could break the barrier into PARALLEL UNIVERSES. It obviously worked, as ACE was able to visit our own universe, meeting his counterpart here.

DISCO LIGHTING: LISTER claims it is only due to inefficient examples of these that he has dated worse than the warty yeti lookalike he encountered on the GELF MOON.

DISINTEGRATOR: Where Kochanski (2) almost dispatched FRANKENSTEIN. Not doing so resulted in her extended stay in STASIS.

DISPENSER 172: The DISPENSER which fell foul of the now infamous CHICKEN SOUP NOZZLE blockage!

DISPENSERS: Also known as VENDING MACHINES, these handy, time saving apparatus dispense food to – and presumably also prepare food for – the crew of *RED DWARF*.

DIVA-DROID INTERNATIONAL: A corporation which manufactured MECHANOIDS such as the KRYTEN Series III (otherwise known as the Series 4000) and HUDZEN 10 models.

DIXON, REGGIE: One of the many musical artistes whose only actual fan seems to be ARNOLD RIMMER. His albums apparently include the unappetising 'Tango Treats'.

DNA: RIMMER searched long and hard for an example of his own, in the hope that the DNA MODIFIER could then provide him with a body. One sneeze from CAT, and that hope was lost. However, using equipment discovered in ESCAPE POD 1736 he was able to populate RIMMER-WORLD with an army of clones; it is likely that either the genetic code was present in his LIGHT BEE's programme or that it is possible to synthesise DNA using material from his hard-light body.

DNA MODIFIER: A machine which could turn any living thing into any other living thing by altering its molecular structure. Amongst other things, it turned LISTER into a CHICKEN and KRYTEN into a human. It also formed a MUTTON VINDALOO BEAST out of a curry.

DOBBIN: The drummer with SMEG AND THE HEADS, who later joined the police-force and the masons.

DOG: Much to the CAT's frustration, his PARALLEL UNIVERSE counterpart was not female, and if that wasn't bad enough, was a dog! Although evolved into humanoid form and reasonably intelligent, the dog still retained many canine characteristics, and was particularly scruffy, smelly and flea-ridden, with a predilection for sniffing others' behinds.

DOG FOOD: Having been forced to eat some when marooned on an ICE PLANET, LISTER realised why DOGS licked their testicles.

DOGS: When CAT first learnt about these creatures, via a photograph of LISTER's stepfather's dog, HANNAH, he became intent upon finding one to chase. LISTER disabused him of this notion by claiming that they were eighteen feet long with teeth as big as your leg. Upon divorcing his parents as a teenager RIMMER was granted access to the family dog every fourth weekend. *See also* DOG.

DOGS' MILK: Used for necessity when the cows' milk ran out. Dogs' milk has the distinct advantage of lasting much longer – because, as Holly quite rightly pointed out, no bugger'll drink it!

DOLLARPOUNDS: Never mind the ECU – the dollarpound ($£) is the standard unit of world currency in the twenty-second century. RIMMER was the proud owner of twenty-four thousand of them, but when LISTER became marooned on an ICE PLANET, he had to burn the lot just to stay alive.

DOM PERIGNON '44: LISTER drank this in his BETTER THAN LIFE fantasy – out of a pint mug, of course.

DONALD: A hypnotherapist who regressed RIMMER to a previous incarnation as ALEXANDER THE GREAT'S CHIEF EUNUCH.

DONATELLA, DON: No, not a mutant turtle, a ZERO GEE FOOTBALL player in the ROOF ATTACK position.

DORKSVILLE: RIMMER's suggestion for a town to be named after KRYTEN following his creation of the TRIPLICATOR.

DOUBLE POLAROID: A euphemism for the strange appendage KRYTEN found on his body after turning human – so called because, after a quick look through an electrical appliance catalogue, he had to take two photographs to fit it all on so that he could show it to LISTER.

DOVE PROGRAM: In order to create this antidote to the ARMAGGEDON VIRUS, KRYTEN linked himself to *STAR-BUG*'s computer. To better cope with the task at hand, his subconscious saw fit to perceive it as a Wild West confrontation.

DOWNTIME: KRYTEN's equivalent of sleep.

DOYLE, BILLY: One of DUANE DIBBLEY's party and the brother of the highly successful SEBASTIAN DOYLE, this down-at-heel vagrant was actually how RIMMER perceived himself when under the influence of the DESPAIR SQUID's ink.

DOYLE, SEBASTIAN: The Section Chief of CGI and Head of the MINISTRY OF ALTERATION in a FASCIST state. The mass murdering VOTER Colonel Doyle was a HALLUCINATION of LISTER's; in this hated guise he was pushed to the brink of SUICIDE.

DREAM RECORDER: The machine which automatically records the dreams of everybody on board *RED DWARF*. It enabled LISTER to ascertain the fact that KOCHANSKI dreamt about him three times. CAT also used it to re-live those dreams in which he'd had a particularly good time.

DRESSING GOWN, PINK: Along with fluffy white pig slippers and dental floss wood-glued to his teeth, this is how LISTER appeared when he met KRISTINE KOCHANSKI (2) for the first time. Bet she was impressed.

DRIVE PLATE: Had RIMMER repaired this item efficiently, he might well have prevented the leakage of lethal CADMIUM 2 RADIATION that wiped out the entire crew of *RED DWARF*.

DRIVE ROOM: The bridge, by any other name. It was here that RIMMER met his death, whilst he was busy explaining to CAPTAIN HOLLISTER why he had failed to mend the DRIVE PLATE. LISTER's son BEXLEY is also destined to die here in his mid-twenties, following an accident with the NAVI-COMP.

DROID ROT: An unfortunate disease that caused the deterioration of KRYTEN's third SPARE HEAD.

DUBOIS BROTHERS: The legendary toy makers, who hand-carved RIMMER's treasured ARMIES DU NORD.

DUKE: (1) Another of the nicknames that RIMMER would rather like to have (*see also* ACE). When he first met CAMILLE, he claimed that his friends often used this, but asked her not to mention it in front of them, just in case they'd forgotten. *See also* IRON DUKE and CAPTAIN A. J. RIMMER, SPACE ADVENTURER.

DUKE: (2) *See* FRANK.

DUKE OF DORK: *See* DUANE DIBBLEY.

DUMPLINGS: The taste notwithstanding, RIMMER's dumplings can be distinguished from the usual sort by their unique ability to bounce. *See also* STOMACH PUMP.

DUNCAN: A friend of LISTER's who introduced him to the use of MIRRORS on his toe-caps for looking up girls' skirts. When LISTER was ten, Duncan had to move to Spain because of his father's job – a bank job, as it happens. LISTER never saw him again.

DUREX VOLLEYBALL: *See* GAMES.

DUST STORM: A self-explanatory space phenomenon, which *RED DWARF* ran into shortly after LISTER's CONFIDENCE and PARANOIA manifested themselves on board.

DWARFERS: A no longer fashionable term referring to the *RED DWARF* crew. Not to be confused with the word's twentieth-century usage, which denotes a particularly unpleasant sexual practice.

E

EARTH: (1) A language understood by SIMULANTS: it sounds a lot like English.

EARTH: (2) The birthplace of LISTER, to which he hopes one day to return – even if it's been taken over by giant ants or dolphins. KRYTEN was surprised to discover that the planet was far shorter than he'd expected(?!). *See also* BACKWARDS EARTH.

EASTBOURNE ZIMMER FRAME RELAY TEAM: Allegedly somewhat faster than *STARBUG*.

ECO-ACCELERATOR ROCKETS: Twenty-fifth-century TERRAFORMING devices which created RIMMER-WORLD in six days.

E5A908B7: The machine code equivalent of the word 'LOVE', utilising Z80012, using hex rather than binary notation and converting to a basic ASCII code. Sweet-talking KRYTEN wooed CAMILLE with its use.

EGYPTIAN WHISKEY: As smooth as one of KRYTEN's landings it seems.

EJECTOR SEAT: *STARBUG* is fitted with this gadget, as KRYTEN accidentally discovered. During his 'driving test', he managed to eject his instructor – RIMMER – out into the CARGO BAY. RIMMER managed to eject himself when he first attempted to take off in Ace's ship.

ELECTROMAGNETIC PHASING FREQUENCY 434: Required to re-establish the linkway between dimensions in order for KOCHANSKI (2) to return home. KRYTEN was well pleased when they found it.

ELECTRONIC BIBLE, THE: The fictional work in which ANDROIDS are programmed to believe. This states that 'the iron will lie down with the lamp,' and explains the concept of SILICON HEAVEN.

ELLIS, MICHAEL: Or rather Leahcim Sille, who had the generous occupation of bank raider on BACKWARDS EARTH.

EMOHAWK: A POLYMORPH spayed at birth and half domesticated. The one sent to sort out the DWARFERS after they cheated its KINITAWOWI masters out of an O/G unit transformed itself into several items, as you might expect from a shape-changer, and we suppose you'd like a list, eh? Here goes then: a rabbit, a lamp, a stick, LISTER's deerstalker, a CHICKEN, a can of beans, a FROG, a paper dart/plane, a microphone, a slinky, a toy car, a THERMOS FLASK and a GRENADE.

ENFORCEMENT ORB, CLASS A: The SPACE CORPS EXTERNAL ENFORCEMENT VEHICLE which intercepted *STARBUG* and accused its crew of looting.

ENIG: KRYTEN's enigmatic last word in a TIMELINE which, fortunately, was later wiped out of history. As it transpired, this seemingly incomprehensible message was meant to tip KRYTEN's slightly younger self off to the fact that the programming of THE INQUISITOR's TIME GAUNTLET worked on a variation of the ENIGMA DECODING SYSTEM.

ENIGMA DECODING SYSTEM: *See also* ENIG (though if you're reading this section in the correct order you should just have done so) and TIME GAUNTLETS.

ENLIGHTENMENT: A HOLOSHIP crewed by the holo-gramatic cream of the SPACE CORPS – 2,000 of them to be exact.

EPIDEME VIRUS: Wacky but charismatic, this intelligent manmade parasite was conceived as a rival to the nicotine patch. Indeed it successfully blocked the neural signals relating to nicotine cravings. Unfortunately it also blocked the ones telling the body it needed blood and oxygen, with fatal consequences for its host. Having consumed the body and absorbed its knowledge, the epideme seeks out a fresh victim.

EQUAL-RIGHTS-FOR-MEN MARCHES: Demonstrations which took place in the female dominated PARALLEL UNIVERSE. These protest rallies consisted of thousands of men burning their jockstraps, in an attempt to achieve equality.

ERASURE: A fate suffered by HOLLY after his defeat at CHESS by QUEEG – except that it was all a joke!

ESCAPE POD: Looks rather similar to an ORE SAMPLE POD; identical, in fact. The one on *STARBUG* escaped when LISTER used the release mechanism as a bottle opener. Nevertheless a replacement had been fitted by the time ABLE had to make a hasty exit from the vessel. It was presumably an afterthought anyway, as there were none present when the shuttle crash-landed on an ICE PLANET. Perhaps the idea was inspired by the one which didn't contain BARBRA BELLINI.

ESCAPE POD 1736: Originally looted from a twenty-fifth-century seeding ship, RIMMER used it, much to the annoyance of the others, as his exclusive means of escape from the doomed SIMULANT battle-cruiser. Its program took it to the nearest S3 PLANET where RIMMER used the TERRA-FORMING devices aboard to create RIMMERWORLD.

ESCORT BOOTS: An unusual feature of JUSTICE WORLD. Visitors have to wear these items of footwear, which then transport them through to the CLEARANCE ZONE for their crimes to be assessed. Anybody who is granted clearance is able to step out of the boots and walk freely around the complex. Anybody who isn't is sentenced and taken by the boots into the JUSTICE ZONE. CAT wasn't too happy at being made to wear something of such uncool design, describing them as 'Frankenstein's hand-me-downs'.

ESPERANTO: A language which RIMMER has devoted a great deal of time to learning over eight years. It is a great frustration to him that even LISTER is actually better at it than he is.

EXAMS: The means by which SPACE CORPS technicians of LISTER and RIMMER's ranks could better themselves and become Corps Officers. RIMMER was desperate to do so, and he sat the Engineering exam eleven times, failing each one. He also tried his hand at Astro-Navigation, but failed that too, on no less than thirteen separate occasions (although he'll only admit to ten – and then only if you count the time he had his spasm!). LISTER, meanwhile, had never had much time for academic subjects. However, when the opportunity arose to become RIMMER's superior, he grasped it with open arms. He sat the Chef's exam, and claimed to have passed. He was lying.

EXERCISE: A pastime in which RIMMER would like us to believe he frequently indulges (see also NECROBICS). His sham has been exposed both by his own identical 'twin' and by QUEEG, both of whom put him through punishing exercise routines which he was unable to take. LISTER, of course, has never put up any such pretence.

EXISTENCE: The imaginary Western town in which KRYTEN fought the FOUR APOCALYPSE BOYS – as in 'You are now leaving . . .'

EXPERIMENTAL PILE SURGERY: One of LISTER's ideas for a practical joke was to put RIMMER's name on the waiting list for this treatment.

EXPIRY DATE: All ANDROIDS are fitted with these in order for the manufacturers to sell newer models. In

KRYTEN's case, the arrival of his triggered both his SHUT-DOWN DISK (with which he was easily able to cope) and the arrival of his replacement, HUDZEN (with which he had rather more trouble!).

EXTRA-BROWN RUBBER SAFETY PANTS: Required by RIMMER when entering a soon-to-disintegrate SIMULANT Battle Class Cruiser.

F

FALCONBURGER, BLAIZE: The American TV presenter of LIFESTYLES OF THE DISGUSTINGLY RICH AND FAMOUS.

FAMINE: Corpulent member of the FOUR APOCALYPSE BOYS.

FANCY-DRESS PARTY: One of these bashes was in full swing when LISTER, RIMMER and CAT went back in time to visit *RED DWARF* on 2 MARCH 2077. CAPTAIN HOL-LISTER's chosen costume caused a great deal of problems for RIMMER. *See* CHICKEN.

FASCIST: The political party which was hoping for a third glorious decade in power when DUANE DIBBLEY and co emerged from *RED DWARF* – THE TOTAL IMMERSION VIDEO GAME.

FASCIST DICTATOR MONTHLY: A magazine read by RIMMER, which once featured ADOLF HITLER as Mr October.

FASTER-THAN-LIGHT DRIVE: We're not too sure about this one, but think it might be a drive which enables spaceships to travel faster than the speed of light.

FAT BOY: Lister's nickname at school between the ages of eleven and thirteen. He was called this because he was fat.

FEAR: The emotion the POLYMORPH stole from LISTER. Consequently, LISTER thought it would be quite a good idea to strap a nuclear bomb to his head so that he could nut the smegger into oblivion.

FELICITUS POPULI: The good-luck virus developed by the hologramatic Doctor HILDEGARDE LANSTROM. LISTER used it to good effect in combating a HOLO-VIRUS infected and totally psychopathic RIMMER.

FELIS SAPIENS: The highly evolved race of CATs. HUD-ZEN's corrupted data banks mistakenly identified the CAT as being of the species *Felix sapiens*. *See* CAT PEOPLE.

FICTION SECTION: That area of the WAX-DROID THEME PARK in which Droids of fictional characters were kept. One of these was Father Christmas, who was posted to HERO WORLD to help in the WAX WAR.

FIELD MICRO-SURGERY: A skill in which, like most others it seemed, ACE RIMMER was particularly well-versed. It allowed him to save the CAT's leg from amputation after a particularly nasty accident in *STARBUG*.

FIFTH DIMENSION: The HOLLY HOP DRIVE took *RED DWARF* through this, and into a PARALLEL UNIVERSE. LISTER didn't quite understand the concept – he thought of the Fifth Dimension only as a pop group, who got to number six with 'Baby I Want Your Love Thing'.

FIJI: The place where LISTER dreamt of settling down with KRISTINE KOCHANSKI. His hopes were not diminished by the fact that it had flooded, and was three feet under water.

FILM FUN MAGAZINE: A periodical which the SKUT-TERS collected. It was delivered to *RED DWARF* by mail order.

FILMS: *See* VIDS.

5517/W13 ALPHA SIM MODEM: An interface circuit with a built-in 599XRDP. HOLLY modestly claimed it was just intuition that led her to choose this perfect gift for KRYTEN's last day present.

FIRE-AXE, MEDIUM SIZED: The implement that RIMMER deposited in KRYTEN's spine when he acquired telekinetic abilities.

FIRE EXTINGUISHER: Kept on stand-by for CURRY NIGHT.

FISH: The CAT is obsessed by these creatures, and was delighted when RIMMER showed him how to get as many as he wanted from the DISPENSERS. RIMMER seems to be partially obsessed too, as his tenth attempt at passing the Engineering EXAM consisted of the words 'I am a fish', written five hundred times. See also HADDOCK, HERRING, KIPPERS, MIMEAN BLADDERFISH and GOLDFISH, ROBOT.

FISHER, MICHELLE: The girl to whom LISTER lost his virginity on BOOTLE MUNICIPAL GOLF COURSE at the age of twelve.

FISHING: An activity enjoyed by all of the crew – although the others would prefer it if RIMMER wasn't quite so insistent on joining their expeditions. LISTER also used to indulge in CONDOM FISHING when he was younger. Of course, that sometimes just isn't possible in deep space – which is where JUNIOR ANGLER and that Magnetic Fishing GAME come in.

FLAMINGO-UP: Like a cock-up, only much much bigger.

FLIGHT RECORDER: Each *STARBUG* is fitted with one of these. When *STARBUG 1* crashed on BACKWARDS EARTH, LISTER was able to use a homing device to locate its recorder.

FLIGHT SCHOOL: An academy run by the SPACE CORPS for aspiring TEST PILOTS. Of course, RIMMER had aspirations of attending – and of course, he never did!

FLINTSTONE, WILMA: A cartoon character much desired by LISTER and the CAT. Unfortunately, she'll never leave Fred and they know it.

FOOD ESCAPE: The fate which CAT suffered after being introduced to the DISPENSER and obtaining at least six FISH.

FOOTBALL – IT'S A FUNNY OLD GAME: A book by Kevin Keegan which, having read every book ever written, HOLLY considered to be the worst one. We can imagine!

FOSTER, MISS: LISTER's geography teacher, who didn't believe that men were better than machines – one machine in particular.

FOUR APOCALYPSE BOYS: Dream-state manifestations of the ARMAGEDDON VIRUS, who wanted to wipe KRYTEN out of EXISTENCE.

FOUR-SIDED TRIANGLE: One of the instruments that HOLLY theorised would be used for playing DECIMALISED MUSIC.

14B: A small instrument used in the maintenance of *RED DWARF*, with uncanny similarities to the 14F.

14F: A small instrument used in the maintenance of *RED DWARF*, with uncanny similarities to the 14B.

1421: The year in which, on 16 August, the *STARBUG* crew arrived to drink in the heady medieval atmosphere of deep space, thanks to their newfound TIME DRIVE.

4X2C: Codeword with which SERIES 4000 MECHANOIDS are able to access the truth about their creator and JOHN WARBURTON.

FOX FUR: The 'ferocious' creature with which CAT found himself engaged in battle in the reception area of the GANYMEDE HOLIDAY INN.

FRANK: (1) Along with DUKE, one of the cowboys who, at JIMMY's behest, went for their pieces in the LAST CHANCE SALOON, only to be outgunned by the RIVIERA KID and outfought by DANGEROUS DAN McGREW. *See also* FRANK TODHUNTER, FRANK RIMMER (1) and FRANK RIMMER (2).

FRANK: (2) Local who discovered the box containing LISTER left in the AIGBURTH ARMS.

FRANK: (3) *STARBUG*'s washing machine. KRYTEN believes it works better if things are put on a more personal level.

FRANKENSTEIN: In legend, the HOLY MOTHER of the CAT PEOPLE, whose miraculous VIRGIN BIRTH spawned their race. In reality, LISTER's pet cat, who was impregnated by a BIG BLACK TOM on TITAN.

FREAKY FUNGUS: The common name for TITAN MUSHROOMS.

FRENCH: A subject (presumably one of many) in which LISTER came bottom at school. When his grandmother found out, she nutted the Headmaster.

FRIDAY THE THIRTEENTH 1649: *See* VIDS.

FRIDGE: RIMMER's weapon of choice when LISTER's nostril hair plucking became too much to bear.

FROGS: Generally, these amphibious creatures go ribbit, ribbit – or noises to that effect. In THE SWAMP OF DESPAIR, however, they tend to comment on how useless RIMMER is. On WAX-WORLD the soapy kind were a vital component of the torture which the WAX-DROID of Caligula had in mind for LISTER and CAT. The treatment also involved the removal of their trousers, although beyond that, we can only speculate.

FRONTAL LOBES: A SIMULANT's idea of a xylophone.

FUCHAL: The PROMISED LAND, to which the CAT PEOPLE believed CLOISTER THE STUPID would lead them. In fact, Fuchal is a corruption of FIJI, where LISTER wanted to take his pet cat FRANKENSTEIN.

FUCHAL DAY: A festival of the CAT PEOPLE, on which anybody who didn't eat hot dogs was stoned to death with stale doughnuts.

FURSDAY: *See* HAVE YOU GOT A GOOD MEMORY?

FUTURE ECHOES: Images of the future, which could be seen on *RED DWARF* as the ship broke the LIGHT BARRIER. The faster the ship travelled the further into the future the reflections originated.

G

GAMES: Amongst those played by LISTER and CAT to while away the years are Scrabble, Table Golf, JUNIOR ANGLER, unicycle polo, DUREX VOLLEYBALL, soapsud slalom, tiddleywinks showjumping and a computer adventure game featuring GANDALF THE MASTER WIZARD. Poker is also an option (although perhaps not the strip version, as they once claimed to HARRISON), whilst further entertainment can be found in the POINTY STICK GAME and the weekly crap game. HOLLY used to enjoy CHESS, competing both against QUEEG and postally with GORDON, whilst RIMMER played war games – RISK, especially – cheated at draughts against the SKUTTERS, considered himself a master of hide and seek and indulged in the occasional round of GOLF. LISTER and CAT played GOLF too, notably during their BETTER THAN LIFE fantasy; BETTER THAN LIFE being, of course, the ultimate in TIV games. Less sophisticated TIVs such as GUMSHOE and STREETS OF LAREDO were made available to LISTER via an ARTIFICIAL REALITY MACHINE. The whole crew believed they'd been playing in *RED DWARF* – THE TOTAL IMMERSION VIDEO GAME, but this was actually a HALLUCINATION. LISTER is an avid spectator of ZERO-GRAVITY FOOTBALL and a self-proclaimed expert at POOL, and we're led to believe that the crew will one day play canasta and mixed doubles with ADOLF HITLER and friends. One game to avoid is CAT AND MOUSE, especially with a ship full of genocidal rogue SIMULANTS, and particularly if you're the mouse. *See also* PARTNERSHIP WHIST.

Decision time for Lister! Confidence . . . or Paranoia?

Best of friends, really.

Lister and Cat search for hot babes in Pride and Prejudice Land.

The Duke of Dork. Cat loses his cool, to become the dreaded Duane Dibbley.

Ace Rimmer, the first of many. What a guy!

Wedding bells! The happiest day of Lister's life . . . but for one not-so-small detail.

Clearly, this isn't from an actual episode. But it's a nice photo.

Call him Legion. Nigel Williams guest-stars as the gestalt entity.

'Dinner is served!'

It's those 'Parallel Universe' shots again – well just you try finding some new Season Two stuff. Matthew Devitt and Suzanne Bertish guest-star.

The saga continues . . .

GAMES NIGHT: With KOCHANSKI (2) now a fully fledged crew member, the others realised that they might have to get a little more sophisticated in their choice of evening GAMES, with the likes of Match the Body Part to the Crew Member and Armpit Name That Tune not perhaps entirely appropriate in mixed company. Her suggestion that they play the opera-based game, Magic Flute, didn't go down as well as she hoped, but Guess Whose Botty is Sticking Through the Hole in the Curtain was quickly added to the slate.

GANDALF THE MASTER WIZARD: *See* GAMES.

GANYMEDE HOLIDAY INN: The hotel in which the CAT became locked in mortal combat with a FOX FUR, and where LISTER found KOCHANSKI, already married to his future self. Judging by the reception area, this Holiday Inn was a dead ringer for its twentieth-century Manchester counterpart.

GARBAGE POD: The type of vessel in which *RED DWARF* ejected its waste into space. When one of them was picked up by the ship on its way back to EARTH, RIMMER was convinced that it was an ALIEN craft.

GARDEN: KRYTEN's dream was to have one of these, which he had planted himself. He left *RED DWARF* on a SPACE BIKE to achieve his ambition, but crashed straight into an asteroid.

GAZPACHO SOUP: An expensive dish, intended to be served cold. This caused RIMMER a great deal of humiliation as, having been offered the privilege of dining at the CAPTAIN'S TABLE, he insisted on sending this course back to be warmed up. He has never quite lived the incident down, and blames it in part for his subsequent lack of success.

GAZPACHO SOUP DAY: 25 NOVEMBER – the day on which the GAZPACHO SOUP incident took place, forever commemorated in RIMMER's diary as the date of his greatest humiliation.

GAZZA: SMEG AND THE HEADS' bass player, who later went into insurance.

GELDOF: All right, here we go – the Lyons/Howarth theory of *Red Dwarf* continuity, tucked away in the index where nobody (least of all our editor) will find it. Okay, so we know that LISTER and RIMMER came from the twenty-second century – yet RIMMER referred to CAPTAIN HOLLISTER as MR FAT BASTARD 2044, and when he and LISTER visit their own past in 'Stasis Leak', the date is given as being 2 MARCH 2077. This date, LISTER says, falls only three weeks before the accident in which the crew of *RED DWARF* are killed – yet in 'Me²', he says that 25 NOVEMBER was only six weeks before said event. The solution? Obvious, really. The development and common usage of inter-planetary travel has forced humans to re-evaluate their calendar, or possibly even to introduce several different versions of it (since years are different lengths on each planet, right?). By simply removing January and February (the last two months to appear, after all), we can solve half of those supposed discrepancies in one swoop. And the proof? The month of Geldof, which the HOLOGRAMATIC NEWSREADER does in fact refer to. So there we are. All sorted!? . . . Oh well, please yourselves.

GELFS: Acronym for Genetically Engineered Life Forms. Created by mankind with a variety of, mainly suspect, purposes in mind, GELFS come in all shapes and sizes with just as many abilities. The DWARFERS have encountered several variants, some more hostile than others. For details see CAMILLE, EMOHAWK, KINITAWOWI, HECTOR, MRS LISTER, POLYMORPH, PSIRENS.

GELF BATTLECRUISER: KINITAWOWI ship sent by the missus to find LISTER.

GELF MOON: Home of the KINITAWOWI.

GELF ZONE: A region of space populated by (wait for it) GELFS.

GEMINI 12: Derelict test ship aboard which the TIME DRIVE was discovered.

GENETIC CLONING: The process by which all human life on RIMMERWORLD was created. *See also* DNA.

GENNY: Beautiful female persona of the POLYMORPH, used to purloin the CAT's VANITY.

GERMAN LANGUAGE COURSE: A disk belonging to KRYTEN, which features HITLER's Nuremberg speech.

GERONIMO: RIMMER's sole contribution to the conversation which took place while he was having sex with NIRVANAH CRANE.

GIANT FLAMING METEORITE: The technical term for a giant meteorite covered in flames.

GILBERT: (1) LISTER's manservant in the alternate past he created for himself with the TIMESLIDES.

GILBERT: (2) An ANDROID once known to KRYTEN which, becoming slightly deranged, preferred to be known as Ramases Niblick the Third Ker-Plunk Ker-Plunk Whoops Where's My Thribble.

GILL, ANNE: A Mapping Officer on board the *NOVA 5*. The *RED DWARF* crew discovered her body when they answered a distress call from the ship's MECHANOID, KRYTEN. *See also* AIR, JANE and JOHNS, TRACEY.

GIMBOID: A mild insult, presumably in common use at the time that LISTER and RIMMER left EARTH. *See also* GIMP and GOIT.

GIMP: Another mild insult, similar in meaning to GIMBOID and GOIT.

GIVE QUICHE A CHANCE: The motif emblazoned on RIMMER's T-shirt when he attempted to devise a peaceful solution to the POLYMORPH problem.

GLOW-IN-THE-DARK TAMPONS: An example of the kind of thing RIMMER discovered while playing the LOCKER-ROOM GAME.

GOALPOST-HEAD: *See* RIMMER, ARNOLD.

GOD: RIMMER found the idea of God preposterous – but LISTER ended up as the God of the CAT PEOPLE. *See* CLOISTER THE STUPID and RELIGION.

GOIT: Another insult!

GOLDFISH, ROBOT: LISTER owned two of these pisciform automata, which the CAT found a constant temptation. He named them LENNON and McCARTNEY.

GOLF: A GAME enjoyed by LISTER and CAT during their BETTER THAN LIFE fantasy. Their scores would have been rather difficult to assess, due to CAT's rather unique style of play, which involved throwing the club rather than hitting the ball. RIMMER used to play golf himself, and was therefore quite annoyed when LISTER confessed that, in the process of losing his virginity, he had left a large buttock crevice in the tenth hole of the BOOTLE MUNICIPAL GOLF COURSE. Occasionally suitable planetoids, such as TRAKA 16, allow for a proper round of golf, but most of the time table golf has to suffice.

GONE WITH THE WIND: The XPRESS LIFTS 'in-lift movie' on the day that LISTER, RIMMER and CAT journeyed down to the STASIS LEAK on Level 16.

GOOD KNIGHT: Chivalrous defender of the QUEEN OF CAMELOT's, erm, honour and challenger of LISTER OF SMEG at CAMELOT. He was believed to have escaped from the AR SIMULATION SUITE and fought RIMMER. But it was actually LISTER in some armour and a put-on voice. Good trick.

GOOD PSYCHO GUIDE: When LISTER finally gets around to writing this handy reference work, LEGION's institute will rate four and a half chainsaws.

GOOD SCHOOLS GUIDE: A publication much perused by MRS RIMMER; not that it did ARNOLD RIMMER much good.

'GOODBYE TO LOVE': A song sung by HOLLY prior to his fake ERASURE. But he's no Karen Carpenter and if he had been wiped, at least the others would have been spared from a further performance.

GORBALS: The trendiest part of Glasgow in which KOCHANSKI was brought up.

GORDON: The SCOTT FITZGERALD's eleventh-generation AI computer, with an IQ of 8,000. Gordon is involved in a postal CHESS GAME with HOLLY, and is winning by virtue of the fact that so far only one move has been made.

GRAV-POOL: Twenty-second-century game played in pubs if not anywhere else.

GREER, JEREMY: The author of *THE MALE EUNUCH*.

GRENADE: The item with which the CAT expressed a wish to play 'fetch' when he met THE DOG in a PARALLEL UNIVERSE.

GREY, MILITARY: Indistinguishable from OCEAN GREY, this was the colour to which RIMMER attempted to change *RED DWARF*'s internal corridor walls. No sooner had he begun the job than his double (*see* RIMMER, MRS (2)) changed them back.

GREY, OCEAN: The colour of *RED DWARF*'s internal corridor walls.

GRIT: HOLLY mistook five specks on the scanner scope for five BLACK HOLES. Understandable, considering the similarity in colour.

GROINAL SOCKET: One of KRYTEN's more useful features, into which a multitude of attachments can be fitted, ranging from a vacuum cleaner to an egg whisk. Unfortunately, very few people will eat his omelettes! KRYTEN apparently experienced the nearest emotion he has had to sexual excitement when he accidentally welded the socket to a front-loading washing machine.

GROOVY CHANNEL 27: The funky TV channel which had a HOLOGRAMATIC NEWSREADER, which screened the minority soap opera *ANDROIDS* and whose weather girl performed obscene actions with her pointy stick – in LISTER's imagination, anyway. *See* POINTY STICK GAME.

GUIDANCE BEAM: The malfunctioning device which drew *STARBUG* to LEGION's military research base.

GUILT: The emotion the POLYMORPH stole from KRYTEN.

GUILT CHIP: With this removed KRYTEN is without behaviour protocols. Just call him Bad Ass!

GUITARS: LISTER has possessed several guitars, which is just as well considering his crewmates' ongoing efforts to destroy as many as possible. Believing himself to be the ghost of Hendrix when it comes to performing, he is nevertheless banned from doing so unless he puts on a space suit and goes outside. He has become very protective about his remaining instruments, particularly the genuine Les Paul copy with five strings which was given to him by his stepfather. His attempts to preserve an earlier model led to RIMMER filing a charge against him for MUTINY. As of now, it seems there are no guitars left on *STARBUG*; the final one was broken in a particularly nasty crash, as the CAT would no doubt swear blind.

GUMSHOE: Chandleresque AR GAME which enabled participants to experience a realistic simulation of America's underworld of the 1940s. Naturally, LISTER used it to experience simulated SEX.

GWENLYN, KYLIE: The producer and director of the TV soap opera *ANDROIDS*. Her surname has also been used on occasion as a term of abuse.

H

HAÇIENDA: A club on MIRANDA, where RIMMER instigated a fight with McWILLIAMS and four of his friends, then promptly left.

HADDOCK: A species of FISH very similar to the one that was discovered to have committed suicide as a result of coming into contact with its fellow marine creature, the DESPAIR SQUID.

HAGGIS, IRRADIATED: There are 4691 examples of this foodstuff aboard *RED DWARF*. Now wasn't that worth knowing?

HAIRCUT LENGTH: It is a source of frustration for RIMMER that CAPTAIN HOLLISTER never put forward his suggestion of reducing the required SPACE CORPS haircut length by a quarter of an inch. He was acting with the best of motives too: every major battle in EARTH's history, RIMMER contends, was won by the side with the shortest hair. No wonder he didn't appreciate HOLLY's little hair related jape which, in RIMMER's own words, left him looking like 'a complete and total tit'.

HAIR DRYER: The device with which the CAT inadvertently deactivated every instrument in the scanning room, while the others were trying to track a UFO. It also came in useful for frying eggs when *RED DWARF* lost all power – except that it was powered by LISTER using an EXERCISE bike, and he was knackered long before the first egg turned white.

HALLUCINATIONS: LISTER became prone to these when he caught a mutated PNEUMONIA virus. Worse still, his hallucinations became solid. *See* CONFIDENCE, PARANOIA, HERRING and MAYOR OF WARSAW. RIMMER, meanwhile, is no stranger to hallucinations either, thanks to the voyage to TRIP-OUT CITY which an accidental dosage of TITAN MUSHROOMS induced him to take. The whole crew suffered from potentially fatal hallucinations when the four of them encountered the DESPAIR SQUID.

HAMMOND ORGAN MUSIC: A type of music of which RIMMER is a big fan, enjoying especially the works of REGGIE WILSON in this field. When still a soft-light HOLOGRAM, he encouraged the SKUTTERS to practise this skill instead. See also AMATEUR HAMMOND ORGAN

RECITAL NIGHT and HAMMOND ORGAN OWNERS SOCIETY.

HAMMOND ORGAN OWNERS SOCIETY: The organisation in which RIMMER served as treasurer, a post of which he is extremely proud.

HAMSTER: The second animal into which LISTER was turned by the DNA MODIFIER. *See also* CHICKEN.

HANDMAIDENS: Although manacled to a pillar on the PSY-MOON, RIMMER thought his luck was in when two of these scantily-dressed ladies began OILING his nearly naked body.

HANDSHAKE: A term used to denote a radio greeting between space ships.

HANEKA: The principal time measurement used by the KINITAWOWI. Its exact equality to the standard EARTH minute caused CAT all manner of mathematical problems.

HANGERS: CAT was quite pleased when LISTER bequeathed him anything from his wardrobe – he needed some more hangers.

HANNAH: A DOG belonging to LISTER's stepfather, which features prominently in the only photograph he has of him.

HAPPY DEATHDAY: The song sung to RIMMER on the anniversary of his death. When the celebrations were over, a few verses of 'Show me the way to go home' were considered in order.

HARD-LIGHT DRIVE: The revolutionary type of HOLOGRAM drive which, created by LEGION, was bestowed upon RIMMER. Unlike his previous soft-light drive, this gave him a solid presence, thus necessitating the immediate use of a PUNCTURE REPAIR KIT.

HARD-LIGHT REMOTE BELT: The means by which RIMMER sustains his hard-light hologramatic presence away from *STARBUG*.

HARLEY DAVIDSON: The type of motor-cycle chosen by LISTER as his mode of transport in his BETTER THAN LIFE fantasy.

HARRISON: A potential replacement HOLOGRAM, chosen when it was believed that RIMMER was to join the crew of the HOLOSHIP. She declined the offer, deciding that remaining dead was preferable to spending any length of time with LISTER, KRYTEN and CAT.

HAVE YOU GOT A GOOD MEMORY?: A quiz in a magazine which LISTER was annoyed to discover had been filled in by someone. As it turned out, it was him –well, who else would spell Thursday with an F?

HAZARD APPROACH LIGHTS: On *STARBUG*, these can mean anything from 'the ship is under attack', to 'the baked potatoes are burning'.

HEAD SEX-CHANGE OPERATION: Performed by an erratic HOLLY upon himself so that he resembled HILLY, his counterpart in the female-dominated PARALLEL UNIVERSE.

HEAD-BANGER HARRIS: The likeliest owner of the FREAKY FUNGUS that LISTER gave RIMMER.

HEADLINES: RIMMER's wall contains a selection of these, all of which are about people called either Arnold or RIMMER. None of them are about him, but the intention is to make it look like they are.

HECTOR: A HUGE GREEN BLOB who turned out to be the husband of CAMILLE.

HEIDEGER: *See* LEGION.

HEIMLICH MANOEUVRE: Despite KOCHANSKI's protestations, KRYTEN was convinced that this was the correct method of stopping someone from crying. Though this idea was obviously the result of a corrupted memory, it worked.

HERO WORLD: An area of the WAX-DROID THEME PARK in which Droids of history's heroes were kept.

HERRING: The type of FISH which rained down in the bunk room during LISTER's bout of a mutated PNEUMONIA virus which made his HALLUCINATIONS solid. This particular image was inspired by an incident in twelfth-century Burgundy.

HEX VISION: A lethal symptom of the HOLO-VIRUS. Fortunately, the *RED DWARF* crew never meet anyone who can shoot straight.

HIGHS: The perfect version of *RED DWARF* and its crew, patterned by the TRIPLICATOR. Aboard the High *RED DWARF* a pure, aesthetic life was earnestly adhered to, the pursuit of culture and beauty providing the prime motivation for its exalted crew – unlike those bastards, the LOWS.

HILLY: *RED DWARF*'s on-board computer in the female dominated PARALLEL UNIVERSE. HOLLY fell madly in love with his counterpart, and later performed a HEAD SEX-CHANGE OPERATION on himself in order to look like her.

HISTO CHIP: A piece of KRYTEN's workings that informed him that President J. F. KENNEDY was shot from the Texas Book Depository. He was more than a little shocked to discover that he was at that moment standing in the Texas Book Depository.

HITLER, ADOLF: Leader of the runners-up in World War II and not such a bad chap after all, according to the future *STARBUG* crew who used to pop in for the odd GAME of canasta, or mixed doubles with the Goerings. Our own LISTER met him twice, once (along with CAT) as a WAX-DROID and once thanks to the TIMESLIDES. On BACK-WARDS EARTH, Hitler really wasn't so bad: his armies retreated to where they came from, bringing people to life in the process. *See also FASCIST DICTATOR MONTHLY*.

HOLDEN, FRED (THICKY): A particularly stupid classmate of RIMMER's, who was destined to become a multi-millionaire and marry LADY SABRINA MUL-

HOLLAND-JJONES, all due to his invention of the TENSION SHEET.

HOLDER: *See* LEGION.

HOL ROCK: The name which HOLLY applied to his own invention of DECIMALISED MUSIC.

HOLLISTER, CAPTAIN: The Captain of *RED DWARF*, who ordered that LISTER be confined to STASIS.

HOLLY: The *RED DWARF*'s tenth generation AI hologrammic computer, now lost along with the ship.

HOLLY HOP DRIVE: A device constructed by HOLLY, which looked rather suspiciously like a box with start and stop buttons. It was theoretically capable of instantly transporting *RED DWARF* anywhere in the universe, but on the one occasion it was used, it actually deposited the ship in a female dominated PARALLEL UNIVERSE.

HOLOGRAM: A computer-generated light image of a person, into which his or her brain patterns can be projected. This technology is used primarily for bringing people back from the dead. HOLLY can sustain one HOLOGRAM at a time, and currently this is ARNOLD RIMMER, although in the past GEORGE McINTYRE and KRISTINE KOCHANSKI have also had this distinction.

HOLOGRAM DISKS: Also known as PERSONALITY DISKS. The pieces of equipment on which are recorded the details necessary to generate HOLOGRAMS of particular people. *RED DWARF* holds both disks and back-up disks for each of its former crew members.

HOLOGRAM PROJECTION SUITE: The room from which HOLOGRAMS are created, monitored and controlled.

HOLOGRAMATIC NEWSREADER: One of these late broadcasters was employed by GROOVY CHANNEL 27.

HOLOGRAMMIC PROJECTION CAGE: An apparatus which must be used to sustain a HOLOGRAM away from *RED DWARF*, when conditions make it necessary.

HOLOGRAMMIC PROJECTION BOX: The apparatus from which HOLOGRAMS are created. Not surprisingly, these are located in the HOLOGRAM PROJECTION SUITE.

HOLOSHIP: A computer generated space craft crewed by HOLOGRAMS. Composed of tachyons, it is entirely without mass or volume and as such is capable of travelling through worm holes and star gates. *See ENLIGHTENMENT.*

HOLO-VIRUS: A disease so unpleasant that it can kill people that are already dead. The main symptom of the illness is complete insanity, but there are potentially lethal side effects. By stimulating various unused areas of the brain it endows its victim with psychic powers such as telepathy, telekinesis, and HEX VISION, but the energy used to sustain these abilities drains the life force. The disease can be transmitted by radio waves as RIMMER found to his cost when he contracted the virus from Doctor LANSTROM.

HOLOWHIP: A weapon which can apparently be used by humans in order to inflict pain on HOLOGRAMS. Presumably, *STARBUG*'s Munitions Cabinet doesn't contain one of these, but the threat of its use certainly had Commander BINKS worried. Alternatively the device can certainly be used by HOLOGRAMS on humans as LISTER painfully discovered aboard the LOW version of *RED DWARF.*

HOLY BOOK: The bible of the CAT PEOPLE, which told the story of CLOISTER THE STUPID and the parthenogenesis of the CAT race.

HOLY CUSTARD STAINS: Thanks to LISTER, these became items of religious significance to the CAT PEOPLE, and were worn by the CAT PRIESTS. *See also* SACRED GRAVY MARKS.

HOLY MOTHER: The title by which the CAT PEOPLE refer to LISTER's former pet, FRANKENSTEIN.

HOLY WARS: The millennia-long battle that broke out between the CAT PEOPLE over what colour the CARDBOARD HATS in FUCHAL should be.

HOME SWEET HOME: The motto which is mono-grammed on to RIMMER's pyjamas.

HOMING POD: The means by which HUDZEN arrived on *RED DWARF*.

HOODED LEGIONS, THE: Acolytes of the Dark One, RIMMER's SELF-LOATHING. Encountered on the PSY-MOON, they were the negative aspects of RIMMER's psyche personified. Counted among their number were Bitterness, Self-Doubt, Mistrust and Loneliness.

HOOVER, J. EDGAR: Mafia-controlled, transvestite President of the USA in an alternate time-stream created by LISTER's single-minded quest for a CURRY.

HORSES: One of the types of animal that LISTER wanted to breed when he got his farm on FIJI.

HOT DOG AND DOUGHNUT DINER: LISTER's desire to open one of these on FIJI became the CAT PEOPLE's idea of Heaven.

HOT WAX DRIP UNSIGHTLY HAIR REMOVER: One of CAT's beauty aids, which he adamantly refuses ever to unplug.

HOW TO PICK UP GIRLS BY HYPNOSIS: A book used extensively, but to little avail, by RIMMER. *See* LORRAINE.

HOWDY DOODLY DOO: A term of greeting used constantly by TALKIE TOASTER. Like most other things about this appliance, LISTER found this particularly irritating.

HUDZEN 10: The state-of-the-art MECHANOID sent to replace KRYTEN. Thousands of years alone in deep space had taken their toll on his sanity CHIP, however, with near fatal consequences for the *RED DWARF* crew.

HUMANS: Lovely with mint sauce in the opinion of the Rogue Simulant captain of the SS *GEMINI*. Perhaps if there had been some mint sauce to hand in mid-sixties Dallas

KRYTEN's cooking might have been a little more palatable. *See* CANNIBALISM.

HUMMING: An activity in which LISTER indulges – maliciously and persistently, according to RIMMER.

HYDROGEN RAM DRIVE: LISTER (2) offered to update *STARBUG*'s to a tachyon-powered engine core. In return CAT volunteered to unscrew all those old pickle jars they couldn't open.

HYPERWAY: A link through NON-SPACE to a parallel dimension when the membrane between the two realities has collapsed. Here the *STARBUG* crew encountered alternate versions of themselves, who appeared to be slightly more sophisticated.

I

ICE AGES: LISTER's preferred time unit for calculating the period since he last had SEX. 'Four' sounds so much better than the alternative, and in leap ice ages, it's only one.

ICEBOX: A handy storage space for LISTER's spare sneakers.

ICE CREAM VANS: Like the SS *CENTAURI*, most of these can travel at speeds that the *STARBUG* crew can only dream of.

ICE PLANET: The unnamed world where LISTER and RIMMER were marooned for several days when *STARBUG* crash-landed.

IDLEWILD AIRPORT: Airport that didn't become Kennedy International in an altered time-stream.

INCINEREX: Destructive substance with which LISTER hoped to kill the EPIDEME VIRUS.

INDLING SONG, THE: A song composed by LISTER, and much admired by the personification of his own CONFIDENCE – if by nobody else.

INFLATABLE INGRID: RIMMER's Polythene Pal who, unbeknownst to him, was LISTER's pal too. *See also* RACHEL.

INFLATABLE SHARK: Just one of the useful items found on the planetoid that was once *RED DWARF*.

IN-FLIGHT MAGAZINES: These are present in *STAR-BUG*, their only purpose being to provide an anaesthetic effect which keeps the body relaxed in the event of a crash. CAT found that one of them worked particularly well when KRYTEN had to re-set his broken leg.

INFULLIBLE: HOLLY claims to be the nearest thing to infullible – i.e. infallible.

INTELLIGENCE TEST: LISTER conned PETERSEN into believing he'd passed one of these.

INTERSTELLA ACTION GAMES: Makers of AR role-playing games such as GUMSHOE and STREETS OF LAREDO.

INQUISITOR, THE: A self-repairing SIMULANT which, having survived to the end of time, concluded that GOD did not exist and that the purpose of life was to lead it in a worthwhile manner. Building a time machine, it travelled throughout eternity administering its own particular brand of punishment to those who did not live up to their potential. Those it considered unworthy were erased from history and replaced. Needless to say, the Inquisitor's arrival aboard *RED DWARF* prompted a certain degree of worry among the crew.

IO AMATEUR WAR-GAMERS: RIMMER was once a member of this group, and felt that his commanding role in the WAX WAR would have earned him their respect.

IO HOUSE: RIMMER's old school, at which he was rather less than happy. He always resented his parents for not sending him to a private school and, as with most things, he believes this to be one of the factors which prevented him from achieving his ambitions. It is not clear whether or not this school is actually based on the Jupiter moon of Io itself.

IONIAN NERVE-GRIP: The non-existent, painless method by which KRYTEN promised to render RIMMER unconscious. RIMMER became suspicious when KRYTEN actually smashed him over the head with a vase.

IQ: HOLLY professes to have an intelligence quotient in the region of six thousand, this being equivalent to that of either 6,000 PE teachers or 12,000 car park attendants. In reality, an advanced case of COMPUTER SENILITY has reduced this figure greatly. Although KRYTEN did try to rectify the problem, the raising of HOLLY'S IQ to 12,000 also brought about an exponential reduction in her life-span, leaving her with only 3.41 minutes of run-time left.

IRANIAN JERD: According to the CAT, this animal can do fifty pelvic thrusts per second. He considers his own record to be somewhat higher.

IRON DUKE: The radio code-name which the unhinged RIMMER gave to himself during the WAX WAR.

J

JACKSON POLLOCK: Euphemism for being sick (as in 'I feel a Jackson Pollock coming on'). This was used by KRYTEN after hearing LISTER telling of the time he was sick off the top of the Eiffel Tower. The result was apparently sold as a genuine example of the pavement art of this painter.

JACQUENAUX, LIEUTENANT GENERAL BARON: The commander of RIMMER's treasured ARMIES DU NORD.

JAGUAR, E-TYPE: The mode of transport selected by RIMMER in his BETTER THAN LIFE fantasy – complete with FURRY DICE.

JANE AUSTEN WORLD: AR GAME. KOCHANSKI was a real fan of this; much more so than, say, Name That Smell or How Many Marbles Can You Fit Up Your Nostril? Women eh?

JAPANESE MEAL: NIRVANAH CRANE felt that RIMMER's sexual technique was akin to one of these – it came in incredibly small portions, but there were plenty of courses.

JAVANESE CAMPHOR-WOOD CHEST: Given to him by his father, this is RIMMER's most cherished possession – or at least it was, before it acquired a GUITAR-shaped hole.

JAZZ FM: A radio station favoured by KRYTEN, who can pick it up with his left NIPPLE NUT.

JIGSAW: LISTER possesses one of these, which shows *RED DWARF* itself. Having wiped his own memory of the day on which he finished it, its completion became a bizarre mystery to him.

JIM: Jim and BEXLEY were LISTER's twin sons both named after JIM BEXLEY SPEED. They were conceived in the female-orientated PARALLEL UNIVERSE, but born in our own, where the differing physical laws caused them to age eighteen years within three weeks of being born. They were returned to their home dimension, where they currently live with their 'father' DEB LISTER. In another such dimension – the one from which ACE RIMMER hailed – LISTER's counterpart, SPANNERS, had a Jim and BEXLEY of his own, by KRISTINE KOCHANSKI. Unscrupulous PSIRENS tried to lure our own LISTER to his death by claiming that his KOCHANSKI had likewise borne his children, this time by breaking into *RED DWARF*'s sperm-bank whilst LISTER was in STASIS. *See also* BEXLEY.

JIMMY: A regular of the LAST CHANCE SALOON, whose expertise with a whip was no match for BRETT RIVERBOAT's knife throwing.

JMC IDENT CODE: Using this KRYTEN was quickly able to identify CAROLINE CARMEN.

JOE: No other name given. A member of the *RED DWARF* crew, known to GEORGE McINTYRE.

JOHNS, TRACEY: A Mapping Officer on board the *NOVA 5*. The *RED DWARF* crew discovered her body when they answered a distress call from the ship's MECHANOID, KRYTEN. *See also* AIR, JANE and GILL, ANNE.

JOHNSONS BABY BUD: The most romantic thing RIMMER ever had down his ear.

JONATHAN: The middle name with which RIMMER claims to have been bestowed. In fact it's really Judas.

JOVIAN BOOGLE HOOPS: Yet another form of cutlery which KRYTEN is skilled in the use of.

JOZXYQK: A word used by CATS when they get their sexual organs trapped in something – if the CAT is to be believed when playing Scrabble.

JUGGLING: CAT thought that the one-armed, EPIDEME-VIRUS-infected LISTER could perhaps spend his remaining fifty-eight minutes left alive with half a lesson.

JUMP-LEADS: The devices which RIMMER expresses an interest in attaching to KRYTEN's NIPPLE NUTS, should he fail to 'shape up'.

JUNIOR ANGLER: All the thrills and spills of fresh-water fly-fishing in your own home, and as such, a favourite game with LISTER and the CAT. CAT has, however, had to lay down the law, telling LISTER that Junior Angler is the nearest he's going to come to making LOVE to him. LISTER was doubtless quite relieved.

JUNIOR COLOUR ENCYCLOPEDIA OF SPACE, THE: The source of all HOLLY's knowledge – or so QUEEG alleged.

JUNIOR D: When RIMMER was seven, his Headmaster considered keeping him down a year in this class, but decided against it. In a PARALLEL UNIVERSE, his decision was different, and the Head's foresight led to Arnold's development into Commander ACE RIMMER.

JUNK MAIL: Even in THREE MILLION YEARS' time, this still constitutes the greater proportion of all post. In the case of *RED DWARF* in particular, the problem was an even

greater one, due to LISTER's habit of sending off for everything he possibly could, simply to ensure that he got some
letters.

JUPITER MINING CORPORATION: The company to
which *RED DWARF* belonged. The corporation ran merchant
vessels on behalf of the SPACE CORPS, crewed by Corps
personnel.

JUPITER RISE: The photograph which all the tourists take.

JUSTICE COMPUTER: The mechanism which administers
JUSTICE WORLD.

JUSTICE FIELD: This covers the whole of the JUSTICE
ZONE on JUSTICE WORLD, and once within its influence,
it is impossible to commit a crime of any kind without the
effects of that crime rebounding against you. In this way,
prisoners are expected to get into the habit of not committing
crimes and to continue this habit upon release.

JUSTICE WORLD: The site of a high-tech, completely
automated penal colony. *See also* anything else in this index
that starts with 'Justice'.

JUSTICE ZONE: That area of JUSTICE WORLD in which
prisoners are kept, and which is covered by the JUSTICE
FIELD.

K

KAY, JEFF: Not in fact a former King of America, despite
what LISTER and RIMMER may think to the contrary.

KEELAN, CHARLES: A schoolmate of LISTER's, who
later achieved a certain amount of notoriety by eating his
wife.

KELLY: A character in the *ANDROIDS* soap opera, presumably married to BROOK. She shocked him with the
revelation that her son, Brooke Jnr, was not his. She was
played by ANDROID I 4762/E.

KENDALL, FELICITY: A twentieth-century personality, whose bottom was, not surprisingly, much admired by the *RED DWARF* crew. They once discovered a moon which bore a startling resemblance to said object, and spent a great deal of time flying around it.

KENNEDY, J. F.: The man behind the grassy knoll; the second gunman who assassinated US President J. F. Kennedy, i.e. himself. Mystery solved!

KETCHUP: LISTER wanted some to pep up his LOBSTER. This lack of condimentoral refinement resulted in KRYTEN literally blowing his top.

KEYRING: Jealous KRYTEN imagined that LISTER was going to go off with KOCHANSKI and leave him alone once more, and to add insult to injury they presented him with a keyring with a C on it.

KIDNEY: A form of punctuation, or perhaps just an accident, for a luckless GELF victim.

KING: Ruler of CAMELOT in an AR simulation. He was never identified as King Arthur, though he may as well have been.

KING OF THE POTATO PEOPLE: Someone who was apparently unwilling to let the badly deranged RIMMER release the others from QUARANTINE.

KINITAWOWI: One of the friendlier GELF tribes: not skinning you alive the moment they set eyes on you is one of their warmest greetings.

KIPPERS: ACE RIMMER was perhaps partial to this particular type of FISH, hence his oft-used phrase, 'Smoke me a kipper – I'll be back for breakfast!'

KITTY SCHOOL: A place of learning where CAT was taught the rudiments of the feline method of reading by smells and where, in religious instruction, he heard the story of CLOISTER THE STUPID.

KNICKERS: See WORLD'S STUPIDEST STUNTMEN and LAUNDRY ROOM.

KOCHANSKI, KRISTINE: (1) A Navigation Officer on board *RED DWARF*, and the LOVE of LISTER's life, the girl of his dreams, the object of his desires, etc. So LISTER isn't about to let a couple of minor considerations – such as their relationship being something of a non-starter, and her being dead – stand in the way of true happiness. And in fact one day he will discover a way back through time and they'll be married. Ah . . . isn't it romantic? However, in the meantime he'd quite like to have seen Krissy's HOLOGRAM replace RIMMER's, but as RIMMER always considered her to be rather a snooty cow and had her disk well and truly hidden there wasn't too much chance of that happening. *See also* PSIRENS.

KOCHANSKI, KRISTINE: (2) Parallel-universe counterpart of LISTER's true love, although she looks quite different and doesn't possess a Scottish accent. She is the latest member of *STARBUG*'s crew.

KRISPIES: A type of food favoured by CAT (aren't they all?!), and fed to him by LISTER.

KRYTEN 2X4B 523P: Formerly the service ANDROID on the *NOVA 5*, and brought on board *RED DWARF* by LISTER.

L

LABORATORY MICE: The only organisms on *RED DWARF* that had to obey orders from DAVE LISTER. Like every other form of life on the ship, these perished in the RADIATION leak, but the CAT still searches the CARGO DECKS in hope.

LAGER: A drink of which LISTER is a great admirer, particularly as milkshake flavouring or served hot with croutons. That proved to be his salvation when he faced the MUTTON VINDALOO BEAST, as, after all, lager is the only thing that can kill a CURRY. *STARBUG*'s entire supply was wiped out along with the CURRY. But not to worry, at least there was plenty of CINZANO BIANCO and advocaat left.

LANDING DECK B: The place on *STARBUG* from which RIMMER in his newly assumed guise of Ace attempted to take off in his recently acquired dimension-spanning ship, but succeeded only in engaging the EJECTOR SEAT.

LANSTROM, HILDEGARD: A hologramatic Doctor at a VIRAL RESEARCH DEPARTMENT. The crew believed that she might be a valuable asset aboard *RED DWARF* so they considered having both her and RIMMER on a time share basis. Unfortunately the Doctor had fallen prey to her own genius and had been infected by the HOLO-VIRUS. The malady eventually killed her but not before she had made a good attempt upon the lives of our heroes.

LASER BONE SAW: Piece of medical equipment that proved useful for removing LISTER's RIGHT ARM.

LASER CANNONS: Useful devices fitted by considerate SIMULANTS to *STARBUG*, so as to provide themselves with a little sport. Had they carried out this alteration earlier, then one of CAT's amazing plans might actually have become feasible.

LAST CHANCE SALOON: Established in 1874, this was the best watering hole in EXISTENCE.

LAST, JAMES: Although we never saw him, LISTER claims that he was one of ADOLF HITLER's army of evil WAX-DROIDS. RIMMER is obviously an admirer of this musician, as LISTER recognised him from his companion's record collection.

LAUNDRY: CAT disgusted his shipmates with the revelation that he washes his clothes with his tongue! LISTER, meanwhile, carries out this chore with far less frequency. He did manage to get together a laundry list THREE MILLION YEARS ago, but this ended up being used to line the basket of his pet cat, FRANKENSTEIN. Unfortunately, the CAT PEOPLE later misinterpreted its significance, believing it to be a star chart that would lead them to the PROMISED LAND of FUCHAL. One of the two ARKS in which they eventually left *RED DWARF* tried to follow its directions, and collided with an asteroid.

LAUNDRY ROOM: One of KRYTEN's favourite places and the venue for the fourth most popular pastime on *STAR-BUG*: watching KOCHANSKI's KNICKERS spin-dry.

LAXO: Good for indigestion and stomach upsets, but presumably no match for RIMMER's DUMPLINGS.

LEAGUE AGAINST SALIVATING MONSTERS, THE: One of the names put forward by RIMMER in his ANGER-free campaign against the POLYMORPH. *See also* CLITORIS.

LEARNING DRUGS: Illegal drugs that increase the capacity of the memory. RIMMER used them to improve his chances of passing his many EXAMS, although he never did so. LISTER did likewise, stealing the drugs from RIMMER's locker when he wished to enter the Chef's EXAM.

LECLERK, HENRY: A member of the REVOLUTION-ARY WORKING FRONT, who was arrested in France whilst attempting to poison the source of all the world's Perrier water. Had he been successful, it was estimated that the entire middle class would have been wiped out within three weeks.

LEECHES: On the PSY-MOON they possessed the features of MRS RIMMER.

LEGION: A gestalt entity, composed in its first incarnation of five of the most brilliant minds of the twenty-third century, amongst them HEIDEGER, DAVRO, HOLDER and QUAYLE. His later combination of LISTER, RIMMER, KRYTEN and CAT was something of a comedown.

LEGO: A toy which the six-year-old LISTER enjoyed playing with. The greatest boost to his collection came when his stepfather died, and sympathetic relatives bought him gifts.

At the time, he hoped a few more people would die so that he could complete the set.

LEIA, PRINCESS: Character from some science-fiction film or other that apparently did reasonably well at the box office. KRYTEN thought KOCHANSKI resembled her when wrapped in a blanket with ear-muffs on.

LEISURE WORLD INTERNATIONAL: A company which didn't exist, but which in the group HALLUCINATION induced by the DESPAIR SQUID became the home of twenty *RED DWARF* – TOTAL IMMERSION VIDEO GAMES.

LEMMING: A type of animal once kept as a pet by RIMMER, until it sank its teeth into him and he had to smash its head in, ruining his helicopter wallpaper.

LEMMING SUNDAY: The name applied by the press to the day RIMMER joined the SAMARITANS and five people committed suicide.

LENNON: One of LISTER's two ROBOT GOLDFISH. *See also* McCARTNEY.

LEOPARD: A brand of LAGER enjoyed by LISTER. Which is just as well as this is the only sort that seems to turn up on salvaged JMC ships. It came in especially useful against the MUTTON VINDALOO BEAST.

LEVIATHAN: Twenty-third-century JMC supply ship. Its crew had been wiped out by the EPIDEME VIRUS. The virus, however, had survived in a frozen state, waiting THREE MILLION YEARS for its next victim. LISTER, as it turned out.

LEVI JEANS: Even in the far distant future these items still retain, along with Swiss watches, strong bargaining power on the black market.

LICKETTY-SPLIT: RIMMER's preferred state of affairs – everything in order.

LICORICE ALLSORTS: Tragically, the only ones left on *STARBUG* are the black curly ones which no-one likes.

LIE MODE: KRYTEN's preferred mode for use whilst addressing RIMMER.

LIFESTYLES OF THE DISGUSTINGLY RICH AND FAMOUS: A TV show presented by BLAIZE FALCON-BURGER, which once profiled LISTER when he altered the TIMELINES to make himself both rich and famous.

LIGHT BARRIER: The theoretical threshold which has to be crossed before attaining LIGHT SPEED. When *RED DWARF* did so, the action caused a series of FUTURE ECHOES to appear to its crew.

LIGHT BEE: A small, highly advanced device which 'buzzes around' inside RIMMER's hologramatic body, maintaining his form. When it isn't doing that, it can still hold his conscious personality – and LISTER found to his delight that it was small enough to swallow.

LIGHT SHIP: A vessel developed in the PARALLEL UNIVERSE of ACE RIMMER – if not in our own – which was capable of travelling at LIGHT SPEED.

LIGHT SPEED: Well, what does it sound like it means?!

LIGHT SWITCH: RIMMER's idea of a work of art.

LIMPET MINES: The explosives which HOLLY used to turn the DESPAIR SQUID into fried calamari.

LINGERIE DATABASE: Erased by KRYTEN since leaving his female mistresses on the *NOVA 5*. He didn't see much point in it unless LISTER ever decided to go to a fancy-dress party as Hermann Goering.

LIQUID DILINIUM: A freezing agent used against the EMOHAWK.

LISTER, DAVID: (1) The last human being left alive. God help Mankind!

LISTER, DAVID: (2) A version of LISTER that might have been born had a different sperm prevailed; he was brought into temporary existence when THE INQUISITOR attempted to remove all traces of the original from history. Unfortunately, for him, he was killed, but fortunately for the other LISTER, his dead hand proved useful for opening doors with.

LISTER, DAVE: (3) A well-dressed, sophisticated hologram LISTER from a universe in which he died and KRISTINE KOCHANSKI (2) survived after being put into STASIS. Being composed of soft light for so long made him sensitive and caring. He enjoys shopping for shoes and having conversations about relationships. Every woman's dream really.

LISTER, DEB: DAVE LISTER's counterpart in the female dominated PARALLEL UNIVERSE, identical to him in all but physical characteristics. She is the 'father' of his twin sons, JIM and BEXLEY, having slept with him after a drunken binge.

LISTER, MRS: Daughter of the KINITAWOWI chief, whose unpronounceable real name sounds like a footballer clearing his nose. Fortunately for the reluctant groom, the marriage was never consummated.

LISTER OF SMEG: Knightly persona adopted by Lister in his libidinous pursuit of the QUEEN OF CAMELOT.

LITHIUM CARBONATE: A gas used as a MOOD STABILISER which reversed the near fatal effects of the DESPAIR SQUID's ink.

LITTLE JIMMY OSMOND: The only thing in the known universe for which HOLLY suspects that there may not be a logical explanation.

LITTLE TOMMY: The boy whom ACE RIMMER nursed back to health after an unspecified illness.

LIVVIES: A derogatory slang term employed by HOLOGRAMS, to describe those people left alive.

LOBSTER: KRYTEN discovered four of these in the SS *CENTAURI*'s STASIS block. He thought that one of them along with a bottle of green wine would be a nice way to celebrate the anniversary of his rescue of the *NOVA 5*. KOCHANSKI had other plans for the evening, much to the MECHANOID's annoyance. *See* KETCHUP.

LOCKER-ROOM GAME: Pastime in which LISTER and RIMMER would take it in turns to open up the lockers of dead *RED DWARF* crew members. LISTER seemed to have more luck at it. *See* 'BAKED BEAN BOMBSHELLS VOL 12'.

LOLA: Barmaid at the LAST CHANCE SALOON.

LOLITA: Nabokov's erotic novel, and one of the books LISTER had to burn to keep warm when he and RIMMER were marooned on an ICE PLANET, though page 61 was spared the flames.

LONDON JETS: A ZERO-GRAVITY FOOTBALL team supported by LISTER, who has the posters, the book and several shirts. Their ROOF ATTACK player, JIM BEXLEY SPEED, is LISTER's particular hero, after whom he named his twin sons, JIM and BEXLEY. It is also known that an un-named member of their team is the man he associates most with CONFIDENCE, as it is in this form that LISTER's own CONFIDENCE manifested itself.

LORETTA: Despite being a psychotic, schizophrenic, serial killing *femme fatale*, she was the sexiest computer sprite LISTER had ever seen. *See* GUMSHOE.

LORRAINE: A girl with an artificial nose, who initially fell for RIMMER's 'hypnotic' chat-up lines. She later came to her senses and, during the couple's first date, escaped through the toilet window. In order to avoid a second date, she claimed she had to move to PLUTO.

LOUIS XVI: According to history, a cruel despot who lived in obscene opulence whilst his subjects starved to DEATH. According to the future *STARBUG* crew, a charming, urbane and witty host with a cute wife, who held a banquet in their honour.

LOVE: Considered 'a short-term hormonal distraction which interferes with the pure pursuit of personal enhancement', the concept was abandoned, along with that of family, in the twenty-fifth century. RIMMER agreed with the philosophy of the LOVE CELIBACY SOCIETY i.e. 'Love is a sickness that holds back your career and makes you spend all your money'.

LOVE CELIBACY SOCIETY: An organisation joined by RIMMER, due to his negative attitude towards the concept of LOVE. LISTER suspected, with much justification, that his true reason for joining was that nobody fancied him.

LOWS: The imperfect version of *RED DWARF* and its crew formed by the TRIPLICATOR. Aboard this vile, putrescent *RED DWARF* could be found all the abhorrent things in life: video nasties, weapons magazines, even toastie toppers. Its sadistic crew consisted of a one eyed LISTER, a clapped out KRYTEN, a sabre toothed CAT and a transvestite RIMMER; between them they were responsible for the deaths of their counterparts, the HIGHS.

LS: An abbreviation for LIGHT SPEED, as favoured by HOLLY.

LUGGAGE, ELECTRONIC: Another miracle of twenty-third century technology, made possible by the development of Artificial Intelligence circuits.

LUIGI'S FISH 'N' CHIP EMPORIUM: Suppliers of LISTER's sausage and onion gravy sandwiches.

LUNAR CITY SEVEN: Presumably a real place, this conurbation is celebrated in a popular song which is particularly enjoyed by LISTER.

LYING: An action of which KRYTEN's programming rendered him incapable. With some help from the movie *CASABLANCA*, LISTER was able to overcome this 'difficulty'.

M

McCARTNEY: One of LISTER's two ROBOT GOLDFISH. *See also* LENNON.

McCAULEY, CAROL: A recipient of 'secret' love letters from RIMMER.

McCLURE, DOUG: Dinosaur battling star of most of the movies left on *STARBUG*. It is notable that, when LEGION provided LISTER with his perfect environment, no such FILMS were present. *See also* VIDS.

McGEE, BEAR-STRANGLER: The meanest, toughest patron of the LAST CHANCE SALOON, and thus the one with whom RIMMER immediately picked a fight.

McGREW, DANGEROUS DAN: A barefist fighter with a great deal of stamina from STREETS OF LAREDO, this role-playing character was portrayed by RIMMER.

McGRUDER, YVONNE: The ship's female boxing champion, and the subject both of RIMMER's dreams and of his BETTER THAN LIFE fantasy. McGruder is the only woman he ever managed to sleep with, and even then, it was due in great part to the concussion she had suffered through being hit over the head with a winch. Apparently, she mistook him for somebody called NORMAN.

McINTYRE, GEORGE: A flight co-ordinator on board *RED DWARF*. He died and was brought back to life as a HOLOGRAM.

McQUEEN: A flight co-ordinator whose mathematical genius proved useful to RIMMER following a mind patching operation – at least it did until RIMMER's unsuitable mind rejected it. *See also* BUCHAN.

McWILLIAMS: A necrophiliac, according to RIMMER, who voiced this opinion to McWilliams' face when he was with his four biggest friends in the HAÇIENDA club on MIRANDA. The outcome was a huge bar-room brawl, which RIMMER deftly avoided.

MACEDONIA: The site of ALEXANDER THE GREAT's palace, which was visited by RIMMER on a school trip. He later discovered that he might have led a past life there.

MAGIC CARPET: The means by which LISTER, CAT and KRYTEN hoped to visit the KING OF THE POTATO

PEOPLE and plea for their freedom – and they say they weren't going mad?!

MAGIC DOOR: The term by which the CAT was able to comprehend the concept of the nature of the STASIS LEAK.

MAGIC FLUTE: KOCHANSKI's preferred choice on GAMES NIGHT. It was popular on her own *STARBUG*, where crew members would take it in turns to hum a section of an aria, and the others would try to guess the character. Fortunately for her new crewmates, GAMES NIGHT was cancelled.

MALE EUNUCH, THE: A masculinist BOOK by JEREMY GREER.

MAMET, PROFESSOR: KRYTEN's creator about whom we know very little. However, a canny PSIREN knew enough to realise that assuming her appearance would render the mechanoid unable to refuse any command it received, even if it meant self-destruction.

MAMOSIAN ANTI-MATTER CHOPSTICKS: The implements with which one is expected to consume MAMOSIAN CUISINE. If any of the DWARFERS hadn't been too polite to ask for a fork they might actually have tasted some of their meal.

MAMOSIAN CUISINE: A uniquely flavoured food, suitable for ANDROIDS, which made up the twenty-fourth-century banquet laid on by LEGION.

MAMOSIAN TELEKINETIC WINE: A drink which can be enjoyed without your ever having to lift the glass. Theoretically, anyway.

MAN PLUS: What LISTER hoped to become, via the DNA MODIFIER, to combat the MUTTON VINDALOO BEAST. In fact, he ended up more like Man Minus.

MANTOVANI: One of RIMMER's musical idols.

MAPLE SYRUP: The comestible substance with which MELLIE promised to cover herself on ACE RIMMER's behalf.

MARCH 2077: The month in which LISTER married KOCHANSKI and the crew of *RED DWARF* were wiped out – but *see also* GELDOF.

MARGUERITA, CHILLED: LISTER's favourite drink, no longer served on *STARBUG* due to the absence of tequila. KRYTEN broke out the last mini-bottle in anguish when he discovered his master's ultimate fate.

MARIJUANA GIN: No comment!

MATTER PADDLE: A prototype transporter discovered by KRYTEN in the research labs. This was capable of converting an individual into digital information and then transmitting him as light beams to another point in space. It could home in on any atmosphere-bearing planet within 500,000 light years. Unfortunately, when the crew used it, the one it homed in on turned out to be WAX-WORLD. The device was later adapted, by KRYTEN, into a TRIPLICATOR.

MAXINE: The twin sister of LORETTA; she murdered PALLISTER and LORETTA took the rap knowing that PHILIP was her alibi. Something like that, anyway. *See* GUMSHOE.

MAYDAY: A distress call. RIMMER finds it difficult to understand why something like Shrove Tuesday or Ascension Sunday can't be used instead.

MAYOR OF WARSAW: According to RIMMER, this dignitary spontaneously combusted in 1546. When LISTER caught a mutated PNEUMONIA virus that made his HALLUCINATIONS solid, he remembered that tale, and the incident was re-enacted outside the bunk room.

MECHANOID MENU: Special ANDROID food, knocked up by HOLLY for what was supposed to be KRYTEN's last day of life. RIMMER recommended the barium hydrochlorate salad nicoise and the helium 3 isotopes de la maison, with a small, radioactive fruit salad for pudding.

MECHANOIDS: *See* ANDROIDS (1).

MEDALS: LISTER was surprised to discover that RIMMER has four of these, although less so when he realised that they were for Three Years' Long Service, Six Years' Long Service, Nine Years' Long Service and Twelve Years' Long Service.

MEDICAL EQUIPMENT: LISTER's attempt to use these items to make a meal a special occasion were met with some trepidation by CAT.

MEDI-COMP: The computer which runs *RED DWARF*'s medical unit.

MEDI-SCAN: The means by which LISTER patched into the security cameras, thus obtaining a view of his future which KRYTEN had wished to keep from him.

MEGAMART: Where LISTER, from the age of seventeen, worked as a trolley-parker.

MELLIE: One of ACE RIMMER's friends in his own dimension, this woman looked suspiciously like HOLLY's female form.

MENTAL EMETIC: A process used as part of the MIND SWAP operation.

MERCURIAN BOOMERANG SPOON: An often lethal type of cutlery.

MERMAID: One of the CAT's fantasies, as provided to him by the BETTER THAN LIFE GAME, was a mermaid called MIRANDA. Naturally, she had the top half of a FISH and the bottom half of a woman. Well, the other way round would be stupid!

MILK RATION: The regular allowance of milk given to all crew members of *RED DWARF* before the accident that killed most of them. LISTER had to use his to feed his secret pet cat FRANKENSTEIN.

MILLENIUM OXIDE: A chemical substance, the presence of which alerted KRYTEN to the fact that there were SIMULANTS about.

MILLER, GLEN: RIMMER believed him to have been kidnapped by ALIENS – and he was worried that they might give him back!

MIMAS, SATURN: In ACE RIMMER's PARALLEL UNIVERSE, if not in our own, this moon is the site of the SPACE CORPS Test Base where he was stationed.

MIMEAN BLADDERFISH: An edible marine animal that, after borrowing LISTER's body, RIMMER selected as the FISH course for his first colossal meal.

MIND PATCHING: An illegal and dangerous process to insert the mind of an individual into that of another, thereby giving the recipient access to the intelligence of the donor. RIMMER had no scruples about undergoing the operation if it would help him gain a place aboard *ENLIGHTENMENT*.

MIND PROBE: The device used in the CLEARANCE AREA on JUSTICE WORLD to ascertain whether any visitors have a criminal background.

MIND SWAP: The process by which an individual's mind is drained and stored on tape, leaving the body free to play host to another personality. Both LISTER and the CAT were unfortunate enough to have their bodies temporarily on loan to RIMMER.

MINIMUM HAIRCUT LENGTH: RIMMER always favoured the reduction of this by a quarter of an inch, but he could never persuade CAPTAIN HOLLISTER to see the matter quite his way.

MINISTRY OF ALTERATION: The Government department headed by Colonel SEBASTIAN DOYLE. The Ministry of Alteration changed people; it changed them from living people to dead people.

MINUTE'S FLATULENCE, A: Suggested by RIMMER in honour of the destroyed CURRY supplies.

MIRANDA: (1) The CAT's MERMAID girlfriend in his BETTER THAN LIFE fantasy.

MIRANDA: (2) The Uranian moon where, whilst on planet leave, RIMMER started a fight in the HAÇIENDA.

MIRRORS: CAT wouldn't be seen without one of these at least not by himself. So when he's at his coolest, he finds almost insurmountable difficulty in tearing himself away from them. LISTER was alarmed when his mirror started to reflect FUTURE ECHOES, and KRYTEN banned him from looking in them altogether when he contracted SPACE MUMPS, presumably thinking that the hideous sight would make him hysterical. LISTER's best use for mirrors so far was taught to him by his best friend DUNCAN, at the age of ten. This was to apply them to your toe-caps, thus allowing you to look up girls' skirts.

MISTER FAT BASTARD 2044: The title with which RIMMER felt CAPTAIN HOLLISTER should have been honoured.

MISTER FLIBBLE: RIMMER's right-hand man – or rather right-hand penguin – when he lost his sanity due to the effects of the HOLO-VIRUS. Sadly the holographic glove puppet vanished when RIMMER was cured.

MODO: A term of abuse, once favoured by RIMMER.

MOGADON CLUSTER: Origin point of the PAN-DIMENSIONAL LIQUID BEAST.

MONKEYS: The way in which the CAT sees human beings.

MONROE, MARILYN: Fifties sex symbol, of whom several posters adorn the locker doors in LISTER and RIMMER's bunk room. The CAT was obviously impressed by her, as not only has he been known to read magazines about the actress, but she also became one of his girlfriends in a BETTER THAN LIFE fantasy (*see also* MERMAID). Another of her fans was obviously PETERSEN, who purchased a Build-It-Yourself kit on CALLISTO. This was eventually assembled by LISTER as a last-day present for KRYTEN. Using only a screwdriver and a tub of glue, LISTER was able to construct a 'droid whose resemblance to the original Marilyn fooled absolutely no-one – except KRYTEN. Finally, Marilyn's likeness was also taken by one of the WAX-DROIDs on WAX-WORLD. Blimey, is she a regular character or what?

MOOD STABILISER: *See* LITHIUM CARBONATE.

MOONBOOTS: *See* DAY-GLO ORANGE MOONBOOTS.

MOON HOPPING: An activity indulged in by both RIMMER and KRYTEN, on occasion. A relatively harmless pastime providing the moon hopped on to is not of the Psy variety. *See* PSY-MOON – if you hadn't figured that out already.

MOONQUAKE: These destructive and dangerous occurrences are to be avoided at all costs. Unless they coincide with RIMMER's rendition of the SPACE CORPS ANTHEM, in which case they are likely to come as a great relief.

MORALE OFFICER: RIMMER's self-appointed position on *STARBUG*. He feels he can boost the spirits of his comrades by routinely insulting them on a weekly basis.

MORRIS DANCING: An activity enjoyed by RIMMER, who is frequently disappointed by his colleagues' refusal to accompany him.

MOTIVATOR: A type of alarm clock, presumably internal, used by RIMMER.

MOTORBIKE, ROCKET-POWERED FLYING: Useful piece of machinery secreted away by ACE RIMMER (2). It aided his escape from the NAZIS.

MOTORHEAD: A twentieth-century rock band whose music is considered, by the people of the twenty-third century, to be classical in content.

MOUSTACHE, BIG: LISTER reckons he can't be gay because he can't grow one of these.

MUGS MURPHY: A cartoon character, whose screen exploits were mistaken by RIMMER for the classic FILM *Citizen Kane*.

MULHOLLAND-JJONES, LADY SABRINA: A jet-setting model, and eldest daughter of the Duke of Lincoln. She was married to FRED 'THICKY' HOLDEN, but in an alternative version of the past, she became LISTER's bird.

MURRAY, SAM: A Deck Sergeant who was an odd choice of candidate for the post of replacement HOLOGRAM. *See also* HARRISON.

MUTANTS: Anyone on RIMMERWORLD who wasn't the spitting image of RIMMER. *See also* NORMS.

MUTINY: RIMMER filed a COMPLAINT against LISTER on this charge – for jumping on his foot when RIMMER was trying to snap his GUITAR in half. He also warned KRYTEN that he was committing mutiny by diverting *STARBUG* in an attempt to rescue CAMILLE from an exploding planet. Apparently, this is just cause for an ANDROID to be dismantled. A more serious mutiny on board a prison ship carrying SIMULANTS to JUSTICE WORLD led to the escape of one of the creatures, who was later inadvertently picked up by *RED DWARF*.

MUTTON VINDALOO BEAST: Half man, half CURRY, this was what HOLLY ended up with when she tested out the DNA MODIFIER with one of LISTER's curries. The creature was impervious to BAZOOKOID fire but, fortunately, was no match for a can of LAGER.

MY INCREDIBLE CAREER **BY ADMIRAL A. J. RIMMER:** A BOOK which RIMMER would have liked to have written, and which featured in his BETTER THAN LIFE fantasy.

N

NANOBOTS: Subatomic robots from KRYTEN's self-repair system. They break down objects into their component atoms and reconfigure them. It transpired that it was the nanobots who stole *RED DWARF*; having tired of remaining inside KRYTEN they left to explore the universe, or at least the part of it within LISTER's laundry basket.

NAPOLEON: RIMMER idolises this man, describing him as his 'all-time favourite FASCIST dictator'. He would like little better than to travel back in time to the nineteenth century, and become one of his marshals. Ironically, when a WAX-DROID of Napoleon fought in the WAX WAR on WAX-WORLD, RIMMER never actually got to meet him. He was on the opposite side.

NAPS: The CAT has to take nine or ten of these per day, as preparation for his main evening snooze.

NASAL ALERT: An impending disaster which has set CAT's nostril hairs vibrating.

NAVI-COMP: An integral part of *RED DWARF*'s guidance system, situated in the DRIVE ROOM. A malfunction in this unit is destined to cause the death of LISTER's son BEXLEY, at some time in the future. There are also smaller navi-comps fitted in *RED DWARF*'s shuttle-craft.

NAZIS: Enemies of ACE RIMMER (2) in a parallel dimension.

NECROBICS: Hologramatic exercises for the dead, with which RIMMER once dabbled.

NEGA-DRIVE: A unit containing all KRYTEN's negativity: his jealousy, anger and resentment. ABLE routed its energy through an ESCAPE POD's thrusters and fired it towards the SS *CENTAURI*.

NEGATIVE EMOTIONS: POLYMORPH snacks. *See* ANGER, FEAR, GUILT and VANITY.

NEUTRAL AREA: The area of JUSTICE WORLD in which visitors are received. They are then fitted with ESCORT BOOTS and taken to the CLEARANCE AREA to be judged.

NEWS CHRONICLE: A newspaper which, during the 1940s, featured LISTER on its front page after the TIME-SLIDES allowed him to meet ADOLF HITLER at that time.

NEWSWEEK: The fabulously wealthy LISTER appeared on the cover of this magazine after inventing the TENSION SHEET.

NEW TOKYO: A city on twenty-third-century EARTH where RUBBER NUCLEAR WEAPONS had to be deployed against a rioting crowd.

NEWTON-JOHN, OLIVIA: According to HOLLY, anything is better than listening to an album by this singer.

NIGHTINGDROID, FLORENCE: KRYTEN's nursing skills have on separate occasions prompted both LISTER and KOCHANSKI to name him thus.

NIGHT SCHOOL: RIMMER once attended such an establishment, where he did a film course. He apparently learnt nothing whatsoever.

NIGHT WATCHMAN: The job to which HOLLY was demoted when QUEEG took over the running of *RED DWARF*.

NIPPLE NUTS: One of KRYTEN's more useful features. He was particularly upset at their loss when he was changed temporarily to a human. The left nut was used mainly to pick up short-wave radio transmissions such as JAZZ FM, whilst the right one regulated his body temperature.

NIVARO, RANDY: The Second Officer aboard the HOLO-SHIP, *ENLIGHTENMENT*. His PROMOTION PROSPECTS were presumably pretty slim, due to his IQ being a mere 194.

NODNOL: A city on BACKWARDS EARTH, looking suspiciously like our own Manchester.

NON-SPACE: An abyss of infinite nothingness where time doesn't seem to exist. A bit like one of RIMMER's organ-recital nights.

NORMAN: According to LISTER, this is the name by which YVONNE McGRUDER referred to RIMMER while the two were engaged in copulation. This no doubt has something to do with the concussion she was suffering at the time.

NORMS: Anyone on RIMMERWORLD who *was* the spitting image of RIMMER.

NORWEB FEDERATION: An organisation invented by HOLLY, NORWEB standing for the (real) North Western Electricity Board. He claimed that they had been tracking LISTER through space to obtain payment for electricity used by a light he had left on in the bathroom, THREE MILLION YEARS ago. However, it was all a jape.

NOSTALGIA NIGHT, 1990S: A party which took place on *RED DWARF* shortly before the accident in which the entire crew were wiped out.

NOVA 5: A crashed spaceship from EARTH, aboard which KRYTEN was discovered, still functioning as servitor for the long-dead Mapping Officers JANE AIR, ANNE GILL and TRACEY JOHNS.

NOW. . .: The only passage from SHAKESPEARE that RIMMER is able to quote.

NOW IRRADIATE YOUR HANDS: Correct procedure after using an ELECTRONIC TOILET.

NOW VOYAGER: KOCHANSKI (2) gets emotional when watching romantic movies. This particular movie once got KOCHANSKI so choked up she couldn't speak for twenty minutes. KRYTEN intends to keep it on standby.

NUREEK, RUTUTT, HUNUNGA: The correct sequence of noises from the sewage processor pipes, according to KOCHANSKI (2), who was kept awake by them – squalookle just doesn't come into it.

O

OCEAN MOON: The culpable party in the case of *STAR-BUG*'s ruptured reserve fuel tank.

ODOUR EATERS: LISTER was reputedly the only person ever to receive a refund from the makers of these items.

OFFICERS' BLOCK: That part of *RED DWARF* in which the quarters of all the officers were situated. LISTER mistakenly entered here while it was still contaminated by RADIATION, and contracted a mutated form of PNEUMONIA. Once they had finally got around to decontaminating the area, LISTER and RIMMER vacated their own rather basic bunk room and relocated to these more up-market surroundings.

OFFICER BUD BABE: CAT's respectful, friendly and flattering nickname for KOCHANSKI (2).

OFF-SIDE: In order to fit in with the others KOCHANSKI (2) attempted to learn what this rule was.

OH BOY, WAS I SUCKERED: The message which, if not for the intervention of his crewmates, CAT would have ended up spelling out with his intestinal tract, following an encounter with BRAIN-sucking PSIRENS.

OILING: As mentioned under the entry for HAND-MAIDENS, RIMMER thought his luck was improving when the two girls began to oil him. Unfortunately, he discovered that the process was intended merely to increase his electrical conductivity.

OM: A song by SMEG AND THE HEADS that was never the hit they expected, though LISTER changed that when he altered the TIMELINES and bought three million copies, sending the disc to number one in the charts.

ONE-ARMED MAN, THE: Character from *The Fugitive* who murdered Dr Richard Kimball's wife . . . Hmm, wrong book.

ONION SANDWICH: Following a night of being kept awake by noisy pipes LISTER used one of these in a failed suicide attempt.

OREGON: A ship on which, according to CAPTAIN HOLLISTER, a nasty problem was caused by a number of unquarantined RABBITS.

ORE SAMPLE POD: A Pod for transporting ore samples in; unless of course it's referred to as an ESCAPE POD.

OSWALD, LEE HARVEY: Accidentally turned into a GIANT PIZZA after being knocked out of a window by the time-travelling *STARBUG* crew. So it wasn't him who did it after all!

OUROBOROS: Everlasting circle of life that has no beginning and no end, symbolised by a snake eating its own tail. This word was written on the box in which the baby LISTER was abandoned – so he wasn't supposed to be called Rob or Ross then?

OUROBOROS BATTERIES: So called because they're everlasting.

OUTLAND REVENUE: The tax people, owed $£8,500 by RIMMER. His BETTER THAN LIFE fantasy became corrupted when they arrived to collect.

OXFAM SHOPS: Charitable outlets suspected of employing women with nostril hair.

OXTAIL SOUP AND ORANGE JUICE: What you'd probably get if you requested Coke from a vending machine serviced by RIMMER.

OXY-GENERATION UNIT: The life-saving device which the DWARFERS purchased from the KINITAWOWI. The price: DAVE LISTER.

P

PADRÉ, THE: A good friend of ACE RIMMER's from his own dimension. He was the chaplain at the MIMAS test base and greatly resembled our own CAT.

PALLISTER: A character in the GUMSHOE murder mystery game, who unfortunately got the worst part.

PAN-DIMENSIONAL LIQUID BEAST: A visit from this creature ensured that Christmas wasn't merely the usual bout of cracker pulling and watching *The Great Escape*.

PARALLEL UNIVERSES: Dimensions similar but not identical to our own. ACE RIMMER hailed from one of these, in which one small incident during ARNOLD RIMMER's childhood had changed the course of his life drastically. In another such universe, to which HOLLY accidentally transported *RED DWARF*, the roles of the sexes had been completely reversed. It was there that DAVE LISTER and ARNOLD RIMMER met DEB LISTER and ARLENE RIMMER, their female equivalents. *See also* HILLY and THE DOG.

PARANOIA: One of the imaginary beings that LISTER and CHEN theorised lived inside their heads. He became frighteningly real when LISTER caught a mutated PNEUMONIA virus which allowed his HALLUCINATIONS to become solid. However, he was murdered by CONFIDENCE – his counterpart – who didn't want to see him holding LISTER back.

PARROT'S BAR: Situated on *RED DWARF*'s G Deck, this is one of the more stylish relaxation areas on board the ship. As such, it is the site that KRYTEN chose for his first date with CAMILLE. As he told her when she left, they'd always have Parrot's . . .

PARTNERSHIP WHIST: An activity which, on the whole, KRYTEN finds preferable to SEX.

PAWN SACRIFICE: The radio code-name used by KRYTEN during the WAX WAR. This was presumably given to him by RIMMER, and it reflected the use to which he was put.

PD: The Punishment Detail on *RED DWARF* had the duty of painting the exterior of the ship.

PEEPHOLE BRA: A revealing item of lingerie which is a recurring object in RIMMER's unhealthy fantasies.

PERITONITIS: *See* APPENDIX.

PERSONAL DATA FILES: *RED DWARF* holds one of these for each of its crew members.

PERSONALITY DISCS: *See* HOLOGRAM DISCS.

PESTILENCE: Unhygienic member of the FOUR APO-CALYPSE BOYS.

PETERSEN, OLAF: A catering officer aboard *RED DWARF*, and a great friend of DAVE LISTER. RIMMER thought of him as a Danish moron, and this opinion was only confirmed when Petersen's holographic arm accidentally replaced his own, and launched a vicious assault on his private parts.

PETE TRANTER'S SISTER: The object of LISTER's lust throughout puberty. He wanted nothing more than to squeeze her buttocks together, thus forming one juicy, giant peach. An unscrupulous PSIREN once turned this desire against him.

PHASING COMET: Also known as a shiny thing with a long silvery glimmery thing behind it. Guess who by?

PHILIP: Private eye role assumed by LISTER when playing GUMSHOE.

PIANO: An instrument that KRYTEN wished to play. During his visit to our dimension, ACE RIMMER took the time to show him how.

PINKY AND PERKY: Names applied to the SKUTTERS by RIMMER.

PIPELINE 22: The place in which RIMMER chose to hide LISTER's CIGARETTES, and from which CAT recovered them.

PIZZA, GIANT: Appetizing bumper feast that turned out to be the splattered remains of LEE HARVEY OSWALD.

PIZZAS: The type of food in which RIMMER likes to indulge after sex – which probably means he hasn't had that many. His preferred type is a large quattro-formaggio, with extra olives. LISTER, on the other hand, doesn't care for pizzas at all – at least not unless they have CURRY on them.

PLANET OF THE NYMPHOMANIACS: It seems a terrible shame that this world was only a product of the HALLUCINATION caused by the DESPAIR SQUID. Still, perhaps somewhere in the universe . . .

PLATINI, HERCULE: Captain of the HOLOSHIP, *ENLIGHTENMENT* with an IQ of 212, going someway towards proving the old saying: 'Nobody loves a smart arse'.

PLATO: According to everyone else, a Greek philosopher. According to HOLLY's data banks, the inventor of the plate.

PLAYBOY: Since he is his own father and his ex-girlfriend is his mother, if LISTER wrote a letter to this magazine *CAT* is sure they'd print it.

PLAYING AWAY AT LEEDS: Not recommended according to LISTER.

PLAYZOMBIE: Hypothetical periodical in which CAROLINE CARMEN could no doubt be the Playmate of every month.

PLEASURE GELF: A Genetically Engineered Life Form programmed to appear to each individual as the object of his or her desires. One such GELF was CAMILLE, who KRYTEN saw as an ANDROID, RIMMER saw as a hologram – looking very much like his sister-in-law JANNINE RIMMER – and LISTER saw as the last woman alive. The object of CAT's desires, it turned out, was himself.

PLUTO: A planet which was first conquered by a woman. And was possibly also visited by LORRAINE, in her attempts to avoid the affections of ARNOLD RIMMER.

PNEUMONIA: LISTER fell victim to a mutated form of this virus after entering the contaminated OFFICERS' BLOCK. The disease caused him to have HALLUCINATIONS, which then became solid.

POCKETS, THE DEFINITIVE HISTORY OF: Another worthy piece of research undertaken by RIMMER.

POINTY STICK GAME: In order to play this you'll need a pointy stick and a TV weather girl. Beyond that you'll have to use your imagination.

POLYGRAPHIC SURVEILLANCE: The type of lie detection system used by the JUSTICE COMPUTER on JUSTICE WORLD, to assess whether or not LISTER was telling the truth when he acted as a witness during RIMMER's trial.

POLYMORPHS: The product of a failed genetic experiment. Originally developed for warfare, these emotion-devouring, shape-shifting mutants proved to be insane. Two of them found their way aboard *RED DWARF*, and, if you're really interested, some of the forms assumed by the first one included: a small ALIEN, a teddy bear, a plastic bucket and spade, some flowers, a toy truck, a flamenco dancer doll, a telephone, a model elephant, a top hat, a baseball mitt and ball, a boxer doll, a plant pot, a flashing beacon, a model Volkswagen, a roller skate, a TRAFFIC CONE, a light shade, an inflatable penguin, a yellow pig, a male doll, a po, a clock, some cheese, an old trainer, a small bucket, a pom-pom, a scrubbing brush, a metal pail, a small inflatable FROG, a Chinese ornament, a light bulb, a light stand, a yellow ball, a sock, a RABBIT, a BEACHBALL, a shami-kebab, boxer shorts, a SNAKE and a large creature with plenty of teeth. There are no prizes for spotting any we might have missed. *See also* EMOHAWK.

POOL: The GAME at which LISTER considers himself a master. He claims that his friends at the AIGBURTH ARMS knew him as **CINZANO BIANCO**, because once he was on the table, they couldn't get him off. His skills came in useful when he was called upon to pot a planet into a WHITE HOLE, thus sealing it up.

POPEYE: When KRYTEN became temporarily human, he borrowed from the wisdom of this cartoon character, with LISTER's encouragement. He decided 'I am what I am', and returned to his ANDROID form.

POP-UP KARMA SUTRA, THE – ZERO GRAVITY EDITION: A BOOK owned by LISTER. Who else?

PORKMAN, DOCTOR BOB: Inventor of the condom that calls you back.

POST POD: The means by which the mail arrives aboard *RED DWARF*.

POT NOODLE: One of the few items of food left aboard *STARBUG* when it crash-landed on an ICE PLANET. Fortunately for LISTER, there was also a can of DOG FOOD present, which he could eat instead. LISTER did eventually find an edible pot noodle, aboard the HIGH version of *RED DWARF*.

POWER PACKS: If possible avoid the cheap Martian ones.

PREGNANCY: LISTER thought, quite justifiably, that this could never happen to him. But when he slept with DEB LISTER in the female-dominated PARALLEL UNIVERSE, he was shocked to discover that the laws of that universe made it a very real possibility. Needless to say, all happened as feared, and DAVE LISTER shortly became the proud mother of twin sons, JIM and BEXLEY.

PREHISTORIC WORLD: The area of the WAX-DROID THEME PARK directly between HERO WORLD and VILLAIN WORLD, in which Droids in the shape of prehistoric creatures were kept. KRYTEN was not too impressed by the likeness, but still ran for cover when he and RIMMER accidentally found themselves right in their midst.

PRIDE AND PREJUDICE LAND: Part of JANE AUSTEN WORLD and certainly Chick City with those five BENNET SISTERS all hotter than a Mustang's exhaust.

PRINCE OF DORKNESS: *See* DUANE DIBBLEY.

PRISCILLA, QUEEN OF DEEP SPACE: What KOCHANSKI (2) thought LISTER looked like in his PINK DRESSING GOWN; she obviously wasn't impressed after all.

PROJECTION ROOM: That area of *RED DWARF* where slide shows are presented. This is presumably avoided by most of the crew members, due to RIMMER's penchant for giving such shows on the subject of TELEGRAPH POLES.

PROMISED LAND: *See* FUCHAL.

PROMOTION PROSPECTS: CAPTAIN HOLLISTER described LISTER's as being zero – and RIMMER's as being comical.

PSIRENS: As if from a futuristic version of the legend from the country big on curly shoes and hummus, these GELFS telepathically altered the perception of space travellers in order to lure them to their deaths. They first tried to entice CAT by masquerading as a couple of temptresses needing seed spreaders on a planet inhabited solely by women. Gullible as ever, Cat would have fallen for it if not for the others' assurance that the girls were in fact BRAIN-sucking Psirens – even the brunette. More sophisticated disguises were used against LISTER and KRYTEN, including KRISTINE KOCHANSKI and PROFESSOR MAMET.

PSI-SCAN: A vital piece of equipment, which may well save the lives of all the crew yet, if only KRYTEN can get it to work properly. The model he has is a 345, which out performs the 346 in nine out of ten bench tests, and was consequently voted Psi-Scan of the Year Best Budget Model three years running.

PSI-VIRUS: See HOLO-VIRUS.

PSY-MOON: An artificial planetoid capable of structuring its landscape according to an individual's psyche. One such moon, its terrain derived from RIMMER's mind, was not a very nice place to visit at all – no indeedy.

PUDDINGS, HOMOGENISED: One of the many food-stuffs stored on *RED DWARF*'s CARGO DECKS.

PULSE MISSILE: Launched on *STARBUG* by a SPACE CORPS EXTERNAL ENFORCEMENT VEHICLE.

PUNCTURE REPAIR KIT: Placed on stand-by status when RIMMER regained the ability to touch. See RACHEL.

PURPLE ALERT: An invention of HOLLY's deranged mind, this alert status is used for situations which are not quite bad enough to merit a RED ALERT, but which are a bit worse than a BLUE ALERT.

PUSHKIN, NATALINA: The First Officer aboard *ENLIGHTENMENT*. She considered it worth mentioning that her IQ was 201.

Q

QUADRANT 4, SECTOR 492: The area of space where *ENLIGHTENMENT* was discovered.

QUAGAARS: The name RIMMER made up for the race of ALIENS he believed he had discovered.

QUARANTINE: A subject on which RIMMER has always been strict. When HOLLY picked up an unidentified object, he insisted on it undergoing the standard quarantine procedure, a procedure which LISTER immediately broke. Likewise, when LISTER, KRYTEN and CAT came into contact with a HOLO-VIRUS, RIMMER made doubly sure that they were confined. But since LISTER was the only official crew member, all three were made to share room 152. When LISTER broke the quarantine imposed upon KOCHANSKI's quarters following the RADIATION leak, he fell victim to a mutated strain of PNEUMONIA.

QUASARS: After eleven attempts at passing his Engineering EXAM, and ten at Astro-Navigation, RIMMER was alarmed to find that he didn't actually know what one of these was.

QUAYLE: *See* LEGION.

QUEEG 500: *RED DWARF*'s back-up computer, or so everyone was led to believe. In fact, Queeg was an elaborate hoax on HOLLY's part.

QUEEN OF CAMELOT: French-accented royal babe who bestowed her favours upon LISTER OF SMEG.

QUEEN OF SPAIN: The role which RIMMER was allowed to take when his brothers were playing THE THREE MUSKETEERS.

R

RABBITS: According to CAPTAIN HOLLISTER, these animals caused an unspecified problem for the crew of the *OREGON*.

RACHEL: RIMMER's latest polythene pal after IN-FLATABLE INGRID did the dirty on him with LISTER. She spent three million years in need of a PUNCTURE REPAIR KIT, until RIMMER acquired his HARD-LIGHT DRIVE.

RADIATION: The crew of *RED DWARF* died when the ship was contaminated with this. *See also* CADMIUM 2.

RAM CHIP: Contains all KRYTEN's memories and personality; it was fortunate that it survived the explosions that accounted for all his SPARE HEADS.

RASTA-BILLY SKANK: The type of music favoured by LISTER. Despite the fact that it carries a Government Health Warning.

REAGAN, RONALD: On BACKWARDS EARTH, KRYTEN wore a mask of this former US President, in order to look inconspicuous.

REALITY CONTROL: Something which THE IN-QUISITOR was a self-appointed administrator of.

REALITY MINEFIELD: Defence mechanism fitted to highly important SPACE CORPS test ships. Pockets of unreality are used to disorientate potential looters by creating false realities, such as the one in which LISTER was perceived to be a SERIES 3000 MECHANOID.

REAPER, JIM: An employee of the DIVA-DROID INTER-NATIONAL Corporation, specifically Head of Sales, Space Division.

REAR ADMIRAL LIEUTENANT GENERAL: The rank by which MRS RIMMER knew her youngest son, due to his reluctance to admit to any EXAM failures.

RECHARGING SOCKET: KRYTEN is equipped with one of these, fitted with the standard three-pin adaption. It was a cause of consternation to him upon becoming temporarily human that, although he seemed to have located his new socket, he couldn't keep the recharging lead in there.

RECREATORS OF THE BATTLE OF NEASDEN SOCIETY: A group of which RIMMER was once a member. He felt that his commanding role in the WAX WAR would have earned him their respect.

RECUPERATION LOUNGE: Provided by the fictional LEISURE WORLD as a place to recover after playing one of their TIVs.

RED ALERT: One step up from a BLUE ALERT, and rarely engaged by the *STARBUG* crew, as it unfortunately means changing the bulb.

RED AND WHITE CHECKED GINGHAM DRESS: The mode of attire, complete with matching hat and army boots, that the HOLO-VIRUS infected, totally unhinged RIMMER selected for himself. The others later donned similar apparel in which to 'entertain' the now cured HOLOGRAM.

RED DWARF: A ship the size of a city, the postal address of which is apparently Deep Space, RE1 3DW. Of the myriad wonders it contains, we have seen the DRIVE ROOM, the medical unit, the CINEMA, the teaching room, the refectory, the science room, the HOLOGRAM PROJECTION SUITE (on Level 592), the scanning room, the observation room, the observation deck, the photographic lab, the supply pipes, part of the CARGO DECKS, the storage bay, the hold, the QUARANTINE bay (47), the locker rooms, the Officers' Club and a drinking establishment called PARROT'S BAR – plus, of course, various parts of the habitation decks, particularly LISTER and RIMMER's original bunk room and the sleeping quarters in the OFFICERS' BLOCK to which they later relocated. We also know that the ship has a penthouse suite on A Deck and research labs on Z Deck, as well as its own CARGO BAY, PROJECTION ROOM, science lab, ammunition stores, security deck, brig and botanical gardens. Its thousands of corridors are coded by colours (including red, blue and white) and numbers. The vessel went missing for quite some time having been stolen by KRYTEN's NANOBOTS. *See also STARBUG*, SPACE CORPS, JUPITER MINING CORPORATION, WHITE CORRIDOR 159 and in fact most of the rest of this index.

RED DWARF: (2) Sub-atomic version created by KRYTEN's NANOBOTS and found on a voyage of discovery around LISTER's laundry basket.

RED DWARF SHUFFLE, THE: A rap routine performed by LISTER and the CAT, the self-proclaimed 'smart party'.

RED DWARF – THE TOTAL IMMERSION VIDEO GAME: The TIV in which after four years DUANE DIBBLEY's party managed to score an astonishing 4% (using, if you really want to know, number sixteen of the LEISURE WORLD INTERNATIONAL arcade's twenty machines). Their poor performance, it seems, was due in no small part to RIMMER who failed to realise that he was in fact a special agent for the SPACE CORPS who had had his mind erased. LISTER also fared particularly badly, as he not only failed to get KOCHANSKI, but also to become creator of the SECOND UNIVERSE. At least three of the 'players' were crestfallen to learn they had missed the opportunity to land on the PLANET OF THE NYMPHOMANIACS, but fortunately, for their egos, the whole experience had been a HALLUCINATION induced by the DESPAIR SQUID.

REDDY MOON: Crimson-hued and circular-shaped body passed by *STARBUG*. LISTER hoped that mentioning it in his log might assist potential rescuers in locating them.

RED HOT WEST INDIAN PEPPER SAUCE: For the want of one more crate of this substance, LISTER kept the *STARBUG* crew on board a disintegrating SIMULANT cruiser for one second too long: the ship wasn't yet empty.

REHYDRATION UNITS: An internal mechanism which helps to keep ANDROIDS such as KRYTEN functioning.

RELATIVE TIME DILATION: The first visible effect of the WHITE HOLE that threatened *RED DWARF*. Simply put, this meant that time was running faster in some parts of the ship than in others.

RELIGION: Like all MECHANOIDS, KRYTEN is programmed to believe in the ELECTRONIC BIBLE and the concept of SILICON HEAVEN. LISTER is sceptical of this, confessing to being a pantheist, but not a frying pantheist. RIMMER on the other hand, doesn't have a religious bone in his hologramatic body, and considers Jesus to be nothing more than a hippy – well he had long hair and didn't have a job, after all! And perhaps it's just as well, considering where the CAT PEOPLE's belief in CLOISTER THE STUPID got them.

REMOTE PROJECTION UNIT: A device which enables RIMMER's HOLOGRAM to be sustained on *STARBUG* and elsewhere away from *RED DWARF*.

REPORT BOOK: RIMMER's constant companion. *See also* COMPLAINTS.

RETRO-HOUSING: Doubles as a makeshift bath when cleaned out.

REVENGE OF THE SURF-BOARDING KILLER BIKINI VAMPIRE GIRLS: LISTER's inspiration for his cunning plan to escape LEGION. By draping his clothing over a misshapen sculpture, he hoped to delude the entity as to his true position. Unfortunately, LEGION had seen the film too.

REVERSE BROTHERS, THE SENSATIONAL: A variety act formed on BACKWARDS EARTH by RIMMER and KRYTEN.

REVERSE THRUST TUBE: KRYTEN's suggestion that he be shot from this into the path of an oncoming missile was warmly accepted by RIMMER. LISTER, however, vetoed the idea, being unprepared to do his own ironing.

REVISION TIMETABLE: Meticulous as always, RIMMER found that after seven weeks painstakingly preparing this chart, he only had one night left in which to actually revise. He was not therefore very pleased when LISTER dropped a curry on it. On another occasion, he was even less happy to find that LISTER had swapped around the symbols, causing him to go swimming when he should have been taking his Engineering EXAM.

REVOLUTIONARY WORKING FRONT: A fanatical left-wing group, opposed to the middle class.

RICHARD, CLIFF: A pop star who would doubtless have been going strong for centuries to come had someone not had the good sense to shoot him.

RIMMER, ACE: (1) The ARNOLD RIMMER of a PARALLEL UNIVERSE, who had grown up to be totally different from his counterpart in our reality. Brave, handsome, resourceful and popular and holding the rank of Commander in the SPACE CORPS, he instantly earned our RIMMER's jealous hatred. Under that macho exterior, he was sure, lurked women's underwear. Sadly he caught the business end of a neutron tank in Dimension 165.

RIMMER, ACE: (2) A hard-light hologram and one in a long line of Aces. He inherited the mantle from the Ace of a parallel dimension and upon his death he too passed on the Ace persona to another RIMMER – simply because the multiverse has need of someone to right wrongs, and just generally be brave, handsome and all-round magnificent. Not sure he's made the right choice though.

RIMMER, ACE: (3) Formerly our ARNOLD RIMMER. It can't last. Can it?

RIMMER, ARLENE: ARNOLD RIMMER's female counterpart in the PARALLEL UNIVERSE, and just as sad an excuse for a human being as he is.

RIMMER, ARNOLD: A total failure in life, and now a total failure in death as well, as HOLLY has chosen to resurrect this sad character in HOLOGRAM form. References to RIMMER in this guide generally mean this one.

RIMMER DIRECTIVES: The fictional set of rules with which RIMMER sometimes counters KRYTEN's oft-quoted SPACE CORPS DIRECTIVES. Given the rule: 'In an emergency power situation, a hologramatic crew-member must lay down his life so that the living crew members might survive,' for instance, the corresponding Rimmer Directive is: 'No chance, you metal bastard.'

RIMMER EXPERIENCE, THE: Part-musical AR simulation created by KRYTEN using RIMMER's diaries, the purpose of which was to see to it that LISTER never missed his former roommate again.

RIMMER, FRANK: (1) Presumably named after an uncle on his father's side (*see* RIMMER, FRANK (2)), Frank was one of ARNOLD RIMMER's three older brothers. He was 6′ 5″ by the time he was eleven, due to his father's use of a TRACTION MACHINE to stretch his sons to the regulation height for joining the SPACE CORPS. We also know that he later got married and that he bore an uncanny resemblance to Arnold himself.

RIMMER, FRANK: (2) ARNOLD RIMMER's uncle, and the father of twin girls, ALICE and SARAH. He gave RIMMER his first French Kiss, albeit unintentionally. He had confused MRS RIMMER's room with her son's.

RIMMER, HOWARD: One of ARNOLD RIMMER's three older brothers, also in the SPACE CORPS.

RIMMER, JANNINE: ARNOLD RIMMER's sister-in-law, who was a model. In spite of their relationship to each other – or perhaps because of it – RIMMER fancied her a great deal. When CAMILLE mirrored his heart's desire, there was an uncanny resemblance between the two.

RIMMER, JOHN: ARNOLD RIMMER's eldest brother, who was a TEST PILOT in the SPACE CORPS by the time Arnold was seven.

RIMMER, MRS: (1) The only name by which we know ARNOLD RIMMER's mother, who both despised him and disappointed him with her constant sexual liaisons. She was impersonated by the POLYMORPH in order to arouse RIMMER's ANGER. She accomplished this by indulging in an indecent act which involved DAVE LISTER and ALPHABETTI SPAGHETTI.

RIMMER, MRS: (2) The nickname LISTER used for the double of himself that RIMMER once created. The second RIMMER had to be switched off when the two found that they were incapable of living together.

RIMMER WORLD: The lush and verdant paradise, created by RIMMER using ECO-ACCELERATOR ROCKETS. He then proceeded to spoil the place somewhat with the use of GENETIC CLONING.

RISK: A war GAME particularly enjoyed by RIMMER – so much so that he even went to the trouble of noting down his every dice score in his 'Risk Campaign BOOK'. One of his fondest memories is of the campaign he won against his CADET SCHOOL Training Officer, CALDICOTT.

RIVERBOAT, BRETT: LISTER's STREETS OF LAREDO alter ego, whose knife throwing skills were unparalleled.

RIVIERA KID, THE: A highly charismatic STREETS OF LAREDO character whose identity was taken, not surprisingly, by CAT. The Kid used a Colt 45 as his weapon of choice; his skill with it was matched only by his dancing ability.

ROBERT HARDY READS *TESS OF THE D'URBER-VILLES:* A chewed-up tape of Thomas Hardy's classic once provided an enjoyable musical experience for the CAT and LISTER.

ROCKET PANTS, ROBBIE: A fictional character whose jet powered trousers, the CAT considered, would provide a useful means of escape when the *STARBUG* was stuck on the PSY-MOON.

ROEBUCK, PORKY: Considered by RIMMER to be his best and only friend, until the fateful SPACE SCOUTS camping trip when Porky led the pack in an attempt to cook and eat RIMMER, choosing for himself the right buttock. RIMMER should have realised what sort of 'friend' Porky really was when he threw his shoes with the animal tracks into the sceptic tank – RIMMER was wearing them at the time. Porky's father was also one of the many intimate friends of MRS RIMMER.

ROGUE SIMULANT HUNTING GROUND: Best avoided really.

ROLL-OFF DEODORANT: An invention of BACKWARDS EARTH, this helps you stay wet and smelly for up to twenty-four hours.

ROOF ATTACK: The position in which LISTER's hero, JIM BEXLEY SPEED, played for the LONDON JETS ZERO-GRAVITY FOOTBALL team.

ROOM 008: The honeymoon suite of the GANYMEDE HOLIDAY INN.

RUBBER NUCLEAR WEAPONS: A twenty-third-century crowd control device. These were put to use in NEW TOKYO, when discontented shoppers rioted outside a store which had sold out of BETTER THAN LIFE.

RUBBER PLANT: LISTER possessed one of these and, according to HOLLY, spoke more words to it than he ever did to KRISTINE KOCHANSKI.

RUBBER ROOM: Put on metaphorical standby when LISTER began to miss RIMMER.

RUBBER SHARES: In the alternative dimension of ACE RIMMER, his popularity was such that his return to EARTH always positively affected their value.

RUBBLE, BETTY: Next-door neighbour of WILMA FLINTSTONE. Although the CAT would go with Betty, he'd be thinking of Wilma.

RUDE ALERT: An impending disaster which has affected HOLLY's vocabulary units.

RUN FOR YOUR WIFE: A twentieth-century play, which LISTER's older self advised him never ever to see.

RUSTY GATE: During those long dull evenings, the *STAR-BUG* crew were glad even of LISTER's anecdote about the time he mended his gran's rusty gate; of course he never let slip the fact that KOCHANSKI also made a sound like a rusty gate when making love. Unfortunately, however, she did. KRYTEN filed the anecdote for future blackmail opportunities.

S

SACRED GRAVY MARKS: Thanks to LISTER, these became items of religious significance to the CAT PEOPLE, and were worn by the CAT PRIESTS. *See also* HOLY CUSTARD STAINS.

SACRED LAWS: According to the Holy Bible of the CAT PEOPLE, CLOISTER left five of these commandments to his people, including 'It is a sin to be cool.' When CLOISTER – or rather LISTER – actually read them, he commented that he had already broken four of them himself – and that he would have broken the fifth if there had been any SHEEP on board!

ST FRANCIS OF ASSISI: A WAX-DROID of this worthy formed part of RIMMER's army in the WAX WAR. RIMMER later attributed to him the quote 'Never give a sucker an even break!' although KRYTEN was convinced that, if he really did say that, it was strictly off the record.

SALADS: In deep shock at the loss of the CURRY supplies, LISTER thought he might have one of these instead.

SALAD CREAM: KRYTEN believes it should be kept in the fridge, while KOCHANSKI (2) insists it be put in the cupboard. It has become the sauce of much friction.

SAMARITANS: An organisation to which RIMMER belonged for one morning. The five people to whom he spoke killed themselves. One unfortunate had actually dialled the wrong number, and only wanted the cricket scores. The event reached the newspapers, who dubbed the day LEMMING SUNDAY.

SAMMY THE SQUIB: Machine-gun-toting GUMSHOE persona assumed by KRYTEN in order to interrupt LISTER's Artificial Reality SEX session.

SAND PIT: The place where, as children, RIMMER's brothers playfully hid a landmine. RIMMER apparently escaped unscathed when it went off.

SANDRA: A girl from CADET SCHOOL to whom RIMMER claimed to have lost his virginity in his brother's BENTLEY V8 CONVERTIBLE.

SARAH: RIMMER's cousin; daughter of his uncle FRANK RIMMER (2), and twin sister of his cousin ALICE. Unlike ALICE, RIMMER was absolutely sure that Sarah fancied him. However, she probably didn't either!

SATSUMA: Not only can LISTER not understand Mandarin, he is also at a loss to comprehend this language.

SATURN TECH: An educational establishment where RIMMER took a maintenance course.

SAUSAGE, GOLDEN: One of the items by which, it is said, the CAT PEOPLE will know their GOD, CLOISTER. Several simulacra of this holy item can be found in the CAT PEOPLE's former living areas on the CARGO DECKS, and it was with one of these that LISTER was able to convince the last CAT PRIEST of his identity.

SAUSAGE PATE, RECONSTITUTED: Another useful fact – *RED DWARF* currently carries seventy-two tons of this foodstuff.

SCAN PROBE: See SCOUTER.

SCANTILY CLAD KUNG-FU FIGHTING VAMPIRES: Found in all of LISTER's favourite horror movies.

SCARPER CITY: A good place to visit when a SPACE CORPS ENFORCEMENT VEHICLE arrives.

SCHOOL CABBAGE: The vegetable on which RIMMER lays the blame for his lack of sexual prowess, having been force-fed it at IO HOUSE.

***SCOTT FITZGERALD*, THE:** The spaceship aboard which GORDON served as the primary computer.

SCOUTER: A surveillance device. True to form RIMMER insists that it is his responsibility, and his alone, to order its launch. The others of course take no notice whatsoever. *See also* SEARCH PROBE.

SCRAMBLE: From bed to battle stations, it takes LISTER and CAT one hour, seventeen minutes and thirty-nine seconds, though LISTER's sure it'd only take one hour and sixteen minutes if they were to cut out their fourth round of toast.

SCRUMPING: An activity in which LISTER indulged during his childhood in Liverpool. Apparently, he went scrumping for cars. He admits, however, that he was caught every time.

SCS PIONEER: A vessel which fell victim to PSIRENS and took up permanent residence in their SPACE-SHIP GRAVEYARD.

SEARCH PROBE: A device with a similar purpose to a SCOUTER, although strictly speaking it's used for searching for things instead of scouting them. Presumably once you've found something with your SEARCH PROBE you can then send in your SCOUTER to have a scout round. Look, if you want detailed technical information, buy a *Star Trek* manual or something.

SEAT TILT CONTROL: No longer squeaky, thanks to the generosity of a crew of xenophobic, genocidal SIMULANTS.

SECOND-DEGREE MURDER: The crime with which RIMMER was charged – on 1,167 counts – by the JUSTICE COMPUTER. He received a sentence of eight years for each count, making a total of 9,328 years of penal solitude. Fortunately for him, KRYTEN was able to reverse the computer's decision at the appeal stage, by proving that he was nothing more than a complete dork.

SECOND TECHNICIAN: RIMMER's rank aboard *RED DWARF*. Not the most impressive of positions!

SECOND UNIVERSE: See *RED DWARF* – THE TOTAL IMMERSION VIDEO GAME.

SECTOR 12: The part of space where ACE RIMMER (2) arrived from his dimension.

SECURITY CLEARANCE CODE: A very useful thing to have, unless you happen to be erased from history, when it becomes totally worthless, as LISTER himself discovered when – courtesy of the INQUISITOR – that particular fate befell him. His number is 000169 – another piece of vital information.

'SEE YA LATER, ALLIGATOR': The song played – by his own request – at the funeral of GEORGE McINTYRE.

SELBY: One of LISTER's friends aboard *RED DWARF*.

SELF-CONFIDENCE: A positive aspect of RIMMER's psyche, believed to be dead and buried alongside his generosity, his humour and his charm. With RIMMER's SELF-CONFIDENCE at its side it manifested itself as a dashing swordsman in order to do battle with THE HOODED LEGIONS, before hope succumbed too.

SELF GAMUT MIXING IN-VITRO TUBE: Thanks to this LISTER was conceived.

SELF-HYPNOSIS TAPES: RIMMER went through a phase of playing these every night, in order to learn such subjects as ESPERANTO and quantum theory whilst he slept. This irritated LISTER, as it simply meant that neither of them could get any sleep.

SELF-LOATHING: The emotion which dominated RIMMER's mental landscape. Personified as a hideous creature it became the ruler of the TERRAFORMed PSY-MOON, intent upon torturing the man who spawned it.

SELF-REPAIR UNIT: Considering his encounter with the waste compactor, it is fortunate for KRYTEN that he possesses one of these.

SELF-RESPECT: *See* SELF-CONFIDENCE.

SENSO-LOCK FEEDBACK TECHNIQUE: The technology which makes TOTAL IMMERSION VIDEO GAMES such as BETTER THAN LIFE possible.

SERIES 3000: A line of ANDROIDS deemed too human-like for comfort. They soon fell out of favour and were superseded by the series 4000 who, equipped with heads resembling a freak formation of mashed potato, could never be taken for human.

SERIES 5000: A superior model ANDROID to KRYTEN, a mere series 4000; fortunately favourable trade-in terms are available.

SERVICE DUCTS: There are two miles of these aboard *STARBUG*! They're so cramped that CAT reckons if he were dead you wouldn't be able to swing him round in there.

SERVICE ROBOTS: Presumably another name for the SKUTTERS. LISTER mentioned that there were four of these aboard *RED DWARF*.

SET-SQUARE: The device which, much to KRYTEN's despair, LISTER didn't even bother to use when making triangular sandwiches.

SEVEN: A number with which HOLLY admits to having a blind spot. It is also the number of children with which RIMMER's mind saddled himself during his BETTER THAN LIFE fantasy.

SEVENTH DAY ADVENT HOPPISTS: Due to a misprint in their Bible which they took literally, RIMMER's parents' particular form of religion was based on 'faith, hop and charity', and required them to hop each Sunday. According to RIMMER, this made it necessary for sou'westers and asbestos underpants to be worn when Sunday dinner was being served.

SEX: An activity that most of the crew of *RED DWARF* would like to indulge in more often. Unfortunately, stranded alone in deep space, they have to be content with going for runs, watching gardening programmes and playing JUNIOR ANGLER. RIMMER in particular only ever had sex once in his life, this being with the concussed YVONNE McGRUDER. He was therefore delighted to discover that the regulations of the HOLOSHIP, *ENLIGHTENMENT*, stipulated that sexual congress be undertaken at least twice a day. Having managed in death what he only managed once in life, he resolved to stay on the ship with his latest love, NIRVANAH CRANE, but the relationship was not to be. LISTER, meanwhile, thoroughly regretted his only sexual encounter since leaving STASIS. Taking place as it did with his alternate self in a PARALLEL UNIVERSE, it left him pregnant – with twins.

SEX DECK: An area on a HOLOSHIP put aside for the purposes of sexual recreation. Ship's regulations require crew members to indulge in sex at least twice a day.

SHAKE AND VAC: Unfortunately, there is none left aboard *RED DWARF*. The implications of this are unknown.

SHAKESPEARE, WILLIAM: Obviously not quite as famous a figure in the future as he is now. LISTER didn't even know who he was – and RIMMER thought his first name was Wilfred. Even so, his plays are obviously still regarded as works of art, hence RIMMER's objections when LISTER realised he had to burn the very last copy in existence to keep himself alive.

SHAKESPEARE, WILMA: The female-dominated PARALLEL UNIVERSE's finest playwright, author of such classics as *Rachel the Third* and *The Taming of the Shrimp*.

SHAM GLAM: A style of dress fashionable when LISTER was a teenager.

SHAMI KEBAB DIABLO: A chilli-based culinary speciality of LISTER's, though whether he has prepared the dish since it was assimilated by the POLYMORPH is uncertain.

SHAPIRO, HELEN: The female singer to whom RIMMER bore a startling resemblance following HOLLY's re-styling of his hair in revenge for an insult.

SHEEP: One of the types of animal that LISTER wanted to breed when he got his farm on FIJI. Given that FIJI was now three feet under water, RIMMER commented that he could corner the market in wet-look knitwear. *See also* SACRED LAWS.

SHEETS: *STARBUG* has at least two kinds: the blue stripey-patterned ones and the ones with green squares.

SHERIFF: A dream-state persona created by KRYTEN's subconscious in order to devise the DOVE PROGRAM. By the time BRETT RIVERBOAT and co arrived in town the lawman had hit the bottle.

SHE'S OUT OF MY LIFE: The first song LISTER learnt to play on his GUITAR. It was taught to him by his stepfather.

SHE WHO MUST BE DROOLED OVER: One of KRYTEN's names for KOCHANSKI (2) – she's not his favourite person.

SHINY THING: A particularly prized possession of the CAT's – in reality, a YO-YO.

SHIPQUAKE: An imminent disaster aboard a SIMULANT Battle Cruiser which threatened to bring the DWARFERS' 'shopping' expedition to a fatal conclusion.

SHIP'S LOG: Lister got as far as log one of his journal of life aboard *STARBUG*: the cameras couldn't cope with his explanation of the paradox relating to the ship's destruction by its future counterpart.

SHOE TREES: RIMMER possessed several of these: Monshoetree, Tueshoetree . . . well, you get the picture.

SIGMA 14D: A desert moon designated by HOLLY to be the rendezvous point for the crew once she had safely navigated *RED DWARF* away from five (non-existent) BLACK HOLES.

SILICON HEAVEN: The final resting place for ANDROIDS and other machines with Artificial Intelligence – or so they are programmed to believe. The promise of a reward in an electronic after-life is all that guarantees machines' servitude to Mankind.

SILICON HELL: The place where the photocopiers go.

SIMULANTS: Created for a war which never took place, these xenophobic, genocidal maniacs are physically the same as ANDROIDS, but lack the same degree of restrictive programming. The main difference between the two types of artificial lifeform is that an ANDROID will never rip off a human's head and spit down his throat. The DWARFERS have encountered several SIMULANTS on their travels; most uniquely, THE INQUISITOR, who was of the self-repairing variety.

SINAL FLUID: RIMMER was the proud owner of a small flask, containing the fluid of General George S. Patton. He had retained possession of it even when a rival collector offered him $£1,000. However, he generously gave it to KRYTEN as a last-day present.

SINCLAIR ZX81: Although she was slow and wouldn't load for him, she was HOLLY's one and only love – at least until he met HILLY, who literally turned his head.

SINGING POTATOES: HOLLY claimed that his collection of these musical root vegetables helped him to retain his sanity.

16 MARCH: The date on which RIMMER spent twelve minutes, minus the time it takes to eat a PIZZA, having sex.

SKATEBOARD: The sight of MICHELLE FISHER totally naked almost caused LISTER to drop his.

SKIPPER: ACE RIMMER's nickname for LISTER.

SKIVE HARD, PLAY HARD: The sometime motto of LISTER and his cronies, SELBY, CHEN and PETERSEN.

SKUTTERS: *RED DWARF*'s rebellious SERVICE ROBOTS. A quirk of their design has left them able to make insulting gestures, which they reserve exclusively for RIMMER.

SLEEPING: The CAT's third favourite activity. Although he hasn't gone into detail about the first two, we can probably guess. *See also* NAPS.

SLIDE-BACK SUNROOF HEAD: A feature of the Series 4000 GTI ANDROID of which KRYTEN, as a mere Series 4000, was particularly jealous.

SLOBBING: LISTER's hobby, to the pursuit of which he devotes most of his time.

SMART SHOES: Shoes with Artificial Intelligence. LISTER claimed that PETERSEN had purchased a pair of these and that, bored with their job, they had taken him from Oslo to Burma whilst he was unconscious. He had tried to get rid of them, but they had always followed him back home.

Eventually, they stole a car and drove it into a canal. No, we didn't believe it either – but RIMMER did.

SME HE: Not surprisingly on many occasions KRYTEN is sorely tempted to throw a few insults in RIMMER's direction. Unfortunately his restrictive programming makes it impossible for him to utter more than a syllable or two and the ensuing abuse is generally lost on the 'thick skinned' HOLOGRAM. He really is a SMEG-head isn't he?

SMEG: A popular twenty-third-century expletive, from which the insults 'smegger' and 'smeg-head' are derived. LISTER demonstrated just about every use of this formidable word in the phrase 'Oh smeg! What the smeggin' smeg's he smeggin' done? He's smeggin' killed me!' But as for its actual meaning – well, we're not going to delve into that here (or indeed anywhere). Try Black's Medical Dictionary if you're curious.

SMEG AND THE HEADS: LISTER's first band, in which he featured as lead vocalist. Also included in the line-up were DOBBIN on drums and GAZZA on bass.

SMOKING: Taken up by KRYTEN following the removal of his GUILT CHIP.

SNAKES: LISTER's second worst fear.

SNOT STREET STATION: LISTER missed the way RIMMER's nostrils flared like two tunnels leading here. No wonder he dreamt about him.

SOCK SUSPENDERS: A type of clothing worn by ARNOLD RIMMER, which ARLENE RIMMER considered to be extremely provocative.

SOCKS: LISTER's are particularly odious, and indeed RIMMER contends that they have in the past set off the SPRINKLER SYSTEM. HOLLY has been known to put *RED DWARF* on alert when her sensors discovered one on the CARGO DECKS, and mistook it for a completely new lifeform. LISTER also bemoaned the fact that, amongst all of his socks, he doesn't have a complete pair – whilst

RIMMER's favourite use for them is to roll them up and stick them down his trousers, thereby hoping to impress any girls he may happen to meet.

SOLAR ACCELERATORS: The power source used to sustain RIMMER's HARD LIGHT DRIVE for the five and a half centuries he spent on RIMMERWORLD.

SOLAR BATTERIES: *STARBUG*'s power source.

SOLAR PANELS: Situated on the outer hull of *RED DWARF*, RIMMER found these useful as his original hiding place for KOCHANSKI's PERSONALITY DISC.

SOMEONE TO WATCH OVER ME: A Gershwin song that RIMMER always intended to share with someone special. Now it's just his song.

SOUTHPORT: The seaside town where RIMMER believed he had made love to LISE YATES six times in one night, when, in fact, she had done it with LISTER.

SPACE: Black with twinkly bits.

SPACE BIKE: Ridden by KRYTEN – straight into an asteroid.

SPACE CORPS: The organisation which RIMMER's father was desperate to join, but was prevented from doing so because of his height. He was adamant that all four of his sons should follow the career path which was closed to him, and he even had each of them stretched on a rack to ensure that they could. RIMMER, however, was only able to enter the Corps at THIRD TECHNICIAN level, aboard the mining ship *RED DWARF*. Although he gradually made his way up the ranks to SECOND TECHNICIAN, he was never able to pass the EXAMS which would have made him a fully-fledged officer. LISTER, meanwhile, joined the Corps by the same route, but was happy to remain as the lowest rank on board the ship.

SPACE CORPS ACADEMY: By far the best route to join the SPACE CORPS, as this involves intensive training and immediate entry at officer level. All three of RIMMER's brothers were able to fulfil the entry requirements for the Academy, but Arnold himself had to be content with joining the Corps by a less direct route. *See* SPACE CORPS.

SPACE CORPS ANTHEM: A song with twenty-three stanzas, all of which RIMMER insists on singing when claiming new moons, etc.

SPACE CORPS DIRECTIVES: The rules and regulations which SPACE CORPS personnel must obey, and which RIMMER persistently mis-quotes. *See also* RIMMER DIRECTIVES and ARTICLES.

SPACE CORPS DIRECTIVES MANUAL: A volume which RIMMER believed to be imaginary, since all the directives contained therein seemed to be levelled against him personally. However, upon being furnished with a holographic copy he saw to it that any rules and regulations that would make things less pleasant for the others were obeyed to the letter.

SPACE CORPS EXTERNAL ENFORCEMENT VEHICLE: Watch out, it's the space filth.

SPACE CORPS SPECIAL SERVICE: An elite branch of the SPACE CORPS to which ACE RIMMER belongs, naturally.

SPACE CRAZY: A state of mind to which some people can be driven by loneliness, during prolonged journeys through space. Having avoided it for THREE MILLION YEARS, it seems unlikely that LISTER or RIMMER will now fall victim to this illness.

SPACE MIRAGES: Judging by the sign which warns of their presence, these phenomena are probably well worth seeing.

SPACE MUMPS: A particularly unpleasant disease which causes an enormous swelling of the forehead. This lasts for about three weeks, after which the swelling bursts – much to the disgust of CAT, who was present when LISTER's bout of this illness ended.

SPACE SCOUTS: An organisation to which the young RIMMER belonged. He almost got eaten by his fellow scouts on a survival expedition.

SPACE-SHIP GRAVEYARD: Created by and inhabited by PSIRENS. The *STARBUG* crew stumbled across it whilst taking a shortcut through an asteroid belt.

SPACE WEEVILS: When these insectoid space vermin invaded *STARBUG*'s food stores, they became ironically the only way of replacing the contents. Despite the near-cannibalism of the situation, LISTER enjoyed his weevil snack, believing it to be crunchy king prawn.

SPANNER: Because in life RIMMER had been a technician, his Deathday cake was baked in the shape of a spanner. HOLLY was relieved that RIMMER hadn't been a gynaecologist.

SPANNERS: The name by which DAVE LISTER was known in the PARALLEL UNIVERSE from which ACE RIMMER hailed. An accomplished Flight Engineer in the SPACE CORPS, he had also achieved LISTER's longed-for desire of marriage to KRISTINE KOCHANSKI. The couple even had twin sons, JIM and BEXLEY. Unlike RIMMER, who was insanely jealous of his other-dimensional counterpart, LISTER was extremely pleased to learn that at least somewhere he was doing so well for himself.

SPARE HEADS: KRYTEN had at least three of these until the KETCHUP incident caused them to explode, although one of them was infected with DROID ROT. Capable of independent thought and speech, the heads took it in turns to become the ANDROID's main head for a month.

SPEAKING SLIDE RULES: Entrants for the Engineering EXAM are positively not allowed to use these instruments.

SPEED, JIM BEXLEY: LISTER's hero, a ROOF ATTACK player for the LONDON JETS ZERO-GRAVITY FOOT-BALL team. LISTER named his twin sons JIM and BEXLEY after this sports star.

SPEED OF REALITY: According to the DIMENSION THEORY OF REALITY, this was the theoretical speed at which ACE RIMMER had to travel to reach a PARALLEL UNIVERSE.

SPIDER-MAN COSTUME: If we are to believe LISTER, he possesses one of these for the purpose of making love in.

SPINAL IMPLANT: A remote control device with which the LOWS forced LISTER into carrying out a successful murderous attack on the HIGHS and then an attack on his own crewmates with the same purpose.

SPRINKLER SYSTEM: *RED DWARF* does have one, although fortunately the only things that have set it off thus far have been LISTER's SOCKS.

SPROUTS: The vegetable that formed the basis of a menu devised by RIMMER, while the others were in QUARANTINE. A typical meal would consist of sprout soup followed by sprout salad with sprout crumble for dessert. Perhaps it had slipped RIMMER's memory that sprouts make LISTER sick.

SQUIRRELS: One of the types of animal kept in *RED DWARF*'s botanical gardens. After KOCHANSKI finished with him, LISTER expressed a desire to become one – and in retrospect, he was glad that the DNA MODIFIER wasn't around at the time.

SSS *ESPERANTO:* A Class D SPACE CORPS Seeding Ship – its mission: to introduce oceanic life into potential S3 PLANETS. The crew were impelled to commit SUICIDE by one of the fruits of their labour, the DESPAIR SQUID.

STARBUG: A class two ship-to-surface vessel, withdrawn from service due to design faults. It is nevertheless the shuttlecraft of choice for the *RED DWARF* crew, who use it in preference to the smaller *BLUE MIDGET* and *WHITE MIDGET*. Originally, there were at least two Starbugs; however, the effort to maintain both was enormous, as they suffered more crashes than a ZX81. Currently, the *RED*

DWARF crew live upon one such vessel (registration Star-bug 1), as they search in vain for their parent ship. Capable of travelling both underwater and through marshy terrain, and fitted with a cloak, a DECOY device and, lately, LASER CANNONS, the ship is at least capable of holding its own.

STAR-DRIVE: Appropriated from LEGION, this device should have enabled *STARBUG* to catch up *RED DWARF* in a matter of nano-seconds. The star-drive made the trip; unfortunately it didn't take *STARBUG* with it.

STASIS: The freezing of time around a person, causing him or her to become a non-event mass with a quantum probability of zero.

STASIS BOOTHS: *See* STASIS ROOMS.

STASIS FIELD: The area in which STASIS takes place.

STASIS LEAK: A phenomenon discovered by the *RED DWARF* crew on Level 16, which enabled them to travel back through time to 2 MARCH 2077. This is even harder to explain than STASIS itself, so let's just accept the CAT's theory that it was a 'MAGIC DOOR', okay?

STASIS PODS: A nest of these life-sustaining chambers was discovered at the VIRAL RESEARCH DEPARTMENT; one of them was occupied by HILDEGARDE LANSTROM who, unfortunately, turned out to be absolutely raving bonkers.

STASIS ROOMS: Also known as STASIS BOOTHS. The two rooms on *RED DWARF* in which the STASIS FIELD can cause STASIS to take place. We hope that's all perfectly clear now.

S3 PLANET: A potentially habitable world, with a similar atmosphere to EARTH (Sol three). As such, it is eligible to be claimed by RIMMER on behalf of the SPACE CORPS.

STELLAR-FOG: Tightly-packed particles, possibly from an exploding super-nova, in which the *STARBUG* crew encountered a REALITY MINEFIELD.

STOCHASTIC CAPABILITIES: The ability to predict the future through the examination of probabilities. STOCKY, the computer on board *ENLIGHTENMENT*, was able to do this to an accuracy of five per cent. KRYTEN's CPU has similar, though more limited, capabilities.

STOCKY: An incredibly advanced computer aboard the HOLOSHIP, *ENLIGHTENMENT*, so called because of its STOCHASTIC CAPABILITIES.

'STOKE ME A CLIPPER, I'LL BE BACK FOR CHRISTMAS': RIMMER's attempt at an Ace-like catch-phrase.

STOMACH PUMP: This was required by the CAT after sampling RIMMER's lamb and DUMPLINGS. One was also used by RIMMER himself in an attempt to rid his body of a dose of FREAKY FUNGUS.

STOPPING DISTANCES: Just as is the case with cars, these have to be meticulously learnt before a spaceship is flown. For instance, the stopping distance for half the speed of light is four years and three months. The thinking time is a fortnight.

STRAWBERRIES: The type of fruit that KRYTEN was able to recreate using the TRIPLICATOR. Upon sampling the fruit LISTER discovered that one of them was succulent and delicious. The other he wasn't too keen on; he didn't care for its taste, its texture or its maggots.

STREETS OF LAREDO: Artificial Reality Western game which enabled the other DWARFERS to patch into KRYTEN's mind, buying him time to create the DOVE PROGRAM.

SUGAR PUFF SANDWICHES: One of the few things that LISTER doesn't mind eating without the addition of CURRY sauce.

SUICIDE: An option which CAT prefers to wearing unfashionable prison clothing. Also the way in which SEBASTIAN DOYLE and company attempted to end their lives when afflicted by a DESPAIR SQUID, and the fate of all those who phoned ARNOLD RIMMER during his SAMARITANS stint.

SUICIDE SQUID: *See* DESPAIR SQUID.

SUITS: Having managed to build up a vast wardrobe of fine apparel, CAT has now become very protective about, and close to, his fashion collection.

SUPER-MARKET TROLLEY ATTENDANT: LISTER's job before joining the SPACE CORPS. He left it after years, because he didn't want to be tied down to a career.

SUPPLIES: RIMMER took a fancy to two brunettes who worked in this section. He offered to take them to TITAN ZOO, but LISTER's sarcastic comments about him, and about his mother's resemblance to the exhibits there, put them off.

SUSPENDED ANIMATION: A term often used instead of STASIS, although not meaning that exclusively. Does that help at all?

SUSPENDED-ANIMATION BOOTH: Just the thing if you can't locate a STASIS ROOM, STASIS POD, STASIS BOOTH, etc.

SWAMP OF DESPAIR, THE: An area of the PSY-MOON located not too far from the WOOD OF HUMILIATION and quite close to the CHASM OF HOPELESSNESS.

SWIMMING CERTIFICATES: *See* BSc, SSc.

SWIRLY THING ALERT: Rarely engaged, as the CAT hates to get so technical.

SYNAPTIC ENHANCER: Used to restore LISTER's memory following 200 years spent in DEEP-SLEEP. Believing RIMMER to be his best mate, LISTER was obviously in great need of a shot.

SYNTHE-SHOCK: What KRYTEN told LISTER he was suffering from when he believed he was a SERIES 3000 ANDROID.

Red Dwarf Programme Guide

T

T-COUNT: The hologramatic equivalent of blood pressure, with the T presumably standing for tachyon. Thanks to a stress-related nervous disorder, RIMMER's T-count tends towards the dangerously high side.

TAIWAN: The country of origin of TALKIE TOASTER; also, KRYTEN once believed, of a mechanical DAVE LISTER, although this was due to the effects of a REALITY MINEFIELD.

TAJ MAHAL TANDOORI RESTAURANT: Located behind the JUPITER MINING CORPORATION offices in London, this was the destination of LISTER and co when they ended up in Dallas, 1963, and accidentally buggered up history.

'TAKE US TO YOUR LEADER': Yep, LISTER actually said it!

TALES OF THE RIVERBANK: THE NEXT GENER-ATION: A follow-up to the more popular *Tales of the Riverbank*, which was a critical failure due to the absence from its cast of Hammy Hamster. Hammy apparently slid into depravity when his series was cancelled; he ended up suffering the ultimate humiliation, as he had to turn to 'Hamster-grams' to make a living.

TALKIE TOASTER: Manufactured by CRAPOLA INC. and made in TAIWAN, this remarkable toaster had been fitted with Artificial Intelligence and speech circuits. That turned out to be a mistake, as the appliance became obsessed with its job. According to LISTER, it threw a major wobbler if he didn't eat four hundred rounds of toast an hour. Eventually, he lost patience and smashed it to pieces with the aid of the WASTE DISPOSAL. He was therefore most disappointed when KRYTEN took it upon himself to repair it – although thankfully, the proximity of a WHITE HOLE altered time in such a way that the repair job never took place.

274

TANDEM: The type of bike stolen by LISTER and CAT on BACKWARDS EARTH – the scoundrels!

TARAMASALATA: Despite being happily married for 35 years, BONGO so admired ACE RIMMER that he offered to cover himself with this substance for his enjoyment. Unfortunately for him, MELLIE had already offered ACE dinner on her – MAPLE SYRUP, in her case.

TARANSHULAS: *See* TARANTULAS. LISTER, on the other hand, should see a dictionary!

TARANTULAS: RIMMER's all-time greatest fear in the whole world is to have one of these creatures crawling up his leg – so naturally, when his mind insisted on dreaming up bad things in BETTER THAN LIFE, this was one of them. This particular phobia is also shared by LISTER, who thought his fear had been realised when his leg was visited by KRYTEN's detached hand. However, worse was to come when the LOWS, controlling his actions with a SPINAL IMPLANT, forced him to eat one; LISTER, as you can imagine, was not best pleased.

TARKA DAL: Monocular ambassador from the great VINDALOOIAN EMPIRE, as created and portrayed by DAVE LISTER.

TATTOO: Despite the one to be found on his inner thigh, LISTER claims he doesn't really love PETERSEN.

TAU, CAPTAIN: Perhaps at some point in the past she really had been the Captain of the SCS *PIONEER*, but when encountered by LISTER and co she turned out to be another PSIREN.

TEAR GAS: A defence mechanism aboard *RED DWARF* as LISTER discovered first hand when, thanks to the INQUISITOR, he was without a SECURITY CLEARANCE CODE.

TEA STIRRING: Just one of many fantastic uses to which KRYTEN's versatile GROINAL SOCKET attachments can be put.

TEA STRAINER: Kept by LISTER's bed in order to strain the cigar butts out of his early afternoon LAGER.

TELEGRAPH POLES, TWENTIETH-CENTURY: A collection of items in which RIMMER is particularly interested. He possesses an extremely large number of fascinating slides and photographs on the subject, which so far, the rest of the crew have not quite got round to letting him show to them.

TELEPORTER: A device found aboard a SIMULANT ship which enabled the DWARFERS to escape from said vessel before it exploded. Later they used it to extricate themselves from a prison cell on RIMMERWORLD, thus denying LISTER the opportunity to put into action his foolproof escape plan, utilising loosened bricks, a pulley system with ropes hewn from hessian strands, a trip wire, uniform swapping and sword-fighting – though not necessarily in that order.

TELETHONS: If RIMMER had realised sooner that life was meant to be lived in a worthwhile manner, he might have used his own credit card number when pledging money during these charitable events.

TENSION SHEET: A small piece of air-bubble packing paper painted red, patented by THICKY HOLDEN, which earned him a great deal of money, along with the affections of the delectable LADY SABRINA MULHOLLAND-JJONES. Using the TIMESLIDES, LISTER changed history so that he would become the inventor instead, thereby creating a TIMELINE in which he lived a fabulously rich and famous lifestyle, eventually dying at the age of 98 whilst making love to his fourteenth wife in a private jet. RIMMER tried to beat him at his own game by doing likewise, but only managed to give away the secret of the device to a younger THICKY HOLDEN, thereby restoring the TIMELINES to normal.

TERRAFORMING: *See* ALIENS (not the entry, the film).

TEST PILOT: The job which RIMMER always desired in the SPACE CORPS. His father wanted this for him too, and both were bitterly disappointed when it became obvious that it wasn't to be. The ambition was achieved, however, by RIMMER's eldest brother, JOHN RIMMER – and, much to his chagrin, by ACE RIMMER, his counterpart in a PARALLEL UNIVERSE.

THERMOS FLASK: A vital component of DUANE DIBBLEY's survival kit, along with extra strong spot cream, anti-dandruff shampoo and a TRIPLE THICK CONDOM; as such it presented a perfect disguise for the EMOHAWK.

THETA 4: Planet from which the *LEVIATHAN* had departed en route to DELTA 7.

THIRD TECHNICIAN: LISTER's rank aboard *RED DWARF* – the lowest of the low!

THREE MILLION YEARS: The length of time LISTER spent in STASIS. Also, according to HOLLY, the average length of time for second class mail.

THREE MUSKETEERS, THE: A childhood game enjoyed by the RIMMER brothers – even Arnold, although he always had to be the QUEEN OF SPAIN.

3.4 INCHES: The average rainfall of the oil-rich coastal lowlands of Venezuela – if you can believe KOCHANSKI.

TIFFANY: The name of the type of girl RIMMER thinks LISTER should go out with: someone who drinks Campari and soda, says 'somefink' instead of 'something', and wears orange crotchless panties.

TIM: KOCHANSKI went back with him after dumping LISTER. He thought Tim was a bit of a poser in his white shirt and floppy hat – though he was a chef.

TIME DRIVE: Discovered aboard the *GEMINI 12*, this device was fitted to *STARBUG*, giving its crew time-travelling capabilities. An encounter with their future selves saw them killed, then resurrected in a subtly altered continuum. This new reality not only significantly increased *STARBUG*'s interior dimensions, but also gave the Time

Drive transportational properties too. Oddly though, LISTER and company never thought of using it to get home.

TIME GAUNTLETS: The formidable weapons employed by the INQUISITOR. Programmed by a variation of the ENIGMA DECODING SYSTEM, they were able to utilise time itself in a number of potentially fatal ways.

TIME HOLE: An orange whirly thing in space, according to the CAT's picturesque terminology. Actually, a portal to another point in time and space, and the means by which the crew of *RED DWARF* travelled to BACKWARDS EARTH.

TIMELINES: The flow of history, which was altered to varying degrees by both LISTER and RIMMER using the TIMESLIDES. THE INQUISITOR sought to do likewise, though the old backfiring TIME GAUNTLET trick reversed his damage. KRYTEN's accidental misprogramming of a TELEPORTER later caused him and his colleagues to jump timelines, arriving both in their own past and in the future. The FUTURE ECHOES, the events of MARCH 2077 and the appearance of the future, time-travelling *STARBUG* crew map out a great deal of the DWARFERS' possible destiny; however, with such forays into the past and future becoming more prevalent, who knows where the timelines will ultimately lead?

TIMESLIDES: Using a mutated batch of DEVELOPING FLUID, KRYTEN was able to create slides into which you could actually step. By using photographs of the past, the *RED DWARF* crew were able to travel back in time – although it was not possible for them to step out of the confines of the original picture.

TITAN: The moon on which a BIG BLACK TOM impregnated LISTER's cat, FRANKENSTEIN.

TITAN DOCKING PORT: The docking port on TITAN, no doubt.

TITAN HILTON: A hotel, missing at least one of its blankets.

TITAN MUSHROOMS: A hallucinogenic fungus which was inadvertently fed to RIMMER by LISTER. Colloquially known as FREAKY FUNGUS.

TITAN TAJ MAHAL: One of the many Indian restaurants which advertises during film intermissions.

TITAN ZOO: Another of this moon's many tourist attractions. LISTER inadvertently offended RIMMER when he mistook his mother's picture for a souvenir from this place. RIMMER also hoped to visit here with two brunettes from SUPPLIES.

TIV: Acronym for Total Immersion Video. See TOTAL IMMERSION VIDEO GAMES.

TODHUNTER, FRANK: A senior crew member on board *RED DWARF*. RIMMER despised him for his affluent background, and was convinced that he was breast-fed on GAZPACHO SOUP and champagne.

TOILET, ELECTRONIC: LISTER was pleased to find an 'electronic lavvy' in his hotel room during his BETTER THAN LIFE fantasy. This apparently did everything for its user, including removing his trousers. A less sophisticated version could be found in LISTER and RIMMER's original bunk room, although since moving to the OFFICERS' BLOCK, they have used the more private facilities available there.

TOILET PAPER: RIMMER always uses three sheets: one up, one down, and one to polish.

TOILET UNIVERSITY: Computer establishment where KRYTEN studied the lavatorial sciences and became a Bachelor of Sanitation.

TONGS: Used by LISTER to pluck his nostril hair.

TONGUE-TIED: A song and dance routine which featured in one of the CAT'S few non-erotic dreams. It was presumably based on a tune written by somebody else, as a musical version was once played at a disco attended by the *RED DWARF* crew.

'TO PEE OR NOT TO PEE?': A universal dilemma: whether or not to get up out of a comfy warm bed when you're bursting.

TOPIC BAR: RIMMER considered that he was probably the only person ever to get one without a hazelnut.

TOTAL IMMERSION VIDEO GAMES: These GAMES require the wearing of headsets, which insert electrodes into the frontal lobes and hyperthalons. This process allows them to create a virtual reality image in the player's mind. BETTER THAN LIFE is the best-known example of this type of GAME. Under the influence of the DESPAIR SQUID's venom induced HALLUCINATIONS, the crew believed they had been playing *RED DWARF* – THE TOTAL IMMERSION VIDEO GAME for four years.

TOTTENHAM HOTSPUR: A football team whose name is, to HOLLY at least, considered to be a term of abuse.

TOUGH LOVE: Doesn't in fact involve dressing up.

TOUPEES: Despite their enormous technical advances, mankind never developed a toupee that didn't look ridiculous. This didn't stop HOLLY from sporting a rug to impress the *NOVA 5* crew, nor the future KRYTEN's attempts at concealing his resemblance to a damaged crash dummy; however, it did lead to a SPACE CORPS DIRECTIVE which forbade all personnel from wearing ginger toupees on duty. More usefully, a larger toupee helped solve the global warming problem when it was fitted over the hole in the ozone layer.

TRACE: According to RIMMER, space jargon for tracking down someone or something. Though HOLLY's never heard of it and is convinced that the HOLOGRAM made it up.

TRACTION MACHINE: The device with which RIMMER's father hoped to ensure that, unlike him, all of his sons would be tall enough to join the SPACE CORPS.

TRAFFIC CONES: Even THREE MILLION YEARS into deep space, you can expect to find one of these after a good night on the ale. But where the policewoman's helmet and the suspenders come from is anyone's guess.

TRAINERS, CHILLED: The discovery of these led KOCHANSKI to the conclusion that she was looking into a boy's FRIDGE.

TRAKA 16: Small planetoid where LISTER and RIMMER once played a round of GOLF. In fact 'a round' is quite appropriate really because the BALL went all the way *around* the planet. Oh, please yourselves.

TRANTER, ADMIRAL JAMES: *See* BONGO.

TRASH FILE: Where KRYTEN dumps his no-longer-required memories in order to create more space. See BAY CITY ROLLERS' GREATEST HITS.

TRIPLE FRIED EGG BUTTY WITH CHILLI SAUCE AND CHUTNEY: A 'state-of-the-art sarnie' enjoyed by LISTER, although HOLLY was more concerned about the state of the floor. A sort of cross between food and bowel surgery, LISTER claimed to have found the recipe in a BOOK on bacteriological warfare.

TRIPLICATOR: A replicating machine cannibalised from the MATTER PADDLE by KRYTEN. Instead of creating two exact duplicates of an original, as intended, it created one improved perfect version and one flawed imperfect version. Set in reverse it constructed HIGH and LOW variants of *RED DWARF* – complete with crews – while destroying the original in the process.

TRIP-OUT CITY: RIMMER's bout with TITAN MUSH-ROOMS sent him on a voyage here. During its course, he attended inspection parade totally naked apart from a pair of mock leather driving gloves and blue swimming goggles. He also attacked two senior officers, believing them to be armed and dangerous giraffes.

TROUT À LA CRÈME: The DISPENSERS' FISH of the Day when RIMMER instructed CAT in their operation. Six

Trout à la Crèmes later, CAT suffered a severe FOOD ESCAPE.

TRUMPER: A pony owned by KOCHANSKI (2) when she was a girl.

T72: Tank from the WWII AR game incorporated by KRYTEN into JANE AUSTEN WORLD in order to gain some attention.

TURNER, TINA: Popular singing star of the twentieth century. CAT sometimes resembled her after particularly bumpy rides.

25 NOVEMBER: *See* GAZPACHO SOUP DAY.

26 NOVEMBER 2155: The night LISTER was left under the GRAV POOL table in the AIGBURTH ARMS.

2Q4B: The middle name that some poor sucker of an ANDROID got lumbered with.

U

ULTRA-ZONE: Circuit-board-corrupting drug addictive to MECHANOIDS. ABLE became a zoney when he discovered the truth about his origins.

UNDERPANTS: LISTER admits to only having one pair of these – and delights in the revelation that RIMMER keeps his on coat-hangers.

UNDERPANTSKI: Rhymes with KOCHANSKI . . . Well in LISTER's songs it does.

UNDERWATER HOCKEY: A game played at both inter-national and inter-planetary levels, hence the England team's tour of TITAN.

UNIVERSAL TRANSLATOR: Quite useful really. Well, *Star Trek* has them . . .

UO: HOLLY's personalised abbreviation for Unidentified Object.

UP, UP AND AWAY: An IN-FLIGHT MAGAZINE carried aboard the *STARBUG*.

URINE RE-CYC: *STARBUG*'s emergency supply, which had been reused so often it was starting to taste like Dutch LAGER. Kryten tried to make it more palatable by making it into wine. Cynically, his comrades argued that a really fine wine shouldn't leave the drinker with a foam moustache.

UTERINE SIMULATOR: A piece of medi-lab equipment in which LISTER was gestated.

V

VACUUM CLEANERS, SUPER-DELUXE: A type of electrical appliance of which KRYTEN is particularly fond. When he temporarily gained human form, he was confused by the strange effect that the sight of these caused in his groinal area. *See* DOUBLE POLAROID.

VALKYRIE WARRIORS, SCANTY-ARMOUR CLAD: A particular fantasy of CAT's, albeit one by which he is not quite as impressed as he is by his own image. The warriors in question generally have cleavages down which ski-ing is a very practical proposition.

VANITY: The emotion the POLYMORPH stole from CAT, playing havoc with his dress sense.

VEG, FRESH: According to LISTER, for health psychos, vitamin freaks and people who exercise. Consequently, not his favourite food.

VENDING MACHINE: Lister and CAT's reaction upon finding one of these on *STARBUG*'s engine deck was perhaps none too clever – given that there was a perception-altering PSIREN on board at the time.

VENUS DE MILO: She lost both arms and still had a highly successful modelling career. Other notable people lacking in the arm department include: Lord Nelson, the Welsh painter Van Gogh, and the notorious Mexican desperado the One-

Armed Bandit. Despite hearing about the achievements of these luminaries from his crewmates LISTER still wasn't happy about the loss of his own arm.

VIBRATING LEOPARD-SKIN WATER BED: LISTER's BETTER THAN LIFE fantasy came complete with one of these – in the shape of a GUITAR.

VIDAL BEAST OF SHARMUT 2: LISTER thought he could impress KOCHANSKI (2) by mentioning this monster, encountered by the *STARBUG* crew before she arrived. But not the one that nearly killed them, the other one.

VIDS: The common term for video tapes, which by the twenty-third century will also be available in triangular shape, though it's unlikely these will ever replace the established VHS format (remember Betamax?). *The Flintstones* is a favourite of both LISTER and CAT, the latter being something of a cartoon devotee. LISTER is a fan of the series *St Elsewhere*, claiming to have seen every episode. He also enjoys classic movies such as *CASABLANCA*, which he introduced to KRYTEN who, although enjoying it greatly, is still an aficionado of *ANDROIDS*, though he did find 'Easy Rider', 'The Wild One' and 'Rebel Without a Cause' quite influential. RIMMER on the other hand is generally hard to please and critical of much that he sees; for example he found 'King of Kings' quite far fetched and had a few ideas of his own for not only adding credibility to the plot but making it more action packed to boot. When the others were held in QUARANTINE, and RIMMER was required, by SPACE CORPS DIRECTIVE 312, to provide entertainment, the video he selected was 'Wallpapering, Painting and Stippling – A DIY Guide'; the choice wasn't popular. New videos sometimes arrive via the POST POD; one such was 'FRIDAY THE THIRTEENTH 1649', which presumably had a storyline identical to parts 1–1648. More extreme video nasties were discovered aboard the LOW version of *RED DWARF*, including 'Revenge of the Mutant Splat-Gore Monster' and 'Die Screaming With Sharp Things in Your Head'. Finally, for a bunch of lonely males far out in deep space, gardening programmes provide a useful antidote to overactive hormones. *See also* DOUG McCLURE.

VILLAIN WORLD: An area of the WAX-DROID THEME PARK in which Droids of history's villains were kept.

VINDALOOIAN EMPIRE: The home of the great TARKA DAL and BHINDI BHAJI . . . not.

VINDALOOS: LISTER is quite a glutton for this type of hot curry, and has been known to experiment with all types – including kippers and caviar! When under threat of death, LISTER's first regret was that he had never eaten a prawn vindaloo; he has presumably now rectified the omission. *See also* MUTTON VINDALOO BEAST.

VIRAL RESEARCH DEPARTMENT: The place of work of Doctor HILDEGARDE LANSTROM, and the place she developed her theory of positive and negative viruses (*see also* FELICITUS POPULI). Unfortunately she also inadvertently created a HOLO-VIRUS, which ended her hologramatic existence.

VIRGIN BIRTH: The CAT PEOPLE believe that this miraculous event happened to LISTER's former pet, FRANKENSTEIN, spawning their race. In fact, the responsibility lay with a BIG BLACK TOM on TITAN.

VOMIT BAGS: According to the log, there are 3,000 left. According to RIMMER, not enough to cope with another visit from ACE.

VON STAUFFENBERG: The German Officer who planted a bomb in ADOLF HITLER's briefcase. By stealing the case, LISTER inadvertently saved the dictator's life.

VOORHESE, CAPTAIN: He took on ACE RIMMER and came off second best – not to mention dead.

VOTERS: The citizens of the imaginary totalitarian state in which DUANE DIBBLEY and his friend found themselves living.

W

WALRUS POLISHING KIT, PORTABLE: Just the kind of junk that LISTER would send off for in order to receive some mail.

WAR: Violent member of the FOUR APOCALYPSE BOYS.

WARBURTON, JOHN: Bioengineer who jilted PROFESSOR MAMET a day before their wedding. She took her revenge by creating a pompous, ridiculous-looking, mother-hen-clucking, irascible buffoon of a mechanoid in his image; the result was the SERIES 4000. KRYTEN is an example of this type of MECHANOID.

WARS: According to LISTER's theory of world history, there were so many of these in the nineteenth century because of the nadger-restricting trousers they wore then.

WASTE COMPACTOR: *STARBUG*'s method of crushing waste before it is ejected into space.

WASTE DISPOSAL: One of the sections in which LISTER worked during his tour of duty on *RED DWARF*. Any waste was loaded into GARBAGE PODS and ejected into space.

WASTE DISPOSAL UNITS: By the simple addition of some rocket fuel and a THERMOS FLASK full of nitroglycerine, KRYTEN transformed one of these everyday shipboard devices into a rather useful garbage cannon.

WASTE GRINDER: A quicker method of WASTE DISPOSAL than the GARBAGE PODS, this machine simply grinds up rubbish and ejects it into space. CONFIDENCE used it to dispose of PARANOIA once and for all.

WATER-WINGS: Items of *RED DWARF*'s survival equipment which KRYTEN sometimes finds useful.

WATUNGA: The KINITAWOWI word for hut. Sheesh, what an absolutely invaluable reference work this is.

WAX-DROID THEME PARK: The use to which the whole of the newly-named WAX-WORLD was put. Presumably a future version of a wax-works museum. *See* WAX-DROIDS for more information.

WAX-DROIDS: Animated wax-works, which the crew of *RED DWARF* encountered on WAX-WORLD. After millions of years untended, the Droids had broken free of their programming, and a brutal WAX WAR had begun between the exhibits in HERO WORLD and those in VILLAIN WORLD. The forces of good included Elvis Presley (to whom RIMMER gave the rank of Sergeant), Abraham Lincoln, MARILYN MONROE, Albert Einstein, Pythagoras, Stan Laurel, Mahatma Gandhi, Mother Teresa, ST FRANCIS OF ASSISI, the Dalai Lama, Queen Victoria, Noel Coward, Jean Paul Sartre and Pope Gregory, all of whom we were introduced to. Father Christmas was also present, having been posted from the FICTION SECTION, and LISTER claimed to have seen the execution of Winnie the Pooh – and we also know that JOHN WAYNE, Sir Lancelot, Joan of Arc, Nelson, Wellington and even Doris Day had already perished in battle. On the side of evil were such despots as HITLER, Goebbels, Goering, NAPOLEON, Caligula, the Boston Strangler, Mussolini, Al Capone, Rasputin, Richard III and JAMES LAST. You can probably see now why we didn't have the room to give all of these their own entries in this index!

WAX WAR, THE: The wax-thirsty conflict which was on-going when the *RED DWARF* crew arrived on WAX-WORLD. RIMMER took command of the forces of HERO WORLD and led them into glorious victory against VILLAIN WORLD. Unfortunately, every WAX-DROID on the planet was wiped out in the process.

WAX-WORLD: Home of the WAX-DROIDS; also a giant WAX-DROID THEME PARK.

WAYNE, JOHN: Movie cowboy, and idol of the SKUT-TERS, who are not only avid viewers of his films but also members of his fan club. When they are not working, they enjoy re-enacting his wild-west battles in the corridors of *RED DWARF*.

WD40: The lubricant with which KRYTEN oils his neck hinges. He also found its aroma particularly attractive when he believed that CAMILLE did likewise.

WELCOME BACK PARTY: A party thrown for GEORGE McINTYRE immediately after his funeral, when he was brought back on to *RED DWARF* as a HOLOGRAM.

WEST SIDE STORY: A musical update of the *Romeo and Juliet* story, and the nearest thing to a SHAKESPEARE play RIMMER has ever seen.

WHAT BIKE: A magazine read by LISTER, who else?

WHIPPED CREAM: Required by LISTER while having SEX with the QUEEN OF CAMELOT. The KING didn't know what exactly he planned to do with it.

WHITE CARD: An imaginary object with which RIMMER signalled to LISTER that a conversation could continue. *See also* BLACK CARD.

WHITE CORRIDOR 159: Quite a problematic area of the ship, as far as LISTER and RIMMER are concerned. The DRIVE PLATE which, inefficiently repaired by RIMMER, caused a RADIATION leak was in this area. Also, this is where LISTER collapsed after catching a mutated strain of PNEUMONIA. Most importantly, it was the site of that now infamous blockage of the DISPENSER's CHICKEN SOUP NOZZLE.

WHITE HOLE: The exact opposite of the more commonly known phenomenon the BLACK HOLE. White holes spew time and matter back into the universe. When the *RED DWARF* crew encountered one, they had to knock a planet into it to escape its influence.

WHITE MIDGET: A shuttle-craft mentioned by LISTER but never actually seen, as he set off in *BLUE MIDGET* instead.

WHO'S NOBODY: The imaginary BOOK in which the CAT considered DAVE LISTER should have an entry.

WIBBLY THING: Spatial phenomenon, not to be confused with a swirly thing.

WICKED STRENGTH LAGER: Another of LISTER's favoured brands of LAGER. This one certainly lives up to its name, as it got him 'pished' after only two cans!

WIG: The only non-hologramatic bit of the latest ACE RIMMER.

WILSON, REGGIE: A purveyor of HAMMOND ORGAN MUSIC – and, much to everybody else's dismay, a particular idol of ARNOLD RIMMER. His albums include *Reggie Wilson plays the Lift Music Classics, Sounds of the Supermarket – 20 Golden Greats, Pop goes Delius* and *Funking up Wagner*.

WINE BAR: One of LISTER's greatest embarrassments is that he once entered one such establishment. He considers himself lucky that he was able to reverse the slide into depravity, preventing himself from 'selling out' and becoming a 'class traitor'.

WINE, GREEN: Ideal with LOBSTER apparently.

WIPE ALERT, 24-HOUR: Brought into effect when LISTER lost an arm. It's not as gross as it first sounds.

W.O.O.: When the seriously loony RIMMER decided to sentence the others to a period Without Oxygen, they, not surprisingly, considered that two hours was just a bit excessive.

WOOD OF HUMILIATION: An area of the PSY-MOON located not too far from the CHASM OF HOPELESSNESS and quite close to the SWAMP OF DESPAIR.

WORLD'S STUPIDEST STUNTMEN: A video that could well serve as an appetiser for the highlight of the evening – watching KOCHANSKI's KNICKERS spin-dry.

WORM-HOLE: A spatial phenomenon which enabled RIMMER's ESCAPE POD to reach what would shortly become RIMMERWORLD. Unfortunately, due to the effects of time dilation, it would take 557 years before DEREK CUSTER, Kit and Titan were able to mount a rescue.

WORMSKIN RUG: The non-existence of such an item is RIMMER's rebuff to the old CAT saying: 'It's better to live an hour as a tiger than a lifetime as a worm.'

WRIST WATCH: A mechanism into which HOLLY can project his/her consciousness, allowing the computer to provide guidance to the *RED DWARF* crew even when they are not on board the ship. Unfortunately, this proved to be rather an unpleasant experience, due to LISTER's predilections for scratching under his arms and putting his hands in his pockets. The latter was made worse by the presence of a large hole in his trousers, which gave the first HOLLY a view that reminded him of ATTACK OF THE KILLER GOOSEBERRIES. In later years, the addition of KRYTEN to the crew has eased the problem, as HOLLY can now project his/her consciousness to a monitor screen on his chest plate, instead.

X

XANADU: LISTER's disgustingly opulent home in an alternate past, named after the hit song by Dave Dee, Dozy, Beaky, Mick and Titch.

XPRESS LIFTS: The elevators provided for long journeys down to *RED DWARF*'s lower levels. As the journeys take a long time, computerised hostesses and inedible food are provided – as are CYANIDE CAPSULES since, in the event of an accident, there is no means of escape.

Y

YADRETSEY: A BACKWARDS EARTH newspaper.

YAKKA TALLA TULLA: The SPACE SCOUT mistress who saved RIMMER from a cannibalistic attempt on his life by the rest of the pack.

'YANKEE DOODLE DANDY': LISTER's 'party piece' is to belch this tune when drunk. He considers it stylish, but was disgusted when he witnessed a similar performance by DEB LISTER, his female counterpart in the PARALLEL UNIVERSE.

YATES, LISE: A girl with whom LISTER once had a particularly special relationship. As a death-day present he transferred the slightly modified memories of the affair into RIMMER's mind. Until he discovered the truth RIMMER was ecstatic, if not a little confused – after all moving to Liverpool and becoming a total slob was a bit out of character and not many people need their APPENDIX out twice!

YO-YO: CAT was delighted to discover one of these on his travels, and kept it as his 'SHINY THING', despite the fact that he didn't have a clue what it was for.

Z

ZEPPO: The fourth Marx brother. Fancy KRYTEN not knowing that. Presumably he doesn't know that the fifth was Gummo.

Z SHIFT: The small contingent of which RIMMER was in charge, aboard *RED DWARF*. We are led to believe that this consisted only of himself and LISTER – and we know that its most important task was ensuring that the DISPENSERS didn't run out of FUN-SIZE CRUNCHIE BARS.

ZERO GEE FOOTBALL: Short for ZERO-GRAVITY FOOTBALL.

ZERO-GRAVITY FOOTBALL: A GAME particularly enjoyed by LISTER, who supported the LONDON JETS. LISTER's hero, JIM BEXLEY SPEED, was an accomplished player in this sport.

ZERO GEE KICK-BOXING: What ZERO GEE FOOT-BALL is to present-day soccer (or maybe that boring

American thing), this sport is to present-day kick-boxing. Bloomin' obvious really.

001100111011100011110011100111100: An old ANDROID saying which, loosely translated, means: 'Don't stand around jabbering when you're in mortal danger.'

ZOOM FUNCTION: A facility inherent within KRYTEN's optical system, the loss of which he was most upset about when he became temporarily human.

SECTION FIVE:

SUPPLEMENTAL LOG

This section covers the adventures of Lister and co that are not part of the official canon, i.e. not seen in the seven television series to date. We'll leave it to you to decide if they're apocryphal tales, stories set in parallel dimensions, or if you couldn't care less either way and simply want to enjoy them as some *Red Dwarf* bonuses.

THE NOVELS

1. *RED DWARF – INFINITY WELCOMES CAREFUL DRIVERS* by Grant Naylor
First published (soft cover) 1989 Penguin Books
(Hard cover) 1991 Chivers Press

2. *BETTER THAN LIFE* by Grant Naylor
First published (hard cover) 1990 Viking Books
(Soft cover) 1991 Penguin Books

3. *LAST HUMAN* by Doug Naylor
First published (hard cover) 1995 Viking Books
(Soft cover) 1995 Penguin Books

4. *BACKWARDS* by Rob Grant
First published (hard cover) 1996 Viking Books
(Soft cover) 1996 Penguin Books

Despite their experience at scriptwriting, when Rob Grant and Doug Naylor decided that they would attempt to write a novel, both were initially unsure if they would be able to tackle the entirely different kind of writing involved in producing such a book.

Surprisingly, landing a deal for an actual *Red Dwarf* novel proved to be quite difficult. BBC Books themselves expressed some early interest in publishing the *Red Dwarf* spin-off, but Grant and Naylor feared that, under the BBC imprint, the book might be considered to be merely the usual novelisation or straightforward adaptation of the TV episodes rather than a proper novel in its own right. Eventually, after the end of Series II, they approached Penguin Books and, armed with a speculative first chapter and outline of the structure, plus eight bottles of Sancerre, Grant and Naylor were able to persuade an editor, Tim Binding, that the series was fantastically popular and that the project was well worth going ahead with.

Red Dwarf – Infinity Welcomes Careful Drivers was faithful to the spirit of the TV series, but only certain elements were retained exactly as they had appeared on the screen originally; ideas were expanded, altered – either slightly or radically – or dropped altogether, and a number of totally new concepts were introduced. If it seemed as if Grant and Naylor were trying to proffer an improved and perhaps definitive version of events, it is because that was exactly the case. While this revised approach to *Red Dwarf* is a treat for the reader, it tends to make life difficult for anyone wanting to make any kind of sense of the continuity. Perhaps the simplest option is to locate the printed adventures of the *Red Dwarf* crew in one of the infinite number of parallel universes that the TV series claims exist, or, more properly, into one of the six – the more conservative estimate of extant alternate dimensions – suggested in the books themselves.

The enormous success of the first novel, published in paperback form only, earnt its sequel, *Better Than Life*, the prestige of a hard cover first edition in the Viking imprint. Once again the content of the book diverged significantly from its small-screen counterpart.

The plot of *Red Dwarf – Infinity Welcomes Careful Drivers* borrowed extensively from the original television episodes 'The End', 'Future Echoes', 'Me^2' and 'Kryten', though not necessarily in that order. The concept of the 'Total

Immersion Video' from the 'Better Than Life' episode was also used for the first book's cliffhanger ending. The idea was carried through into the second novel, where the game was revealed to be a later version to the one featured on television. The book *Better Than Life* also contained elements from 'Marooned', 'Polymorph' and 'Backwards'. In the case of the last of these it was merely the concept of an Earth on which time runs backwards that was utilised. The fourth season's 'White Hole' was previewed in the novel, but in this earlier version the spatial phenomenon's actions were undertaken by its complete opposite – a black hole.

The long-awaited third *Red Dwarf* novel, *Last Human*, finally appeared in 1995, written, due to the partnership split, solely by Doug Naylor, although Doug's acknowledgements reveal that it was actually Rob Grant who first expressed the desire to pen a solo book. Anticipating developments in the TV series, Kristine Kochanski is highlighted throughout, and Rimmer dies a heroic death. Events and dialogue from the TV episodes 'DNA', 'Emohawk – Polymorph II' and 'Psirens' are included.

The following year saw the publication of Rob Grant's solo effort *Backwards*. As in *Last Human*, the events in this book took place directly after the conclusion of its predecessor, in this case *Better Than Life*. In any other series of books this lack of co-ordination might have completely ruined the established continuity, leaving readers to make up their own minds about which set of events is 'real'. However, as both authors include parallel universes and a number of counterparts for their protagonists, it is easiest to assume that both novels are equally valid but set in alternate realities.

Rob's book borrows heavily from the episodes 'Dimension Jump' and 'Gunmen of the Apocalypse'.

In the interests of completeness, quite detailed synopses of all the novels published thus far follow. If you haven't yet read the books but are planning to, the next bit will spoil them, so we suggest you skip it. If you fancy the books but are too lazy to actually read them, why not try Laughing Stock's Talking Books instead?

Red Dwarf – Infinity Welcomes Careful Drivers

In the latter part of the twenty-second century it has proven essential for humankind to look beyond Earth for valuable resources and to exploit the rest of the solar system – rich in mineral wealth. Technology, too, has advanced, to such an extent that death is no longer the impediment it once was; computers are able to project simulated holograms derived from the brain patterns of the dead. Unfortunately for the rank and file, the process is excessive in terms of both cost and energy; only the most essential members of the populace are resurrected as these impalpable beings.

After celebrating his birthday, with a bold attempt to complete a Monopoly Board pub-crawl around London, Liverpudlian Dave Lister wakes up in a McDonald's wearing a woman's pink crimplene hat and a pair of yellow fishing waders, with a passport in the name of Emily Berkenstein and, as if that wasn't bad enough, the burger bar just happens to be located on the Saturnian moon, Mimas.

Completely broke and without a work permit, Lister is forced into stealing taxis in a reckless attempt to earn enough money to buy a ticket home. Unfortunately, the small amount he saves by not paying rent – by living in a left-luggage locker – is either squandered on consolatory drink or forcibly taken by muggers. One fateful night, however, Lister has a brainwave: after picking up a fare wearing a false moustache and claiming to be Christopher Todhunter, an officer in the Space Corps, he decides to enlist.

Upon joining the Space Corps, Lister is posted aboard the mining ship *Red Dwarf* as a technician third class, the lowest rank in the Corps. However, Lister is not at all concerned with his lack of status. He doesn't intend to be around for long anyway. His plan is simple: the minute they get to Earth he'll jump ship and go AWOL. Unfortunately he had reckoned without a four-and-a-half-year round trip. Lister's bad luck doesn't end there: his bunkmate for the duration is none other than Arnold Rimmer, the badly disguised man he'd once taxied to a 'plasti-droid' brothel.

Rimmer is not exactly the most popular man aboard the vessel. He can count his friends on the fingers of one hand and still have five digits spare. His idea of a good night out is to spend it not ageing in a Stasis Booth. It had taken Rimmer six years to achieve the lowly rank of First Technician and so become the leader of Z Shift – an eleven-strong team responsible for routine maintenance, cleaning and sanitation – a squad from whom he commanded no respect whatsoever, least of all from the newest recruit, Dave Lister.

After several months of the same routine, life aboard *Red Dwarf* becomes mind-numbingly boring for Lister. Even the excessive drinking with Petersen, Selby and Chen in the Copacabana Hawaiian cocktail bar seems to lose some of its appeal. But one night he meets Third Console Officer Kristine Kochanski and immediately falls head over heels in love. A glorious, magical, passionate affair follows – lasting until Kochanski goes back to her old boyfriend, just over a month later.

Devastated, the lovelorn Lister concocts a scheme to avoid the rest of the voyage: buying a healthy pregnant show cat on the Uranian moon, Miranda, he is quickly summoned before the Captain for breaking quarantine regulations. The Captain, an American woman with the unfortunate name of Kirk, gives Lister two choices: hand over the cat or spend the rest of the trip in Stasis and forego three years' wages.

Three million years later the ship's computer Holly revives Lister from Stasis and informs him that his unavoidably extended sentence was due to a leak of Cadmium II radiation, which wiped out the rest of the crew and had until very recently been contaminating the ship. Lister promptly cracks up. A probability study conducted by the now erratic Holly reveals that Arnold Rimmer is the best person to keep Lister sane; Lister isn't at all convinced by the findings, but the computer proceeds to restore Rimmer as his hologramatic companion anyway.

Although, in Holly's not entirely reliable opinion, the likelihood of humanity still being around is slim, Lister elects to return to Earth, undertaking the journey in Stasis. The newly resurrected Rimmer doesn't relish the idea of spending the next few million years alone in space, nor does he fancy being turned off – after all, death may have thwarted his chances of promotion but it's all he's got. Fortunately, circumstances provide a reprieve from his potentially solitary existence.

Upon opening the radiation seals, Holly has discovered a non-human life form, and the task of investigation falls to Lister and Rimmer. Travelling down hundreds of floors of supplies, they first find ten floors completely devoid of their original contents and then discover a city composed of igloo-shaped buildings, constructed from some of the missing supplies. In this strange town they meet what looks exactly like a man wearing a neon pink suit. But he isn't a man at all: he's a cat, *the* Cat – the last surviving descendant of Lister's pet, Frankenstein. Safely sealed in the cargo hold, her kittens had bred and bred. It was a case of survival of the fittest and over the course of time the cats had evolved, *Felis erectus* was born followed, eventually, by *Felis sapiens*.

Though, by nature, the Cat is a self-centred egotist, Lister elects to take him into Stasis for the voyage home – they never reach the booths. While the Cat is reluctantly saying goodbye to his home-made collection of immaculately tailored suits and Lister bids farewell to his bunkmate, *Red Dwarf* breaks the light barrier; images from the future appear before the crew. A shocked Rimmer believes he has witnessed the death of his companion, but an aged Dave Lister materialises and reveals that it is in fact one of his six grandchildren that will die. Following instructions from his older self, Lister hastens to the medical unit, where he sees another future echo of himself, complete with twin babies. Realising that it will be interesting to find out how he will eventually get them or, more accurately, who with, Lister decides to wait around and see.

Eons earlier the *Nova 5*, a spaceship on an advertising mission for Coca-Cola, had crash-landed on an unnamed world. The responsibility for the accident lay solely with the ship's service mechanoid Kryten; taking enormous pleasure from his cleaning duties, the conscientious mechanoid had given the on-board computer a good wash with soapy water. The only survivors had been the Captain, Yvette Richards, and two other female officers, Kirsty Fantozi and Elaine Schuman.

A distress call from Kryten is received on *Red Dwarf*. The encouraging message, with its prospect of some female company at last, prompts Lister, Cat and Rimmer to get kitted out in their finery and mount a rescue, but it's all in vain – the girls have been dead for nearly three million years. It takes a while to convince Kryten of the fact, but when it does finally sink in, the inconsolable, guilt-ridden android activates his shutdown disc.

In the week that followed, the wreckage of the *Nova 5* is transported aboard *Red Dwarf* – complete with the essential supplies that were still on the ship. While Lister endeavours to repair Kryten, Rimmer discovers that, although the personality discs of the crew are all corrupted to some extent, the *Nova 5*'s Hologram simulation suite is fully operational. He takes the opportunity to create a new hologram anyway – a duplicate of himself. Now that he has found the perfect companion and doesn't have to put up with Lister any more, Rimmer decides to move in with his double.

Once repaired and functional, Kryten explains that the *Nova 5*'s quantum-drive duality jump could get them back to Earth within three months – providing there was enough uranium 233 available for fuel. Reading up on the subject, Lister discovers that the fuel can be synthesised from the abundantly available thorium 232. Lister, the Cat and Kryten set off, along with twelve skutters, to do some thorium mining on a nearby moon while, on *Red Dwarf* the two Rimmers oversee the remaining eighty-four Skutters in the job of welding back together the two halves of the *Nova 5*. Neither task runs as smoothly as it ought to: the Cat puts in around fifteen minutes' work per day – between naps and meals. Kryten on the other hand is a great help as long as his duties require nothing more responsible than making tea and sandwiches. Back on *Red Dwarf* the two Rimmers are beginning to fall out – even he doesn't like himself very much. They succeed in breaking the *Nova 5* into three pieces before finally restoring it to its proper, single piece construction.

Returning after three months of solid mining, Lister is shocked to discover that the Rimmers have actually completed their work and the *Nova 5* is in one piece; though arriving at its current state *has* been at the expense of most of the skutters. By now the Rimmers actively loathe each other; the copy believes the original has been changed, for the worse, by his association with Lister. It's just as well that it's possible for only one hologram to make the trip back to Earth and Lister must decide which one. Leaving the choice to fate, he tosses a coin; the original Rimmer loses. Lister, however, erases the copy – but not before coaxing, from the first Rimmer, the hugely embarrassing tale of the time he sent back his gazpacho soup to be warmed.

Earth: two years later. Dave Lister has at last found happiness in the peaceful American town of Bedford Falls; the others are doing well for themselves too. Rimmer is the third-richest man on the planet. His wife, Juanita, is the most beautiful woman – true, she is unfaithful and temperamental, but he loves her anyway – and, thanks to a time machine developed by his company, his friends include Julius Caesar and Napoleon Bonaparte. Elsewhere, on an island off the coast of Denmark, the Cat has all the fish, milk and scanty-armour-clad Valkyries he could ever need.

Despite having everything he ever wanted from life, Lister is convinced that something is amiss. It's all too good to be true. His wife – supposedly a descendant of the original – is identical to Kristine Kochanski, his two sons change each other's nappies and Bedford Falls is indistinguishable from the town of the same name featured in his favourite film *It's a Wonderful Life*. His suspicions are confirmed by the painful messages that appear on his arms, spelling out 'DYING' and 'U=BTL'. For the past two years, he realises, he has been living in a fantasy.

Searching out his crewmates, Lister assures them that their

lives are unreal, but it takes the arrival of Kryten for the truth to be fully discovered. The mechanoid explains that all was set for the voyage home in *Nova 5*, or would have been if the Cat hadn't gone missing. He was eventually found linked up to *Better Than Life* – an illegal, addictive game, which utilises hallucinogenic brain implants to create an authentic yet totally imagined environment. Lister had gone in to pull the Cat out; Rimmer had gone in to pull them both out; they had all become game heads. Kryten had reluctantly burnt the messages into Lister's arms to make him aware of his situation and had then gone into the game himself.

Now, fully cognisant of their potentially fatal predicament, all they have to do is get out of the game, and leaving the game is the easiest thing in the world: all the player has to do is want to. But, as its name suggests, the game is Better Than Life.

Better Than Life

A couple of years have passed, the crew are still trapped within the game. Kryten too has succumbed, the temptation of infinite numbers of dirty dishes to wash proving irresistible to a cleaning mechanoid. Lister continues to lead a contented existence with Kristine Kochanski in the fictional town in Bedford Falls. For the Cat a life of eating, preening, cruelty to animals and, of course, constant sex with his economically dressed Valkyries remains indispensable. Meanwhile, in Rimmer's fantasy, the Brazilian Bombshell Juanita has been passed over for the more homely charms possessed by Helen.

Back in reality, Holly's condition has deteriorated – he has become computer senile. To ease his loneliness he finds a companion in the shape of Talkie Toaster – a cheap novelty belonging to Lister, with a degree of artificial intelligence and an obsession for making toast. Reading Holly's manual – which the computer can not now understand – the Toaster discovers a way to intensify his intelligence, while at the same time reducing his operational lifespan; because of his eagerness to be clever again and his current lack of brain power Holly agrees to undergo the intelligence compression process. The procedure is successful – after a fashion. The computer's IQ rises to 12,368, but his running time is drastically reduced to 3.45 minutes. To conserve his precious remaining moments Holly shuts down *Red Dwarf*'s engines, then himself.

In the game salvation was at hand from an unlikely source. Rimmer's psyche decides to make things unpleasant for him: bankruptcy soon follows, his 'Solidgram' body is repossessed and he is sent to prison in the form of a soundwave. Fortunately Rimmer manages to escape in the body of Trixie La Bouche, a prostitute. In turn he finds the others, and his presence corrupts the fantasies of both Lister and the Cat. With nothing left to lose they finally decide to leave the game – along with Kryten, who had eventually managed to drag himself away from the washing-up.

Aboard *Red Dwarf* life is perfect – too perfect. Not only have Rimmer, Kochanski and Petersen survived in Stasis, but there are ice cubes in the ice-making compartment of the fridge. Lister surmises correctly that the game is not quite finished. This discovery induces Better Than Life's designer, Dennis McBean, to make an appearance and offer the crew the opportunity of a replay. They decline the invitation – this time it really is Game Over.

Life is rather less than perfect aboard the real *Red Dwarf*. The years spent in the game have taken their toll on Lister and Cat. Their wasted bodies are put into medi-suits to recover. Much to Holly's annoyance he is temporarily switched back on in order to reveal why the ship is operating on emergency power and not moving. Rimmer and Kryten realise that having the ship up and running would be quite convenient, as a rogue planet is on a collision course with it and is due to hit *Red Dwarf* in about three weeks – the length of time it will take to start up the engines.

Bemoaning the lack of a blast-off button, Rimmer begins work on his half of the procedure. Determined to complete the task well within the allotted time he succeeds only in destroying forty skutters in the piston towers. The only alternative now seems to be to abandon ship.

Kryten thinks it only fair that Holly be brought back on line for his remaining minute or so – quite a fortuitous move as it turns out, for the computer has a plan.

Using the shuttle craft, *Starbug*, a thermonuclear device can be fired into a nearby sun, creating a solar flare that will knock a planet out of its orbit and drive it into the rogue. Lister sees it as playing pool with planets and, believing Holly to have devised a total mis-cue, elects to take the shot himself.

Accompanied by Rimmer in *Starbug*, Lister sets off to save *Red Dwarf* and, surprisingly, his eccentric trick shot actually works. Unfortunately the small shuttle craft encounters the slipstream of one of the planets, the force of which causes it to crash-land. On the frozen world Lister is without warmth and his food supply consists of little more than a tin of dog meat and a pot noodle. Not all his luck is bad though: Rimmer's remote relay fails and the hologram is returned to *Red Dwarf*.

On the mining ship time is behaving oddly: in one part of the ship it's Monday, in another Friday. The source of the trouble is found to be a black hole; although the newly restarted engines are set on full reverse thrust, *Red Dwarf* is being pulled inexorably into it. Holly is reactivated again but can offer no help on this occasion as his terminals are operating in different time zones. The Toaster, however, claims to have a solution to their problem which he will reveal providing everyone eats a great deal of toast.

Meanwhile Lister is having problems of his own: the ice has melted and the planet seems intent on killing him. Wearing a makeshift metal suit he survives a downpour of acid rain, leaps over gaping earthquake-induced chasms and finally avoids suffocation in a torrent of oil before realising – after seeing Mount Rushmore – that the planet is in fact Earth.

Millions of years before, the rest of the solar system had been colonised; Earth had been abandoned and converted into an enormous garbage dump. Eventually a methane explosion had set off a chain reaction which tore the planet out of its orbit and sent it off into deep space.

The planet seems appeased by Lister's promise to make amends for his ancestors' transgression and with the help of the planet's current inhabitants – a colony of eight-foot cockroaches – the last human being begins to set his world to rights.

Travelling at the speed of light, *Red Dwarf* enters the black hole; many of the ship's propulsion jets are destroyed, but enough survive to maintain light speed and carry the vessel through the omni-zone – where the gateways to the six other universes converge at the centre of a singularity – beyond the event horizon and back out into the universe.

With *Red Dwarf* safely navigated through the black hole it only remains to find and rescue Lister. Rimmer and the Cat set off in the transport craft, *White Giant*, while Kryten and the Toaster take *Blue Midget*. It doesn't take long before the remains of *Starbug* are discovered, along with acres of farmed fields. An impatient Lister is there too: instead of spending a few weeks on the planet as the others had thought, thanks to the time-dilation effects of the black hole, he has been waiting for thirty-four years. During the time spent on his home planet Lister has come up with an idea: they'll tow Earth back to its rightful place in the solar system.

A message from Kryten is greeted with a certain amount of surprise: apparently he and the Toaster have found Lister too. The real Dave Lister warns that his double is in fact a polymorph, a shape-changing, genetically engineered mutant which feeds on emotions; he instructs them to initiate the auto-destruct on *Blue Midget* and abandon ship. Unfortunately, by now they are in space en route to *Red Dwarf*, and the polymorph is showing its true colours. Before the creature is able to strangle Kryten, Talkie Toaster decapitates it with a toasted metal ashtray.

Back on *Red Dwarf*, Lister is puzzled over why the polymorph didn't feed and was so easy to kill. Taking no chances, he decides to go ahead with the destruction of *Blue Midget*. He was right to be worried: the polymorph had reproduced itself, and the second mutant was attempting to find a shape in which to escape from the shuttle craft before it exploded. In the form of a light beam it sped across space back to the *Red Dwarf*.

As Lister prepares to eat his first shami kebab in thirty-four years the polymorph attacks – first as part of his meal, then as his boxer shorts. In the guise of a rat it feeds off Lister's fear and then completes its meal transformed into a hideous armour-plated creature with rather a lot of teeth.

The now fearless Lister decides to take on the polymorph single-handed. His shipmates, opting for discretion, choose to sit it out on Garbage World until the emotion-deprived creature starves to death. They get no further than the supply deck. Imagining that the shape-changer is lurking in the shadows, Kryten and the Cat fire off heat-seeking laser bolts from their bazookoids – but the heat that they actually locate is emitted by the Cat himself. Managing to evade the bolts of energy, Cat succeeds in trapping them in a lift. But his luck ends there and, under the pretence of being a beautiful woman, the polymorph is easily able to flatter the narcissistic animal and steal his vanity.

As Arnold Rimmer, the mutant blames Kryten for the Cat's fate and is consequently able to make a meal of the android's guilt. Finally, by entering the hologram's personality disc, it is able to feast on Rimmer's anger.

The emotionally crippled crew are unable to concoct much of a plan to combat the polymorph. The Toaster, volunteering to become their leader, only provokes Kryten into putting him in the waste-disposal. Lister, fearless as ever, is still convinced that a direct approach is best. The mutant is easily tracked down, but assumes the form of a lamp post, against which the bazookoids prove ineffective.

Eventually, when the polymorph begins to transform, Lister launches himself against the creature, but is easily tossed aside. The others attempt to run away. Seeing his only escape in an old lift shaft, Kryten inadvertently unleashes the heat-seeking bazookoid bolts and this time they find their intended target and the polymorph is destroyed.

Dave Lister is dead, the result of a heart attack. His body is placed in a coffin – along with a chicken vindaloo, eighteen cans of lager and a photograph of Kristine Kochanski – then blasted into space.

Reactivated to be given the sad news Holly, once again, has a solution: the casket must be retrieved then taken through the black hole into the omni-zone to a planet in Universe 3 – a universe where time runs backwards.

Lister wakes surprised to find himself restored to life, albeit a life that is in reverse. A newspaper message instructs him to meet the rest of the crew in thirty-six years' time. In the meantime he has his past to look forward to and somehow Holly has arranged for it to be spent in the company of Kristine Kochanski.

Last Human

For crimes against the GELF state, Dave Lister is sentenced to the personal hell of Cyberia, on Lotomi 5. He really shouldn't have worn that tie in court!

Meanwhile, Dave Lister has been awakened from twenty years of deep sleep, following his rescue from Backwards World. He spent thirty-six years on that strange planet, in the company of Kristine Kochanski, and he is pleased to find that she is still around, particularly as she greets him naked to show off her new appendectomy scar.

Having once more traversed the omni-zone, *Starbug* is heading back towards *Red Dwarf* when a familiar ship is encountered: *Starbug*. The crew board the identical vessel, and it is the Cat who first notices that something is amiss when he discovers what looks remarkably like his own severed head. Rimmer is found next, deader than usual, then Kryten and finally Kochanski, who is alive but barely. Only Lister is unaccounted for and, before she dies, the ersatz Kochanski makes our Lister promise to find his alternate self. The crew realise that a wrong turning through the omni-zone has brought them to a parallel reality.

The most logical place to begin the hunt for the other Lister is on Blerios 15, a nearby asteroid populated by a series of pig-based GELFs who seem rather fond of copulation. Upon arrival, the *Starbug* crew are quickly captured by the Blerions and charged with violating their airspace. This serious crime warrants a large fine: 200 barrels of oil or four millilitres of sperm. The latter, a useful commodity where 99 per cent of the male population is sterile, is the one thing that Lister can provide. It occurs to Kryten that there is a war going on in this region of space: a battle for survival between the various GELF tribes, none of whom have been engineered with procreation in mind.

On the way back to *Starbug*, Lister realises that he has been recognised by one of the GELFs – another lead to his other self. The GELF attempts to run but is soon caught and brought down by the speedy Cat. The terrified pig creature admits to knowing Lister and to getting him into trouble with the authorities. He suggests they continue their search at the Forum of Justice on Arranguu 12.

For reasons of safety it is Kryten who makes the trip to the Forum of Justice. After making his way through a mob of angry demonstrators, the mechanoid confronts the Regulator, from whom he learns that Lister's crimes are more serious than expected. As well as destroying the asteroid Cyrius 3, and looting and plundering his way across the entire belt, he was responsible for many deaths, including that of the Regulator. Kryten is a little confused by this, as the Regulator appears to be very much alive – and, when he pursues the matter, he discovers that Lister's crimes have been predicted by GELF mystics and are destined to be committed in the future. On Arranguu 12, the so-called system of justice prevents crime by punishing the 'guilty' before the crime has happened.

Kryten learns where Lister is being held and then leaves, now realising just what the demonstration outside is about. Now that he knows the alternate Lister has been sent to Cyberia without actually committing any crime, he starts to formulate an escape plan.

In Cyberhell, the other Dave Lister wakes to find that all is not as hellish as he'd expected; in fact he appears to be in a very nice villa by the sea. But before he can begin to enjoy it, he discovers he's in the wrong cyberscape. This personal hell belongs to Capote, a hologram who hates champagne and Spanish architecture. The mistake is quickly rectified.

Meanwhile the *Starbug* crew enlist the aid of the Kinitawowi, a nomadic tribe of apelike GELFs with useful items for trade. Unfortunately, their leader is offended by Lister's offer of sperm and decides that the human must show his respect by marrying his daughter. Very, very reluctantly – and in order to obtain a bunch of ramshackle droids and an electricity-destroying computer virus – Lister agrees. The relationship is doomed to failure, however, and, partway through his bride's attempt to consummate the marriage, he makes a run for it.

On Lotomi 5, a two-pronged assault on Cyberia is put into operation, with Cat piloting *Starbug*. The first stage – to load the Oblivion Virus into Cyberia's power grid – is down to Kryten and Kochanski, not so ably assisted by Rimmer. But, as Rimmer's old girlfriend Yvonne McGruder once said of him, he is a brave man trapped inside the body of a coward. Despite the intervention of Cyberian guards, the task is duly accomplished.

The next phase of the operation is a carefully timed commando-style parachute drop into Cyberia itself, with Lister heading a team of clapped-out mechanoids (Rimmer couldn't take part owing to his unfortunate parachute allergy). Things don't go too badly initially, but then the lights go out. One of the unforeseen effects of the Oblivion Virus is the loss of gravity – a big enough problem in itself, but when Lister finds himself immersed in the floating pink liquid that once formed the huge inmate-enclosing cyberlake, the outcome is fatal. Not for the first time, Lister dies.

When he opens his eyes, he notices something quite familiar about the man beating on his chest: it's himself. Although he's alive, thanks to the other Lister, there's a distinct possibility that it may be a temporary reprieve, what with their being some distance above the ground and with the gravity about to come on just as soon as the antidote disk is booted . . .

Gravity is restored and the two Listers fall. As they watch many of their fellow inmates hit the ground in bloody messes, they hope that enough of the pink fluid will have descended before them to break their fall. They are lucky up to a point, but our Lister suffers a badly twisted ankle. As a consequence, he is partly reliant on his other self – and the excessively violent manner in which his doppelgänger expedites their exit makes Lister wonder if this whole venture hasn't been misguided. Ultimately, he is forced to knock his double unconscious to prevent a totally unnecessary and potentially suicidal clash with a battalion of Cyberguards.

Away from Cyberia, Lister questions his other self, now securely bound, about the box of belongings he was so keen to collect on his way out. He discovers, to his horror, that it contains Kryten's scythed-off arm, the hand still clutching a piece of paper on which are written galactic co-ordinates . . . but for what? Before Lister can find out why his other self killed his crewmates (for indeed he did), *Starbug* appears. With this, the alternate Lister throws himself into the campfire, burning through his bonds and charring his flesh in the process. Then he descends upon his rescuer-turned-captor.

The battle is short and decisive, and ultimately it is the quite-badly injured evil Lister who returns to *Starbug* and is nursed by Kochanski. Once he is fully recovered, he intends to receive even closer attention from her . . . Meanwhile, Kryten's research has revealed that the mysterious co-ordinates mark the location of the *Mayflower*, a starship on a terraforming mission to the Andromeda galaxy.

Long ago, in a dimension far away, World Council President John Milhous Nixon learnt that thermonuclear tests close to the sun had fatally affected the star, and that the only long-term hope for humanity's survival lay in relocation to another galaxy. Unfortunately, the planet chosen for humankind's new home was awash with molten lava. A virus expert, Doctor Longman, was sent on a mission to make the place hospitable, along with his two clone assistants, Doctor Longman and Doctor Longman. They were accompanied by sundry GELFs and by star soldier Michael R. McGruder, who hoped that this mission might present him with an opportunity to find his heroic father, missing somewhere in space: Arnold J. Rimmer. But a mutiny en route to humanity's new home caused the ship to be pulled into the omni-zone. The GELFs left to take up residence in the asteroid belt – but the real significance of these events becomes clear when Kryten discovers that the ship was carrying GOD: the Geonome for All DNA. Anyone with access to this could rewrite his own genetic code and make himself immortal. And (the fake) Lister suggests that they should obtain it for themselves.

Meanwhile, the real Lister is back in Cyberia, but this time as a prisoner, charged with being responsible for a mass break-out. At least he has survived being whacked over the head with a spade and being buried alive by his lookalike! After five months of an eighteen-year sentence in Cyberhell (a depressing, soul-destroying artificial reality), he gets an offer.

Planets from this region of space are being sucked through the omni-zone and destroyed. The GELFs have been trying to terraform a world that can resist these pressures and emerge unscathed into another universe. They have been utilising body donors from Cyberia – donors who have lost their individuality to become part of an intelligent gestalt, capable of controlling and vastly speeding up a planet's evolutionary process. The planet is now ready, but more of Cyberia's inmates are required to test that it is safe. The first test ship has failed to return, but Lister is given the opportunity to escape Cyberhell by joining the crew of the second.

Before leaving, he is permitted to spend one night with a symbi-morph, a shape-changing GELF able to hook into its host's subconscious and thus fulfil its sexual desires. Unfortunately, the symbi-morphs are all out – except for one who intends to save that kind of stuff for her boyfriend. However, Lister is able to persuade Reketrebn to help him escape. With the symbi-morph's unique abilities, this proves to be a piece of cake – and the pair are able to stow away on what they believe is a supply ship heading for Arranguu 12. It isn't. It is the ship on which he was supposed to be leaving anyway, and its destination is the gestalt's planet.

Starbug has embarked upon the long journey to find the *Mayflower* and the molten planet to which it took its payload, and the crew have gone into deep sleep. Kryten is revived before the others and, making a routine check of the medicomp's biodata, realises that they've picked up the wrong Lister. Consulting the files from the derelict, alternate *Starbug*, the mechanoid is confronted with a long list of misdemeanours. But, before he can finish reading them, he is interrupted by their perpetrator.

As Lister's doppelgänger attacks Kryten, an alarm sounds. *Starbug* is under attack. It's the Kinitawowi, and they want the errant Lister back to complete his nuptial agreement. Kryten is only too happy to oblige, and he hands over the evil Lister. His pleasure, however, is quickly tempered by the realisation that *Starbug* is on fire and about to plummet into the molten planet.

Cat, Rimmer and Kochanski wake to find themselves in the middle of what Kryten reassuringly describes as a death dive. Even with the Cat at the controls there is no way to prevent *Starbug* from hitting the lava. The heat is unbearable as the small ship ploughs through the molten rock. But then, 500 fathoms below the surface, *Starbug* emerges into a normal ocean.

For four days, the crew search for an escape route, but to no avail. However, they do eventually find the *Mayflower*. Their psi-scan reveals the ship to be deserted, but the device has been known to give inaccurate readings. They board the vessel and search for the terraforming virus, which should eat away a path through the lava. Kryten and Kochanski discover thousands of vials of different designer viruses, but it takes them over an hour to identify just one.

Meanwhile, Cat and Rimmer find the sleeping domes that once contained the various GELFs. In one of these, they find a jacket belonging to a marine named McGruder. Rimmer always hated marines, but the name reminds him of his old girlfriend and how a misunderstanding brought an end to their relationship. Another corridor brings them into a computer-filled room, where Cat's attempt not to touch anything results in Rimmer being transformed into a chicken by a DNA modifier. Four hours and almost three hundred genetic reshapings later, Kryten returns Rimmer to normal; later, he decides to use the machine himself. He will become a human being.

Meanwhile, Lister's ship arrives on the planet of the gestalt and its workings immediately die, rendering it useless. Separating from the rest of the volunteers, Lister and Reketrebn make camp for the night. The following morning, they find the ship destroyed. It is surrounded by the bodies of many of the other volunteers, and it appears that they have all murdered each other. As if that were not enough of a shock for one morning, Lister then comes face to face with another human – Lieutenant Colonel Michael R. McGruder.

Elsewhere, Kryten and Kochanski's viral research is coming along and they've discovered that there are both negative and positive types of virus, the latter causing infections that actually improve the human condition. One such virus is *Felicitus populi*, the symptom of which is good luck. With a shot of this, Kochanski is immediately able to find the virus that will get them through the lava. In the thirty-six hours remaining before the lava becomes traversable, *Starbug* is packed with salvage, and Kryten takes the opportunity to fulfil his dream and become human.

Lister is alarmed to discover that McGruder's father is Rimmer. Having been regaled by tales of his heroic feats, McGruder is convinced that his father is the greatest soldier who ever lived. Believing they'll never see the others again, Lister decides not to disabuse him of this delusion – and anyway, there is the more important matter of the Rage to contend with. The Rage, Lister learns, is the gestalt being formed from all those falsely imprisoned victims, now furious at the injustice that led to its creation. All those with whom it comes into contact are consumed by the same fury.

The only way to survive its passing, McGruder has discovered, is to form the Circle of Sacer Facere – then only one will be sacrificed to it. Along with McGruder, Reketrebn and a party of GELFs, Lister forms the circle and waits for the Rage to hit. When it does, he feels a wave of anger flood over him: overwhelming feelings of being wronged, betrayed – wanting to kill. After it is over, one of the GELFs lies dead. But the Rage has passed on.

The now human Kryten and his shipmates return to the *Mayflower*, for one last looting expedition. It is now that Kochanski finds three occupied Stasis pods, all apparently containing Professor Longman. Her decision to reactivate the pods turns out to be a mistake. Although retaining Longman's brain and face, the things that inhabit them have been genetically modified so many times that their cells have given up. Three misshapen, animal-like creatures emerge, hungry for DNA.

Before he makes a hasty exit with his companions, Kryten – never entirely happy with the facilities on his human body – elects to return to his mechanoid state. Unfortunately one of the Longmans has beaten him to it and used the mechanoid geonome for himself. Even so, his close proximity to the control panel enables Kryten to trap two of the Longmans within the glass cylinders used during the modification process. The third, in a leopard-like form, closes in on Kochanski. But, once again, the luck virus proves invaluable and she manages to incapacitate it with a well-aimed elastic band. Kryten follows this up with a well-aimed cylinder.

Heading out through the lava-turned-water, the *Starbug* crew learn of Lister's escape from Cyberia. Another shot of the luck virus enables them to guess his whereabouts. Unfortunately, the gestalt planet is thirty-two weeks away at current speed. But fortunately, Cat guesses the equation for a hyperdrive and they're off.

On the surface of the gestalt planet, McGruder is finally introduced to his father. He faints. So does Rimmer. However, there is little time to play happy families, as *Starbug* has become inoperable and the Rage will be back within the hour.

The reunited *Starbug* crew take cover. Rimmer takes this chance to tell McGruder the truth about his lack of heroism, while Kryten concocts a plan. All he needs to do is load the Oblivion Virus into his own network, meet the Rage before it reaches the others and contaminate it, sacrificing himself in the process. His plan never comes to fruition – someone locks him in *Starbug*'s storage vault.

As he tries to come to terms with the fact that his father is a complete zero, McGruder is interrupted by a garrotte around his neck. The other Lister is back. Seeing the attack, Rimmer is in a position to pick up a rad gun and actually become the hero his son believed in for so long. But he hesitates too long and is overpowered by Lister, who grabs the gun for himself.

In the storage vault, Kryten discovers four dead Kinitowawi. They had never even left the ship with their prisoner. A dispirited Rimmer is pushed inside with them. However, the mechanoid has another plan: Rimmer's light bee, set on a timer, could be pushed down the oxy-generation outlet pipe and the hologram reactivated once outside – provided the bee doesn't roll into the oxy-generation unit itself, that is. With extreme reluctance, Rimmer takes this chance of redemption and, seconds later, he is outside.

The evil Lister, meanwhile, wants *Starbug*'s solar-powered escape pod. Kochanski declines his offer to accompany him, which only gives him cause to shoot his counterpart in the groin, rendering him sterile. Kochanski still won't go. The evil Lister attempts to kill her, but she uses the luck virus to make his gun jam. It's only a matter of time before her luck will run out, but help is at hand. From out of the sky comes a fiery figure. It's Rimmer, wearing a jet-powered astro paint-stripper. A fight ensues, with the other Lister firing off rad bolts and Rimmer shooting jets of flame. Michael McGruder watches with pride as his old man loops the loop through the air, thoroughly enjoying himself. But the Rage is almost upon them and the evil Lister knows that his only means of escaping is with the astro stripper. He shoots off a rad bolt and hits Rimmer's light bee full on. Its smouldering remains fall to the ground.

The evil Lister is dragged into the circle of Sacer Facere, but grabs the luck virus to ensure that he will not be marked for death. It is a mistake. As the Rage enters them, all in the circle desperately want to be possessed by its awesome power. The evil Lister is 'lucky'. His wish is granted and he dies.

McGruder picks up the battered light bee, which still has a weak signal. In Morse code, Rimmer tells them that he will use his remaining power to transmit the Oblivion Virus into the Rage. And that's what he does. The emerald planet is, at last, pulled through the omni-zone into another dimension. For three weeks, Lister and the others take refuge in the caverns away from the gravitational hammering it takes on the way.

When they emerge, it is to a hospitable world, with signs of new vegetation beginning to show. It would, thinks Lister, be an ideal world on which to raise a family. But the rad gun has put paid to that. However, Kochanski still has a vial of *Felicitus populi*, and with any luck . . .

Backwards

A reminder: Lister has died of old age. His crewmates took him to a version of Earth where time runs backwards, and arranged to meet him thirty-six years later in a souvenir shop near Niagara Falls.

Thirty-six years later:

Two hours late, or possibly two hours early, Rimmer, Cat and Kryten arrive at the rendezvous point on Backwards Earth to meet Lister. He isn't there. In a shopping mall, Kryten is alarmed to spot a police photofit of Cat's face on a TV newsflash, quickly followed by one of Lister; the only word he is able to make out is 'murder'. However, the Cat cannot be the murder victim: he would have arrived dead, were that the case. Whatever has happened, or is going to happen, they need to find Lister and get off this world before the planetary conjunction makes that journey impossible, only a few hours hence.

Lister is sitting in the back of a police van. Having spent eight years in prison, he is now at the beginning of his sentence and is looking forward to finding out what his crime will be.

Suddenly, there is a disturbance in the mall: Lister bursts in, being unbeaten up by several policemen. A reverse chase follows, which ends up with the reunited Dwarfers careering wildly in a stolen car up a mountain road in reverse. To Lister's delight, *Starbug* is quickly relocated and he can finally escape from a world on which he never really felt he belonged.

There were some good times here of course: the years spent with Krissie, and their two children coming home to live with them and growing younger. But then his twin sons had gone back into their mother and eventually he and Krissie were introduced and she promptly left him. After that, things went downhill, particularly when he spent years inside for a murder he didn't know if he'd committed or not.

Lister's joy at finding *Starbug* is short-lived, however. A fuel canister has been purloined by a local pig-fancying hillbilly to make a still, and all the landing jets have been removed. With only five and a half hours remaining until leaving becomes impossible, the crew decide to split into two groups to find the engines and reattach them. Rimmer and Kryten find one, but it's rusted to hell. Returning to *Starbug* for a digging tool, Kryten spots a pickaxe handle but stumbles. As he stands, he finds that his hands are covered in messy goo, then he notices that the pickaxe is buried in the chest of one of their hillbilly neighbours. This, he realises, must be the murder for which Lister went down. As Rimmer appears on the scene, the body returns to life with a horrifying death rattle. Panicking, Kryten helpfully pulls the pickaxe from the man's chest, but the ungrateful mountain man begins to attack the mechanoid. Once he's safely behind a bush, and the hillbilly has forgotten all about him, Kryten replays these events in his mind and, reversing them, realises that he's just killed somebody . . .

Lister and Cat find another corroded jet. With very little

help from the now suicidal Kryten, it is fitted to the underside of *Starbug*, which seems to have a lot of recently welded plates on it. With only this one landing jet attached, *Starbug* attempts its last-minute takeoff, even though Kryten is nowhere to be found. Feeling himself unworthy, he has decided to stay behind. But, from the ground, the mechanoid watches as the small ship spins out of control. Desperately wanting to help, he leaps for a landing leg as it passes overhead, but his reckless action only makes things worse. With the smallest of bumps, *Starbug* lands. All aboard are unhurt, but the flight window has been missed and the next won't come around for another ten years. Ironically, the crew realise that they don't need the landing jets to take off, as they should reattach themselves as they do – in fact, they'll have to remove the ship's single engine and rebury it, hoping it will unrust enough to be functional by the time of the next flight window. Not only that, but they'll eventually have to unrepair *Starbug*'s undercarriage too.

Meanwhile, in another dimension:

Project Wildfire was the code-name given to a spacecraft that could theoretically break the light-speed barrier. Admiral Peter Tranter, the man in charge of the project, faces a dilemma: the Wildfire ship has returned from its inaugural test flight damaged beyond repair, its pilot a charred corpse. But, significantly, it has returned three days before it set off. A ship that can travel through time is good; one that kills its pilot is not so good.

As he looks at his own blackened remains, Ace Rimmer knows that something is not quite right. Perhaps the black box recorder will provide a clue, before he climbs back into the cockpit to face certain death. Scrutinising the flight video, he and Spanners Lister notice the date: 21 March, the day the ship was recovered. This information leads Ace to the conclusion that Wildfire hasn't broken the time barrier at all, but rather that it has the ability to traverse the reality barrier. He postulates that there are an infinite number of alternate realities, each created whenever a life-affecting decision is made. He believes Wildfire was destroyed because it entered a reality too close to the one it departed, and he is certain he can compensate and make a successful test run in Wildfire, albeit one from which there will be no return.

Back in our own dimension, on *Red Dwarf*, Holly has been having problems. He has been able to increase his (previously curtailed) runtime, thanks to a trip to the Backwards universe, but once back in his own universe, he had to reduce his IQ to prolong his life span further. He has done this several times now, until he can no longer work out what IQ means. As he ponders the reason for the number of layers of skin on an onion, a ship lands in *Red Dwarf*'s docking bay.

Ten years later/earlier: Lister and the others have been living in the mountains, regurgitating various small furry animals and keeping out of sight (except for the occasion when Cat, aged fifteen, had sex for the first time, becoming a virgin in the process). The act of using a toilet here does not even bear thinking about, and they are all relieved as the time to depart finally approaches. The flight window is open once more, and *Starbug*'s gaping rents have become shiny and started to suck up smoke. As takeoff approaches, the hole in the ship's belly glows red. Once they're airborne, two landing jets reattach themselves to the burning ship, followed by bits of shielding. Finally a heat-seeking missile, presumably activated by *Starbug*'s unique signals, seals the hull, attaches the last jet and extinguishes the flames.

Spaceborne again for the first time in a decade, *Starbug* sets off to find *Red Dwarf*, but the mining ship is not where it should be. Kryten notices a large amount of debris spread out across several kilometres of space. On closer inspection, it seems to be the components of some great machine; in fact, the mess is Holly. Donning jet packs, Lister and Kryten retrieve as much of the jumble of wires and circuit boards as they can and haul it aboard *Starbug*. Rimmer is more than a little peeved to learn that he will have to be turned off if enough power is to be generated to revive the computer. Brought on line for only a few moments, Holly is able to name those responsible for the theft of *Red Dwarf*: agonoids.

Agonoids were devised by humankind as mechanical

killers devoid of morality or mercy. They took exception to being eventually decommissioned and turned on their creators. The heavily outnumbered agonoids lost the ensuing war, but a few thousand survivors escaped, taking with them a burning desire for revenge. Now, the remainder of the agonoid population are on *Red Dwarf*, turning it into a huge torture chamber and fighting among themselves for the privilege of being the One – the agonoid with the right to slowly and painfully kill the last living human being, who just happens to be Dave Lister.

The options open to Lister and the others are limited: there isn't enough power to get to a habitable planetoid, so they can either drift helplessly in space or attempt to recapture *Red Dwarf* from the virtually indestructible killing machines. Against Rimmer's better judgment, the latter plan is adopted. But, before it is put into operation, something collides with the vessel, throwing its crew violently to the floor and causing the hull to split. With the oxygen being sucked through the gap and Lister's unconscious form being pulled ever nearer to it, Kryten quickly finds something to plug the hole: himself.

This accident has been caused, inadvertently, by Ace Rimmer, his transdimensional ship having been drawn to his counterpart in this reality. Kryten is naturally confused at his first sight of this new, good-natured, handsome Rimmer, and despite their predicament he finds he's suddenly quite relaxed. Realising that the mechanoid might be dragged out of the ship if the hull splits further, Ace – despite a fractured arm – welds a girder across Kryten's chest. That done, he proceeds to give medical attention to Lister and Cat, while explaining the circumstances of his arrival. Rimmer, who has managed to provide no help whatsoever, is unimpressed.

Back on *Red Dwarf*, the cleverest and most inventive of the agonoids, christened Djuhn'Keep (because humans thought such insulting names amusing), has devised the Death Wheel. Basically, this is a series of ever more deadly corridors leading into the Hub of Pain – a dome-shaped room filled with every conceivable piece of equipment with which it is possible to cause pain to a human. The idea is that Lister will be trapped at the Hub, and the agonoids will compete to get through the Wheel. The first one to reach him has the pleasure of torturing and killing him. The trouble is, Djuhn is just about clapped out. Only his inventiveness has thus far saved him from being attacked by the other agonoids and dismantled for spare parts. In a fair fight, he would have no chance of becoming the One. But agonoids don't fight fairly.

First, Djuhn acquires some new parts. He selects M'Aiden Ty-One, tough even by agonoid standards, as a suitable donor. Substituting a drunkenness-inducing scramble card for his own creation, the Apocalypse Virus, he watches as M'Aiden's brain is wiped clean. Then, as the agonoids all gather for the grand opening of the Hub of Pain, he activates the Wheel of Death prematurely. Those who survive it are ejected into space, leaving Djuhn'Keep as the sole survivor of the agonoid race. Or so he believes.

Lister decides it is time to get Kryten loose. He suits up and spacewalks around to where a mechanical backside is protruding from *Starbug*'s hull. As he fires up his laser cutter, he notices that there is something unfamiliar about the rear end (not that he is an expert). Suddenly, a robotic hand grabs his throat . . .

Pizzak'Rapp can't believe his luck. One minute, he was floating through space; the next, he was grabbing hold of a cord linking two small space vessels. And now, the last living human is at his mercy. But the agonoid has reckoned without another human, especially one like Ace Rimmer. Using his jet pack, Ace fires a burst of flame at the agonoid and sends him floating off into space again. But somehow, it manages to grab Ace's boot, pulling him away from *Starbug*. Realising that the agonoid is after his jet pack, Ace has time to jettison it before the infuriated machine can kill him.

Kryten, having been dislodged from *Starbug* by Pizzak'Rapp, is careering through space when, suddenly, he is harpooned in the back. Djuhn has decided that, if Lister won't come to him, he will go and get him – and Kryten's access code and retinal scan will be useful for getting aboard *Starbug*.

The agonoid confronts the *Starbug* crew, and Rimmer

surrenders immediately as it enthuses about the treats that lie in store. Cat is armed with a bazookoid and, knowing that this is useless against Djuhn, he comes up with a surprisingly intelligent plan: he threatens to shoot Lister with it. The agonoid cannot stand the thought of being deprived of the sadistic pleasures for which he has planned for so long. However, the seriousness or otherwise of Cat's threat is never put to the test. The oxygen regeneration unit, already damaged from the battering that *Starbug* has taken, chooses that very moment to pack up. Lister blacks out . . .

. . . and wakes to find himself in *Starbug*'s engine room, where Djuhn is completing his repairs to the OG unit. Kryten is present too, but Djuhn seems unconcerned when the mechanoid picks up a bazookoid. After all, he is programmed not to kill – and a blast from such a weapon wouldn't damage an agonoid anyway. But Kryten fires the gun at the ship's hull, and the surprised Djuhn is sucked through the resulting hole. Not that his threat is over yet. As if the fresh damage to *Starbug* weren't enough, he leaves the ship with a parting gift: his Apocalypse Virus has been loaded into the NaviComp.

Without the NaviComp, *Starbug* will plunge headlong into a planet in seventeen hours. Kryten explains that the only solution is for him to sacrifice himself by contracting the virus himself and then attempting to create a Dove Virus antidote to it.

Inside Kryten's subconscious mind, this task manifests itself as a Wild West scenario, with himself as the town sheriff, Carton, and the Apocalypse Virus taking the form of a gang of desperadoes known as the Apocalypse Boys. But the sheriff quickly becomes a drunkard, forgetting his real identity and purpose. With time running out, the others utilise an Artificial Reality Western game to program themselves into Kryten's mind and come to his aid. They try desperately to sober him up and remind him of his responsibilities, even as the Apocalypse Boys trap them in the scenario and inflict horrible injuries upon them. They are eventually able to get through to Kryten and, with his faculties restored, he constructs his Dove Virus in time to win the final showdown.

Exiting from the AR game, Lister and the Cat spot Rimmer's light bee, melted beyond repair: the virus must have spread to his hologram generation unit. Kryten too is dead, and it turns out that his sacrifice was a hollow gesture. Although the NaviComp is back on line, there is not enough fuel to successfully reverse away from the impending impact. They have just one option left.

Making the near impossible journey across to Wildfire, the two survivors set off in Ace Rimmer's ship on the journey that will take them to another dimension. Upon arrival in this other reality, they are met with an incoming radio transmission from *Red Dwarf*. It is Rimmer, surrendering unconditionally.

Here, it transpires, Lister and the Cat didn't survive their stint playing *Better Than Life*, but Rimmer, Kryten and Holly are all still around. It wasn't quite what Lister was hoping for, but for the time being it is a place that he can call home.

BOHEMIAN RHAPSODY

Last time we cheated and lumped this together with the proper episodes. Now that we've got this new (sort of) section, we feel it sits better here.

In the midst of 1993's Comic Relief event, sharp-eyed *Dwarf* fans were treated to an unexpected appearance by their heroes. 'Comic Relief asked us to do all kinds of things, actually,' Rob Grant says. Doug Naylor adds: 'We were going to do *Red Dwarf* and the Daleks at one point, but because the schedule was so horrific, there just wasn't time to do that.' Fortunately, the telethon organisers had a solution: the possé could still make their way onto our screens by appearing in a specially filmed video of the twice chart-topping Queen hit, 'Bohemian Rhapsody'.

The idea was a simple one, but effective on screen. Any celeb who fancied him or herself a pop star just set the cameras rolling and bopped along to the song. The impromptu performances were then collected and edited into one definitive video – in which you never knew quite who was going to turn up next. Amongst the stars on parade were the assembled casts of *Drop the Dead Donkey*, *Birds of a Feather*, *Jeeves and Wooster* and *Eldorado*. Nor was it only comedy shows which were spotlighted; the residents of Brookside Close contributed a few lines, as did such luminaries as Noel Edmonds, Andi Peters and Esther Rantzen. They even had Gordon the Gopher in there!

The *Red Dwarf* crew made their surprise appearances (seven in all, but who's counting?) towards the end of the montage, seated in the cockpit of *Starbug* and miming with gusto. 'We thought it was just a mime thing,' explains the show's most celebrated musician, Danny John-Jules. 'But in the end we watched it back and of course everyone else was bloody singing it. It looks like maybe we can't sing, or we don't want to sing!' Rob Grant confirms that that isn't the case: 'We've got a quite melodious crew really, with one exception I think . . .'

For those who keep an eye out for such things, 'Bohemian Rhapsody' was the television premiere of the *Red Dwarf VI* crew – that is to say, our first glimpse of the modified *Starbug* set and of Cat and Rimmer's new costumes. The sequence was shot after recording of 'Psirens' (on Saturday 20 February 1993, for those people who really have to know that sort of thing too), although the audience of the night remained unaware of this additional attraction, having already left the studio. Fortunately, Lister had been required to play guitar in the episode, thus the prop was handy for Craig Charles to make use of.

There was one problem though, which led to Robert Llewellyn's Kryten appearing *sans* nose. In what has become an end-of-recording tradition, the plastic proboscis was ripped from Robert's face by co-star Craig, neither realising that there was more filming to be done. Not even a red nose was available to cover the deficiency, and in the end only a dab of red paint could be found to make the mechanoid look more in keeping with the occasion.

Despite such hiccups, Danny at least enjoyed making the

video. 'It was such an easy feeling – we just rolled cameras, played the playback and went for it from top to bottom, and they took out whichever bits they wanted to use. It wasn't like we had to rehearse it or anything, we just did it in one take.'

Incidentally, *Red Dwarf*'s contribution to the most recent Comic Relief was an out-take from 'Back to Reality'.

RED DWARF – USA

American TV producers first noticed that *Red Dwarf* had the potential to be adapted into a series made especially for US television as far back as season two, when the British show aired on PBS. However, the sweeping changes – to both the characters and the format – they insisted upon, were enough to deter Grant and Naylor from making any deals.

Following *Red Dwarf*'s successful run in the Los Angeles area in 1991, further approaches were made to Grant Naylor Productions, with a view to producing a version of the saga originating in the USA. It was a bid from Universal Studios that seemed likely to yield the most desirable end result. And so, on the completion of *Red Dwarf V*, Rob Grant and Doug Naylor flew to California to assist in the making of a pilot episode. They were accompanied on the trip by Robert Llewellyn, who was to be the only member of the British cast to reprise his role. His Kryten make-up would again be applied by Andria Pennell. Incidentally, Chris Barrie was offered the Rimmer part, but declined the invitation.

Although the show was essentially close in structure to its British antecedent, the studio executives insisted on a few changes in order that it might appeal more readily to an American audience. Instead of being a complete slob, the new Lister, played very agreeably by Craig Bierko, was more in the heroic leading man mould. Consequently, had the series gone ahead, the intention was to include a romantic interest for our hero in every episode, a far cry from the enforced celibacy of the original. Incidentally, an early notion of Grant and Naylor had been to include the Pleasure GELF Camille as a regular character, but this idea was quickly abandoned.

The changes to Rimmer were less radical: instead of a letter H to denote his status as a hologram, a red circle would be present on his forehead. The familiar music and logo would also disappear, the latter replaced by pink digital lettering. The script, by Linwood Boomer, was adapted from 'The End', with several ideas from the books and other episodes slotted in. Boomer's task was primarily to give the jokes more of a stateside flavour.

RED DWARF (The Pilot)

Created by Rob Grant and Doug Naylor. Developed and written by Linwood Boomer. Music by Todd Rundgren. Produced by Todd Stevens. Directed by Jeff Melman. Cast: Craig Bierko (Lister), Chris Eigeman (Rimmer), Jane Leeves (Holly), Robert Llewellyn (Kryten), Hinton Battle (Cat), Elizabeth Morehead (Christine Kochanski), Michael Heintzman (1st Officer Munson), Lorraine Toussaint (Captain Tau).

By the latter half of the twenty-second century, humankind had colonised the outer fringes of the solar system. After a night of excessive drinking had caused Dave Lister to wake up on one of the moons of Saturn – a long way from his home town of Detroit – he had little option but to join the 5000 strong crew of *Red Dwarf*, a beat-up Class 5 Miner/Freighter with a cargo capacity of 47 cubic miles. Although assigned to Rimmer's menial work team, Lister isn't disheartened. Not only does he have his dream of owning a farm with various animals, including two pigs, but he's also found love aboard the mining vessel, in the attractive shape of Christine Kochanski. Lister's work mates are a couple of skutters who are none too keen on Rimmer either and, to express their disapproval, they have learnt how to form an offensive gesture using the middle one of their three digits.

While in the process of being dumped by Chris, because of his reckless and carefree attitude to life, Lister encounters the robot Kryten 2XB 517P, who is newly arrived aboard *Red Dwarf* and en route to the Captain. The two strike up an instant friendship and Kryten is introduced to Lister's cat Frankenstein, which he'd rescued from being cooked in a Titan restaurant and now keeps hidden in his bunk room. Kryten reveals that the cat is in fact pregnant, and not putting on weight because of the amount of beer it drinks.

It isn't long before the unquarantined animal is discovered and Lister and Kryten are summoned before Captain Tau. A security camera has exposed the android taking the cat to a new hiding place, but Kryten refuses to reveal her whereabouts. However, the strain of defying a direct order causes him to overload and explode.

Lister too refuses to spill the beans and consequently is sentenced to Stasis. Just as he is about to become a non event mass with a probability of zero, Kochanski arrives to tell him she loves him – Lister says he'll talk after all, but it's too late.

Three million years later Holly 6000, the ship's computer, revives Lister and informs him that the rest of the crew have been killed (by a lethal dose of Cadmium 2, if you hadn't guessed). However, Holly informs him that he needn't be entirely alone. One of the crew's personality discs remains undamaged and using a holographic projection unit a new hologram can be introduced to replace Munson, the ship's previous one. Much to everyone's disappointment the intact disc is that of Rimmer, who was last seen being carried out of an exam, wearing a straitjacket. Kryten too is still around, albeit in pieces. From the shelf where his head has been stored for the last three million years, the android has contentedly passed the time by reading a conveniently placed fire exit sign.

Holly detects one further presence aboard the vessel. But before introducing the others to the Cat, she explains his origins by means of a series of computer generated, animated images. Yet although an entire race of Cat People had evolved from Frankenstein's kittens, a civil war had wiped them all out except the one about to become the final member of the *Red Dwarf*'s new crew.

Despite his companions, Lister is understandably far from

happy, but then something happens to give him renewed hope. He is visited by his future self accompanied by Kryten, the Cat and, best of all, Christine Kochanski. The visitors have some important information to impart to Lister, but the huge amount of power needed to facilitate their presence requires them to be brief. Unfortunately, Rimmer's eagerness to discover what awful thing fate has in store for him prevents them from revealing much, not even the reason for the hologram's absence – though the Cat helpfully suggests that it's not so much awful as disgusting.

Though learning little of his destiny, the knowledge that Chris is to play a part in it is all the encouragement Lister needs. Filled with a fresh sense of optimism he engages *Red Dwarf*'s powerful engines and sets off into infinity, keen to get out there and do some 'space stuff'.

Although not entirely happy with certain aspects of this try out episode – some of the casting in particular – the studio executives still saw enough promise in the project to give it a second chance, this time with Grant and Naylor in charge of the production. Rather than completely refilm the pilot, Rob and Doug decided to make a promo video utilising scenes from the already filmed episode alongside newly made segments spotlighting the new cast members. Strangely, however, the Kryten footage was from the UK episode 'Terrorform'. The two characters recast were Rimmer and the Cat; Anthony Fuscle was Rimmer (with the familiar letter H restored) and Terry Farrell played a very different kind of Cat – a female one to be specific. Craig Bierko and Jane Leeves reprised their roles as Lister and Holly respectively.

Had it proven successful the resulting series would have aired on NBC, the largest of the US network. But, sadly the promotional film too was unable to secure a deal for a full season of episodes. Terry Farrell went on to land the role of Dax in *Star Trek – Deep Space Nine* and Jane Leeves appeared as Mancunian Daphne Moon in the *Cheers* spin-off *Frasier*.

Since Universal's involvement ceased, other companies have expressed an interest in making *Red Dwarf* for American TV. However, as with some of the early proposals, the changes requested were more than sufficient to put Grant and Naylor off. So, for the time being at least, it seems that *Red Dwarf USA* is dead.

SECTION SIX:

CARGO INVENTORY

Anyone who purchased the very first edition of this book back in 1993 may remember us predicting a dearth of *Red Dwarf* items in the specialist stores. However, the profusion of goodies available since then shows just how wrong we were; so in a fit of pique we've decided to give only a cursory mention to most of this stuff.

BOOKS

The *Red Dwarf Omnibus* is basically a slightly edited compilation of the first two novels, with the pilot script and a bit of *Dave Hollins – Space Cadet* thrown in for good measure.

For purists there are two script books available from Penguin. The first, entitled *Primordial Soup*, features Rob and Doug's favourites: 'Psirens', 'Marooned', 'Polymorph', 'Justice', 'Dimension Jump' and 'Back to Reality'. Its sequel *Son of Soup*, includes 'Gunmen of the Apocalypse', 'Holoship', 'Camille', 'Backwards', 'Kryten' and 'Me²'. This second selection was chosen by Rob Grant only.

There have been several reference works on the subject, pre-eminent among them Virgin's fantastic *Red Dwarf Programme Guide*. Other factual books include Titan's *Red Dwarf Companion* by Bruce Dessau and *The Making of Red Dwarf* by Joe Nazarro, this from Penguin.

A couple of *Red Dwarf* cast members have penned autobiographical works that will no doubt be of interest to fans. Robert Llewellyn has two volumes out: *The Man in the Rubber Mask* and *Thin He Was and Filthy-Haired*. The first of these contains a fascinating insight into the making of *Red Dwarf* USA. More recently, Hattie Hayridge has written *Random Abstract Memory*.

Other publications, which aren't easily categorised under fiction or reference, are *The Red Dwarf Quiz Book*, *The Red Dwarf Diary*, and *Red Dwarf – Space Corps Survival Manual* by Mike O'Hagan.

RED DWARF SMEGAZINE

As *Red Dwarf* began its fifth series in February 1992, it also became one of those rare programmes that are awarded the distinction of their own magazine. Like the programme itself (and like this book!), *Red Dwarf Smegazine* (originally titled *Red Dwarf Magazine*) got its start in Manchester, where the misnamed London Editions were the first to spot the potential of the programme. Work began in late 1991, but by the time the finished product saw print, the company had merged with London-based Fleetway (home of Judge Dredd), and the magazine came out under the new label of Fleetway Editions.

Red Dwarf Magazine featured a blend of factual and humorous articles, along with comic strips, which both adapted episodes and told new stories. Interestingly enough, these strips showed Rimmer (and any other holograms which happened to turn up in them) in black and white. This was the result of a request by Rob Grant and Doug Naylor, who confess that they would like to have done this in the series, had the effect been a little easier to achieve. Some of the TV series' peripheral characters took centre stage with their own comic strips, and, if anything, one or two of Ace Rimmer's strip adventures presented more of a logical prelude to 'Stoke Me A Clipper' than did 'Dimension Jump'.

The *Smegazine* sold reasonably well, but its editor, Mike Butcher, believed the potential readership was much higher and after fourteen issues elected to relaunch the magazine in a revamped Volume 2. Sadly, it seems that sales didn't increase significantly enough to persuade Fleetway to renew their contract and the final issue Vol. 29 appeared in December 1993, the month that saw the demise of Dan Dare's *Eagle*, also from the Fleetway stable.

Given the popularity of the series, quite why the *Smegazine* never realised a readership comparable to, say, *2000AD* is impossible to say. On the plus side, the *Smegazine* boasted some fine artwork by the likes of Colin Howard, Glenn Rix and Paul Crompton, as well as some great articles by a couple of handsome and well-endowed writers (modesty forbids us to mention names). Negative aspects were, in our opinion, the oddball comic strips, which had little or nothing to do with the TV series; and, to be fair, there is a finite number of times the same small group of people can be interviewed on the same subject and still find something fresh to say. Had the mag lasted, the three-year gap between *Red Dwarf*s VI and VII wouldn't have helped either.

During the course of its relatively short run, the *Smegazine* had a number of exclusive free gifts stuck to its cover by various means. These were badges, postcards, stickers and a keyring.

TONGUE TIED

The debut single from the Cat (Danny John-Jules) as featured originally in 'Parallel Universe', released by EMI in both seven- and twelve-inch versions as well as on cassette and CD. Canny marketing meant that in order to obtain all the mixes of 'Tongue Tied' and the *Red Dwarf* theme the record had to be purchased in more than one format.

The single peaked at number 17 in the charts and might well have risen higher had Danny not had to cancel his scheduled appearance on *Top of the Pops*.

Uniquely, the video reunited Danny with Craig Charles, Chris Barrie, Robert Llewellyn and *both* Hollys, Norman Lovett and Hattie Hayridge; also featured were the 'Queeg' actor and 'Parallel Universe' choreographer, Charles Augins and Clayton 'Elvis' Mark. The promo video, along with other related bits and pieces, was set for commercial release but was dropped for reasons unknown. Readers of *Red Dwarf Smegazine*, however, were able to send off for a copy in plain packaging.

Both the video and the record sleeve featured a female Cat character called Kit (shades of *Red Dwarf* USA).

VIDEOS

Of course, no matter how many T-shirts you wear and how many books you read, there is still no real substitute for actually watching the programme. Fortunately for *Red Dwarf* fans, BBC Video have realised this, and taken it upon themselves to release the show's classic episodes on tape.

The first set of two videos was released for the 1991 Christmas market, each featuring three episodes from the tremendously popular third season. Each was named after the first of those episodes, these being 'Backwards' and 'Timeslides' respectively – and before you go flicking back to the episode guide in Section 3, we can assure you that yes 'Timeslides' was the fifth story in that particular season. However, having obviously decided that it was a much better cover title than that of the fourth episode, 'Body Swap', the Beeb swapped the two episodes around it make it so.

Red Dwarf III was obviously a success, and as such it was quite logically followed up, in March 1992 by . . . *Red Dwarf II* – that is, *Red Dwarf* Series 2, renamed for the sake of conformity. Again, the series was released on two tapes, each containing three episodes – this time in the right order. The only drawback to this release seems to be that, due to the lack of colour photographs from this season, shots had to be taken from television monitors to provide the video covers. As a result, these look somewhat less than professional, although obviously this couldn't be helped. *Red Dwarf IV* hit the shelves in October and November 1992. The two tapes entitled 'Camille' and 'Dimension Jump' featured the fourth series in the order in which it was originally screened and not in the preferred repeat season sequence.

Incidentally, there was an opportunity to send for an exclusive *Red Dwarf IV* T-shirt with this release.

After being rescheduled a time or two *Red Dwarf I* finally

appeared in Summer 1993. To overcome the problem arising from the lack of early photos artwork covers were provided by Bruno Elettori. The episodes appeared in their original broadcast sequence and Byte One was entitled 'The End', so no surprise there; however, tape two was named after the fifth episode of the series, 'Confidence and Paranoia'. Apparently BBC Video decided against calling it 'Waiting for God' just in case people confused it with another BBC sit-com. Can't think which one . . .

The blurb on the video cases reminded us that the episodes had never been repeated by the BBC, so naturally, everybody rushed out and bought these rare gems – then of course the BBC repeated them.

July '94 saw the release of 'Back to Reality' the first half of season five, though no prizes for spotting that *Red Dwarf V*'s order on video differed from the first TV run. Anyone who bought their copy from Woolworths received a free official metallic *Red Dwarf* badge (subject to availability) and very nice it is too. The second part of season five appeared in August entitled 'Quarantine'.

The next BBC video release was not in fact the first half of *Red Dwarf VI*, but a selection of out-takes entitled *Red Dwarf Smeg Ups*; one or two of the clips contained thereon were almost amusing.

In 1995 BBC video were back on course with the release of *Red Dwarf VI*, on two tapes as usual. Byte One was sub-titled 'Gunmen of the Apocalypse', Byte Two, 'Polymorph – Emohawk II' (which was quite a similar title to that of one of the episodes on it).

Red Dwarf VI was followed by *Red Dwarf Smeg Outs*, another collection of out-takes (where do they find them?) nearly as funny as the first.

Red Dwarf Six of the Best is a two-tape compilation of what are considered to be the finest episodes from each of the first six series, namely 'Future Echoes', 'Queeg', 'Polymorph', 'Dimension Jump', 'Back to Reality' and 'Gunmen of the Aopocalypse'. Presumably this is aimed at people who've worn out those episodes on the original releases by watching them so often. Others might be tempted by the enclosed CD featuring an interview with Rob and Doug, or even the little *Starbug* hologram stuck to the side of the red box that houses the set.

MERCHANDISE

There's quite a lot of this available, although the bulk of it takes the form of T-shirts. Other tasteful items include: baseball caps, surf Jams, sweatshirts, jackets, mugs, keyrings, greetings cards, posters, calendars, badges, several model kits and, last but not least, the sheet music. The aforementioned fripperies are available from shops.

Also available:

I Can't Believe It's an Unofficial Simpsons Guide

Warren Martyn and Adrian Wood
ISBN: 0 7535 0166 X

The Simpsons must be considered one of the most bizarre success stories to emerge from American TV. From its roots as a series of inserts on *The Tracey Ullman Show*, it has gone on to become the longest running animated show in the world.

But just who are the Simpsons? How did they manage to top the charts with 'Do the Bartman' – a song written by Michael Jackson himself? And why do celebrities fight to join a list of guest stars that includes Elizabeth Taylor, Michelle Pfeiffer, Meryl Streep, Winona Ryder, Leonard Nimoy, the three surviving Beatles, and the entire cast of *Cheers*?

This unique book examines the *Simpsons* phenomenon as never before, looking at the high points of all the episodes and the people who made them. Everything anyone would want to know about America's most dysfunctional family is covered – including many things you didn't want to know but will be pleased to find out.

THE BABYLON FILE
Andy Lane
ISBN: 0 7535 0049 3

Babylon 5 is unique: a science fiction TV show with a pre-determined story arc. The closest thing to a SF novel conceived for the small screen, the programme has been hailed by fans and critics alike as one of the best and most complex genre series ever.

Incisive, helpful, comprehensive and occasionally irreverent, this is the book that will unlock the show's secrets as never before. It features an extended essay on the programme's roots by its creator J. Michael Straczynski as well as a detailed episode guide and an exploration of all aspects of the world of *Babylon 5*. This volume is essential reading for all dedicated fans of the show – and an invaluable guide for recent converts who must be wondering what they have missed.

'this is a remarkable feat and is equally entertaining whether read from cover to cover or just dipped into at random.'
–TV Zone

X-TREME POSSIBILITIES
Paul Cornell, Martin Day and Keith Topping
ISBN: 0 7535 0019 1

This book presents a unique analysis of the *X-Files*, the programme that has transformed our perceptions of the paranormal. Though sometimes humorous in tone, it is also a serious study of all the elements that have made the show what it is today. As well as a detailed and complete episode guide, the book pieces together, step by step, the nature of the series' conspiracy – the first attempt to discover just what the 'truth' behind the series is.

From Mulder's astonishing leaps of logic to the tendency of characters not to make it through the pre-titles sequence, this book covers all the hitherto unexamined aspects of one of the world's most popular science fiction shows.

'This is a refreshing change from the usual po-faced attitude of *X-Files* literature. There's an extremely high possibility that you'll enjoy it.'

–Dreamwatch

LICENCE DENIED

Rumblings from the *Doctor Who* Underground
Edited by Paul Cornell
ISBN: 0 7535 0104 X

The untold story of *Doctor Who* is the story of fanzines: the magazines produced by the artistic and anarchistic culture called fandom. These publications are controversial, intellectual and witty. And often offensive, rude and scandalous. Their story could only be told unlicensed, making this collection of snippets from fanzines unauthorised, uncensored and unputdownable.

Included are a no-holds-barred interview with Tom Baker, set visits to 'Carnival of Monsters' and 'The Web of Fear' and as much satire, analysis and ranting as any fan could want. With contributions from all over the world and from three decades of fandom, *Licence Denied* is the book that finally exposes the artistry, rudeness and wit of *Doctor Who* fandom.